TANGLED DESTINIES
LATIN AMERICA AND THE UNITED STATES

Diálogos

A series of course adoption books on Latin America

Senior advisory editor: Professor Lyman L. Johnson, University of North Carolina at Charlotte

TANGLED DESTINIES
LATIN AMERICA AND THE UNITED STATES

By Don M. Coerver and Linda B. Hall

Blair Woodard, Photograph Editor

ALBUQUERQUE

The University of New Mexico Press

Library of Congress Cataloging-in-Publication Data

Coerver, Don M., 1943–
Tangled destinies: Latin America and the United States / by Don M. Coerver
and Linda B. Hall.

    p.   cm.
Includes bibliographical references (p.) and index.

ISBN 0-8263-2118-6 (alk. paper)

ISBN 0-8263-2117-8 (pbk. : alk. paper)

1. Latin America—Relations—United States. 2. United States—Relations—
Latin America. I. Hall, Linda B. (Linda Biesele), 1939– II. Title.

F1418.C662 1999

327.7308—dc21

98–58040

CIP

FOR "THE CHIEF"
RICHARD E. GREENLEAF

CONTENTS

ILLUSTRATIONS

TABLES

MAPS

ACKNOWLEDGMENTS

Scholars incur many debts, particularly in a wide-ranging project such as this one. We are no exceptions. First of all, we wish to thank our students—at the University of New Mexico, Texas Christian University, and the University of California at Los Angeles—who have contributed through their interest and enthusiasm to this volume. In particular, Corinna Reyes, Josette Griffiths, Jennifer Cutcliffe Juste, and Trena Klohe provided information from their own research, and they are cited in the appropriate chapters. Diata Rhodes gathered dozens of quotations for the "Point-Counterpoint" sections of this volume, as did Blair Woodard, and we thank them both. Blair also collected the photographs and images for this volume, tracking them down through collections and acquaintances.

We are also grateful to those photographers who so generously have let us reproduce their own work, providing not only the images but also the context of the stories that these pictures tell. Their encounters with the history of Latin America as it was occurring and their recording of it has enhanced and informed our own understanding. So to David Craven, David Kunzle, M. L. Horner, Tiffany Thomas, Douglas Hecock, and Michael Stanfield, many thanks. We also thank Robert Corrigan, friend and word-person, for coming up with the appropriate title after we had spent several weeks trying to hit the right note.

To those colleagues who contributed their ideas and critiqued various portions of the manuscript—Kenneth A. Stevens, U.S. diplomatic historian, and the late Jim Corder, professor of rhetoric at T.C.U., and especially the editor of the *Diálogos* series, Lyman Johnson of the University of North Carolina, Charlotte—we extend our gratitude. Lyman not only made general suggestions but also meticulously reviewed the manuscript word by word and helped coordinate the preparation of the maps, above and beyond, certainly, the call of duty.

Thanks also to the library staffs who helped us pull everything together, especially Russ Davidson, historian and professor whose attention to the Latin American Collection in the U.N.M. library has kept it among the best in the country, and Stella de Sa Rego, whose tireless pursuit of historical images has made the collection at the Center for Southwest Research so rich.

Finally, our thanks to the scholar to whom this work is dedicated, Richard E. Greenleaf. Professor Greenleaf has provided both academic and non-academic insights on the history of Latin America to several generations of Latin Americanist scholars. He has made major contributions to the field of Latin American history through his scholarship, his teaching, and his administrative activities at Tulane University and in Mexico City. He has been both friend and inspiration to both of us.

TANGLED DESTINIES
LATIN AMERICA AND THE UNITED STATES

CHAPTER 1

THE COLONY AND
THE NEW NATION TO 1848

Vignette: The Louisiana Purchase

Competing dreams of empire collided in the vast wilderness of Louisiana in the early 1800s. The region had been a consolation prize for Spain in 1763 after the disastrous Seven Years' War. Spain, however, found the area an imperial liability—costly to administer and difficult to defend. As settlers from the newly independent United States penetrated the area, Louisiana once again became part of the French empire. In 1800 Spain returned the area to France as part of Napoleon's scheme to resurrect the French empire in North America and reconquer the rebellious French colony of St. Domingue (Haiti). In exchange for Louisiana, Spain received territory in Italy and a promise that France would not transfer Louisiana to a third party. Although the transaction was secret, President Thomas Jefferson learned of the deal in May 1801. Jefferson realized the significance of the transfer of Louisiana from a weak and passive Spain to a strong and aggressive France, commenting that French control of the mouth of the Mississippi meant that "we must marry ourselves to the British fleet and nation."

The French threat and presence disappeared almost as rapidly as it had appeared. Confronted with military problems in reconquering Haiti, an impending war with Britain, and unrelenting U.S. hostility to a French Louisiana, Napoleon decided to unload the property to one of his antagonists, the United States. U.S. and French interests were rapidly converging; in January 1803 Jefferson dispatched James Monroe to Paris to try to purchase New Orleans and the Floridas because the U.S. government incorrectly assumed that Spain had transferred the Floridas along with Louisiana. On 11 April 1803, the day before Monroe's arrival in Paris, French officials conveyed to the U.S. minister, Robert R. Livingston, an offer to sell the entire Louisiana area to the United States. An astonished but pleased Livingston said that a formal reply would have to await the arrival of Monroe.

Once Monroe arrived on the scene, there was no doubt that the U.S. representatives were enthusiastic about the purchase; the only question was what the price would be. Napoleon hoped for 100 million francs but was prepared to sell for as little as 50 million francs. Livingston and Monroe initially offered 40 million francs but soon raised the offer to 50 million. Both parties were in a hurry to conclude negotiations, fearing the outbreak of war between France and England or interference by England or Spain in the transfer. The Louisiana Purchase was completed in three agreements concluded on 30 April 1803. The United States purchased Louisiana for 60 million francs ($11,250,000) and also agreed to assume claims of U.S. citizens against France up to 20 million francs ($3,750,000), making the total cost $15 million.

Although the Louisiana Purchase had doubled the size of the United States, it had the effect of encouraging additional expansionist pressures. To facilitate negotiations, the French had been deliberately vague about the boundaries of the area. When Livingston questioned one of the French negotiators, Talleyrand, about boundaries, Talleyrand is said to have replied: "... [Y]ou have made a noble bargain for yourselves, and I suppose you will make the most of it." Instead of relieving pressure on Spain's frontier in North America, the Purchase soon led to new expansionist pressures based on U.S. claims that the Purchase included parts of the Floridas and Texas. As early as 1805 the United States was officially maneuvering to acquire the Floridas and Texas; when negotiations failed, Jefferson considered military action to obtain what he called "the rightful boundaries of Louisiana."

Based on Alexander DeConde, This Affair of Louisiana *(New York, 1976).*

Introduction

Relationships between the United States and its Latin American neighbors have rarely been untroubled. From the birth of the republics of the western hemisphere, questions of control of territory and resources; of asymmetric economic, military, and political power; of cultural and ideological difference; even of political sovereignty itself have been disputed. Latin America, for U.S. policymakers, has often been a secondary interest, with more time and attention directed toward world areas considered more important or more dangerous. However, the increasing power of the United States has made the relationship of extraordinary importance for Latin Americans. For the United States, it has been possible, for most of two centuries, to get along without understanding much about its neighbors to the South. Latin Americans have never had the luxury of ignoring the United States.

Part of the reason for this longstanding imbalance of power can be found in the timing and nature of the revolutionary movements in the late eighteenth and early nineteenth centuries. All new nations of the Western Hemisphere faced common challenges: the organization of new governments, adjustment to different positions in the international economy, and the sorting out of social conflicts. There were, however, important differences. The United States achieved independence at a time of high prices for its agricultural exports in the Atlantic market; at the time most Latin American countries were gaining independence, the prices in the international market for their exports were in decline. The American Revolution, 1776–1783, preceded independence movements in Latin America, 1808–1826, by more than three decades. By the time Latin Americans moved to throw off colonial rule, the United States had established secure and stable political institutions. This stability would stand it in good stead in the years of population growth, economic development, and expansion, which quickly followed. The nature of their independence efforts also left Latin Americans at a disadvantage. Enormously destructive, characterized by a lack of agreement on political goals, undermined by regional and personal struggles, most Latin American countries were unable to achieve political stability. This failure also jeopardized economic development, making recovery from the terrible devastation left by the independence wars a long and difficult process. While the United States offered a relatively safe environment for investment, Latin America remained troubled. Political instability, economic devastation, continuing internal wars throughout the nineteenth century and into the twentieth left Latin American countries at a disadvantage relative to their northern neighbor.

Initially, of course, the United States was in a relatively weak position itself. In the first two decades after independence, most contact with Latin America was economic, a contact made possible by the European powers' distraction by European struggles. Still, starting in 1803, the United States began to make major acquisitions of territory at the same time that it was expanding trade with Latin American nations, most of them nominally controlled by Spain or another European nation. Through 1845, however, relatively little military activity was required to achieve these ends. Despite some skirmishing over the Floridas, U.S. territorial expansion came easily, and, it must have seemed, almost by default. The 1783–1845 period was one of increasing trade and significant territorial expansion. There was relatively little need to exert military might, military might which the United States did not yet possess. This relative military weakness, however, did not prevent the United States from enunciating in the Monroe Doctrine (1823), a warning to European powers to stay out of the hemisphere.

The remaining years of the nineteenth century, in contrast, involved the United States in one major foreign war — with Mexico — and one significant intervention, in Cuba's own independence struggle against Spain just at the end of the century. It was not accidental that these were the two Spanish-speaking countries in closest geographical proximity to the United States. U.S. expansion in both territory and trade continued, with increasing economic investments, particularly in the same two countries. The ease with which the war with Mexico was won, and the extraordinary amount of territory which was taken, led to the perception that Latin Americans were somehow inferior and could be easily dominated by the U.S. military. Such attitudes — involving race, degree of civilization, and anti-Catholic sentiments — became widespread and were applied beyond the Mexican case, demeaning Latin American countries, their leaders, and their citizens. Thus, between 1845 and approximately 1900, success at warfare, significant territorial acquisition, and increasing economic connections — along with attitudes that depreciated the countries to the south — characterized U.S. relations with Latin American nations.

The years between 1900 and 1917, when the U.S. entered the First World War, saw continuing expansion, but now more in economic than territorial terms. The nation, quickly emerging as a major world power, became firmly involved in the pursuit of an American empire. It sought increasing economic and political power in the hemisphere. Trade and direct economic investment increased, particularly in Mexico and Cuba, but also in other Latin American countries. Theodore Roosevelt, ascending to the presidency in 1901, put the emphasis clearly on U.S. naval power and on policies that would enhance such power. Roosevelt set the tone with the acquisition of rights to a Panamanian canal in 1903. Construction on the canal began the following year and was completed in 1914. Moreover, Roosevelt, determined to develop and maintain U.S. hegemony in the hemisphere, elaborated further on the Monroe Doctrine. The United States, according to Roosevelt's corollary to the Doctrine, would intervene in Latin American countries — especially the Caribbean — should the governments there find themselves unable to manage their finances or to maintain law and order. His concern was that Europeans, tempted to intervene themselves by the region's political and financial instability, would threaten the sea lanes leading to the Panama Canal. Latin American governments were unenthusiastic, correctly viewing this development as a threat to their own autonomy. Their concerns did not prevent the United States from intervening in the Caribbean, as well as meddling in Mexico, however.

In the post–World War I period, the United States had clearly reached great power status. Through 1933, American business abroad continued to expand, focusing more and more on the control of natural resources, especially oil. President Woodrow Wilson's own corollary to the Monroe Doctrine addressed this point explicitly. Extending the Doctrine to the economic sphere, he declared that economic concessions granted to Europeans might threaten the independence of Latin American nations. It seems very likely that he was also concerned about the imperiling of U.S. economic interests. In any case, this new principle enlarged the category of dangerous Europeans beyond political and military leaders to include financiers and businessmen. As formulated in these policies, U.S. dominance over Latin America was essential not only politically and militarily but also economically. At the same time, Wilson sought, in the words of historian Gaddis Smith, "to detoxify the doctrine in the eyes of Latin American governments." In January 1917, Wilson declared that ". . . the nations should with one accord adopt the doctrine of President Monroe as the doctrine of the world: that no nation should seek to extend its polity over any other nation or people, but that every people should be free to determine its own polity, its own way of development, unhindered, unthreatened, unafraid, along with the great and powerful."[1] Wilson, however, never followed such a policy himself.

U.S. interventions through the 1920s in the Caribbean and Central America would help assure the continuance of U.S. political and economic dominance. However, during the 1930s, the economic depression enveloping the

This New York Globe cartoon shows Teddy Roosevelt carrying his "Big Stick" toward Panama aboard a U.S. battleship.

From David McCullough, The Path Between the Seas: The Creation of the Panama Canal 1870–1914. *Simon and Schuster Touchstone: 1977*

world made the continued policing of the region too expensive. The Good Neighbor policy introduced by Franklin Roosevelt ended direct military intervention, but also led the administration to more readily accept dictators who, it believed, would maintain order. This policy shift led, not surprisingly, to the support of military regimes in some instances. Again, the major focus was on those areas closest to the United States geographically. Because Mexico already seemed stable, the Caribbean and Central America were the regions most affected. World War II, following quickly on the heels of the depression, further distracted U.S. policymakers from Latin American questions. Wilson's emphasis on democracy continued to fade.

In the wake of World War II, security interests related to the Cold War came to dominate U.S. relations with Latin America. Again, especially but not exclusively in the Caribbean and Central America, Soviet communism was seen to be the major threat. Through the end of the presidency of Ronald Reagan in 1989, issues of ideology dominated the discourse of U.S.-Latin American relations. Only with the collapse of the Soviet Union and of its Eastern European empire in the early 1990s did the fear of communism cease to dominate the policies and practices of U.S. administrations towards its neighbors. As we approach the end of the twentieth century, it is possible that U.S. policymakers will no longer need to think in terms of dominance in regard to Latin America, and the opportunity to move to a more equal relationship of consultation and cooperation may be at hand. In fact, the largest problems in U.S.-Latin American relations at the end of the twentieth century—the illegal trade in narcotics and the large migration, legal and illegal, of Latin Americans into the United States—require cooperation with the countries to the south.

The Great Powers and the Emergence of the United States

United States-Latin American relations evolved from a complex mixture of imperial rivalries, colonial rebellions, ideological ferment, and changing views on economic development. During the eighteenth century Spain was still the dominant European power in the western hemisphere in terms of area controlled, but shifting power relationships in Europe made Spain a target of, rather than a principal actor in, imperial schemes. By 1800, Spain paradoxically was the weakest power in Europe and, at the same time, the major impediment to U.S. dreams of expansion in the New World.

Frequent warfare between Great Britain and Spain in the eighteenth century culminated in the smashing victory of British forces against combined Spanish and French forces in the Seven Years' War which ended in 1763. The British victory completely reworked the map of colonial North America. The French lost Canada to the British while Spain transferred to Britain the Floridas, an ill-defined piece of real estate stretching from the Atlantic Ocean to the Mississippi River. France, eager to retain its Spanish alliance, transferred the Louisiana Territory to its ally. The British victory had two important consequences: on the one hand, Spain became extremely concerned about its weak northern borderlands, which stretched from Louisiana to California; on the other, Britain's effort to tighten control over its maturing North America colonies led rapidly to the American Revolution.

The American Revolution provided an opportunity for Britain's European enemies to gain a measure of revenge for their losses in the Seven Years' War. France in 1778 officially extended recognition to the United States, signed a military alliance, and completed a commercial treaty. France's ally, Spain — not entirely comfortable with the idea of an independent United States — did not enter the war until 1779 and never became a formal ally of the United States. It did provide limited financial and material aid, primarily through Havana and New Orleans. At the Paris peace conference which ended the war, Spain tried to promote a reconciliation between Great Britain and her colonies. When this untimely initiative failed, Spain tried to prevent the United States from receiving the Mississippi River as its western boundary. Spanish officials foresaw correctly that an expansionist United States was a threat to its own New World empire and provided a dangerous revolutionary example for Spain's own colonies.

European wars continued to provide opportunities for the United States, particularly in the areas of trade and expansion. When fighting broke out again in 1796 between Britain and the revolutionary government of France, Spain was dragged into the struggle as well and was forced by British disruption of Atlantic trade to open its colonies to neutral commerce in 1797. U.S. traders had run contraband to Florida and the Caribbean for some time, and were able to expand further in those areas while initiating trade as far away as the La Plata region. Montevideo and Buenos Aires became important ports of call for Yankee merchants. More importantly, the continuing warfare in Europe led almost immediately to U.S. expansion. The French still dreamed of restoring their New World empire and acquired Louisiana from Spain in 1800.

Spain hoped, in this way, to provide a buffer to protect what was really vital to Spanish imperial interests: Mexico and its precious metals. However, French dreams were dependent on regaining control over its rebellious colony, Haiti (St. Domingue), which was to be a base for expansion into Louisiana. Strong military opposition from the Haitians and an even more implacable foe — yellow fever — thwarted the French attempt. Fearing war with Britain, Napoleon decided to liquidate his Louisiana adventure. He quickly came to an agreement with the United State to purchase the territory for $15,000,000. The purchase was popular in the United States, but the Spanish were left without a northern buffer for Mexico.

After the Louisiana Purchase, the Floridas became the principal focus of U.S. expansionism. President Thomas Jefferson used economic and diplomatic pressure to try to acquire them from Spain, but his overtures were rejected. However, time — or more correctly, population — was on the side of the United States. U.S. immigration into the Floridas was creating a demographic reality that the Spanish government could not ignore. At the same time, U.S. economic penetration of the area was drawing it increasingly into the American sphere. Finally, the Adams-Onís Treaty of 1819 ceded the Floridas to the United States, but Spain still retained Texas. The treaty also extended the boundary line between Spanish and U.S. territory to the Pacific Ocean along the forty-second parallel (the current northern boundary of the state of California). This later helped strengthen U.S. claims to Oregon.

While both sides made concessions, Spain would not have to deal very long with the aftermath of the treaty; just two years later, Mexico would achieve independence and inherit the problem of defending the northern borderlands. Most of the criticism of the treaty in the United States revolved around the so-called loss of Texas. The treaty designed to deal with the unfinished business of the Louisiana Purchase had created some unfinished business of its own — at least in the minds of expansionists in the United States.

The United States and Latin American Independence

While Spain and the United States were maneuvering for control of the Floridas and Texas, Napoleon's invasion of the Iberian peninsula in 1807 provoked an imperial crisis throughout the Latin American colonies. Spain and France had agreed to let French troops march through Spain to attack Portugal, Britain's long-time ally; Spain and France would then divide Portugal. French troops quickly conquered Portugal, forcing the royal family to relocate the court to Brazil in November 1807. Instead of dividing the spoils with Spain, however, Napoleon turned on his former ally, forced the abdication of the Spanish king, Charles IV, and placed his brother Joseph Bonaparte on the Spanish throne. Patriotic juntas were formed in Spain to resist French domination and work for the restoration of the Bourbons; similar organizations appeared in the Spanish American colonies. Several of these colonial juntas became centers of political intrigue and ultimately vehicles for independence movements. The collapse of the last vestiges of peninsular control in 1810 was the signal for revolution in the Spanish American colonies.

Revolution and independence in Latin America presented significant difficulties for the United States in formulating foreign policy. The drive for independence represented a series of movements with differing causes, goals, and leaders. There were at least four distinct geographical movements: New Spain (Mexico and Central America), the La Plata (primarily Argentina), New Granada (Venezuela and Colombia), and Brazil. The duration of the movements (1810–1825) presented an additional difficulty. The old colonial political units often failed to survive the independence movements. For instance, the Spanish Viceroyalty of the Rio de La Plata ultimately broke up into four nation-states: Argentina, Bolivia, Uruguay, and Paraguay. The United States would also have to place any policy toward the independent states in the broader context of its relations with the European powers, particularly its interests in trade and territorial expansion.

Many Latin American revolutionaries assumed that the United States would provide official aid to the independence movements, only to be disappointed by the cautious policy of the United States. While there was widespread sentiment for Latin American independence in the United States, the government officially adopted a policy of neutrality. There was also considerable skepticism about whether or not the liberation of Latin America from European control would lead to free and democratic institutions. In 1813, Jefferson noted that "History . . . furnishes no example of a priest-ridden people maintaining a free civil government," although he expressed some satisfaction that at least they would no longer be embroiled in European problems. He further believed that "America [the United States] has a hemisphere to itself." Secretary of State John Quincy Adams was equally doubtful in 1821, when he declared that he ". . . wished well to their cause; but I had seen and yet see no prospect that they would establish free or liberal institutions of government. . . . Arbitrary power, military and ecclesiastical, was stamped upon their education, upon their habits, and upon all their institutions."[2] Questions of power and hegemony were also involved; the United States was clearly looking to expand into territories currently or formerly held by Spain.

Events in Europe also dictated that the United States adjust its Latin American policy to broader foreign policy objectives. Relations with Britain were deteriorating and would eventually lead to war in 1812. Trade with the Iberian peninsula was booming, making the United States reluctant to offend Spain or Portugal.

Expansion in the Spanish borderlands also took priority over Latin American independence; Spain had drawn a specific connection between negotiations over border questions and U.S. restraint in aiding the revolutionaries. U.S. neutrality laws were strengthened in 1817 in response to Spanish criticism that the rebels were receiving too much unofficial aid in the United States. The U.S. government also feared that extensive U.S. involvement in the independence movements might encourage other European powers to become more actively involved and might even provoke a war with Spain or Spain's allies. The shifting fortunes of the different movements also promoted a cautious response; all of the insurgencies, especially the one in Mexico, experienced major setbacks during the independence process.

A change in U.S. policy, influenced by the increasing success of the Latin American revolutionaries, began in 1817 under the administration of President James Monroe. The Republic of the Rio de La Plata declared its independence in 1816, and there was notable military progress in Chile and Venezuela in 1817. In the years following the Congress of Vienna [1814–1815], Britain increasingly distanced itself from the other European powers and considered a more cooperative approach with the United States in Latin American matters. In the United States there was growing congressional pressure on the Monroe administration to extend recognition to the rebellious colonies. The conclusion of the Adams-Onís Treaty had broken the linkage between borderlands negotiations and a restrained policy toward the Spanish American colonies. There was also the assumption that the independence of Latin America would mean greater economic opportunity for the United States. Then, in 1820, revolts in both Spain and Portugal further weakened imperial control, pushing the United States toward recognition.

In extending recognition, the United States considered cooperating with Britain but decided to take unilateral action. In a special message to Congress in March 1822, Monroe stated that Chile, Colombia, Mexico, Peru, and the United Provinces of the Rio de La Plata had achieved independence and that there was no likelihood of their being reconquered by Spain. Congress responded by appropriating $100,000 to meet the cost of diplomatic missions to these new Latin American nations. The United States formally recognized Colombia and Mexico in 1822, Chile and the United Provinces of La Plata in 1823, and Peru in 1826.

Independence and recognition for Brazil followed a different course. Brazilian independence had its roots in the Iberian upheaval caused by the Napoleonic invasion of 1807. Under British protection, the Portuguese royal family fled—with the royal treasury—to Rio de Janeiro, which became the capital of the Portuguese empire. The United States established relations with the displaced Portuguese court in 1810. The royal family adjusted well to its new situation and was reluctant to return to Portugal even after the Napoleonic threat ended. A liberal revolt in Portugal in 1820 led to a demand that the royal family return. King João, once again with the royal treasury in tow, left Brazil in April 1821, leaving his son Pedro as regent. When the Portuguese government repeatedly pressed Pedro to return as well, he instead declared Brazil independent in September 1822 and had himself crowned emperor of Brazil in December. Pedro—with significant British aid—quickly overcame the limited Portuguese resistance. The next step was to seek recognition by the United States. The U.S. government delayed at first, put off by the monarchical character of the Brazilian political system, doubts about its political stability, and uncertainty about the Brazilian attitude toward the slave trade. The United States soon overcame its initial reluctance and extended recognition in May 1824.

The events and discussions influencing the U.S. recognition process also shaped the environment that would produce the Monroe Doctrine. The United States had extended recognition despite the European powers' opposition to recognition and Britain's refusal to cooperate. The U.S. willingness to pursue a unilateral policy reflected growing conviction about the uniqueness of the "American" (that is, New World) experience and of a hemispheric identity resulting from a common history and aspirations. The U.S. commitment to neutrality exhibited the dual concern of remaining aloof from European affairs and of preventing or reducing European interference in the affairs of the western hemisphere. Some in the United States flattered themselves that the Latin American revolutionaries were following the model of the

American Revolution and that independence would lead to a hemispheric family of democratic nations.

The basic principles that would ultimately take the form of the Monroe Doctrine represented the refinement of this sense of American uniqueness as well as a conviction that the United States was destined to expand. In his so-called "large policy" of 1808 Jefferson envisioned a cooperative effort between the United States and an independent Spanish America to "exclude all European influence from this hemisphere." U.S. officials regularly expressed fears that the chronic problems of Spain might lead to the loss of part of the Spanish New World empire to a more powerful European nation; a British takeover of Cuba was a particular concern. Even U.S. trade attitudes fed into the Monroe Doctrine; the U.S. desire to penetrate Latin American markets included a desire to reduce European—especially British—trade in the region. The unilateral recognition of rebellious colonies in the face of European opposition was a preview of principles which would soon be enunciated more formally.

Actions taken by the European powers formed the immediate background to the formulation of the Monroe Doctrine. The conservative alliance of European powers that grew out of the Congress of Vienna was dedicated to the suppression of liberal movements and sanctioned the intervention by France in 1823 in Spain to put down a liberal movement and restore the Bourbon monarchy to full power. There was fear in the United States that this alliance might take the additional step of helping the Spanish monarchy restore control over its American colonies. While President Monroe and Secretary of State Adams saw little prospect of that happening, they were concerned about British intentions in the hemisphere. Another European threat came from a much different direction. Russia was moving down the Pacific Coast, expanding its North American possessions from Alaska to the northern boundaries of the Spanish empire. This Russian action posed a threat to U.S. plans for the region resulting from the Adams-Onís Treaty of 1819.

As had been the case with recognition of Latin American colonies, the United States at first considered cooperative action with Britain. Britain was distancing itself from the other European powers and had its own trade and territorial plans to defend in the hemisphere. In August 1823, Britain proposed to the United States a joint declaration based on the principles that Spanish recovery of its colonies was unacceptable and that there should be no transfer of colonies to another European power. Monroe gave serious consideration to the plan but finally rejected it after Secretary of State Adams came out in strong support of a unilateral statement. Britain also lost interest in the project after the French government indicated in October that it would not support an effort to reconquer Spain's colonies.

Monroe set down what would become known as his "doctrine" in his annual message to Congress in December 1823. The president did not consider his declaration of principles as a "doctrine" and did not even present them as a coherent package in his message. Basically the doctrine revolved around two principles or concepts: noncolonization and the "two spheres." Monroe declared that the nations of the western hemisphere had achieved a "free and independent condition" and therefore could no longer be considered as "subjects for future colonization by any European power." Included implicitly in the message was the principle that no transfers of existing colonial possessions from one European power to another would be acceptable to the United States.

In his two-spheres principle, Monroe maintained that the political system of Europe was "essentially different" from that of the Americas. Any effort to extend the European system into the western hemisphere would be viewed by the United States "as dangerous to our peace and safety." Monroe, however, also offered to reciprocate. The United States would not interfere in the internal concerns of any European power nor would it interfere with existing European colonies.

The response to the Monroe Doctrine was mixed. While it represented a bold challenge to the European powers, the United States lacked the military and especially naval strength to support this boldness. Indeed, the British Royal Navy was the effective — if unofficial — enforcer of the Doctrine for most of the nineteenth century. While the European powers were generally contemptuous of the pretensions they saw in the Doctrine, they did not respond officially to it. Latin American reaction to the Doctrine was even more uncertain. Many in Latin America linked it to U.S. efforts at expansion and penetration of Latin American markets; others mistakenly concluded that the United States was interested in constructing an inter-American system of alliances. While the Doctrine reflected and encouraged the growing nationalism in the United States, even some of its supporters feared that it might lead to military conflict with the European powers or military alliances with the Latin American nations. A congressional resolution approving the Doctrine died without action in the House of Representatives and was never even considered by the Senate. Monroe himself did not consider the Doctrine a long-term policy and never invoked it in any specific case; in fact, it essentially lay dormant until its revival in the 1840s in connection with expansion.

Trade considerations had played a role in both the U.S. policy of recognition toward Latin America and the formulation of the Monroe Doctrine. The United States equated the European presence in Latin America with restrictions on U.S. trade. Britain—the principal competitor of the United States for Latin American markets—followed the U.S. lead in recognition and implicitly supported the Doctrine for much the same reasons. The opening of Latin American markets did not produce the trade boom which many Americans expected. U.S. exports to Latin America showed a modest upward trend in the early decades of independence, but much of that trade was directed toward Cuba which was still under Spanish control. U.S. exports to Europe were far more important to the U.S. economy than were those to Latin America; in fact, U.S. exports to Britain alone regularly exceeded all exports to Latin America. U.S. imports followed a similar pattern. Although Britain retained the dominant trading role in Latin America, its optimistic views about the trade potential of an independent Latin America were not realized. Both U.S. and British commercial interests encountered the same limitations in trying to expand their trade with newly independent Latin America: restricted domestic demand, antiquated internal transportation, political instability, the pursuit of chaotic economic and financial policies by the new governments, irregularity of shipments, and competition from smugglers.

The Case of Texas

Meanwhile, U.S. expansionism continued unabated. The rapidly growing population continued to push the frontier to the south and west, into a confrontation with Spain's heir in the borderlands, Mexico. Independent Mexico suffered from endemic political instability, chronic financial problems, and an acquisitive neighbor with apparently unlimited territorial ambitions. The next target for U.S. expansionism was obvious: Texas, the "unfinished business" of the Adams-Onís Treaty of 1819.

Just as Spain in the eighteenth century had tried to establish an Indian buffer against expansion in the North, Mexico resorted to a similar policy by trying to establish an Anglo buffer to protect the Mexican heartland. Under the plan, immigrants from the United States would be attracted to Texas by the prospects of cheap land and tax exemptions. Once there, they would be detached from their loyalty to the United States, eventually becoming "Mexicanized" to the extent of embracing Catholicism and giving up their slaves.

This plan went immediately awry. The new arrivals showed great interest in the land but none in acculturation, retaining their Protestantism, their language, and their slaves despite efforts by the national government to abolish slavery. The "buffer" soon turned into a "beachhead," and worried Mexican officials proclaimed a ban on further immigration from the United States in 1830. The ban, however, was weakly enforced and largely ignored. From 1834 on, a general drive for political centralization in Mexico under General Santa Anna added to the increasing restiveness of the new settlers. When Santa Anna attempted to increase his control over Texas, revolution broke out in October 1835; despite major political and military problems, the rebels — including some of the local Mexican population — proclaimed the independence of Texas in March 1836. After a lengthy retreat, the Texas army under Sam Houston inflicted an overwhelming defeat on the Mexican forces at the Battle of San Jacinto in April 1836, capturing Santa Anna. The Mexican leader signed a treaty recognizing the independence of Texas, an action he promptly repudiated after being released to return to Mexico.

The United States had officially followed an ambiguous role in the Texas affair. The U.S. government maintained a neutral position and even ordered strict enforcement of the existing neutrality laws. Nevertheless, Mexican officials as well as opponents of expansionism in the United States were skeptical about these claims of neutrality. Mexican authorities were convinced that the U.S. government had encouraged immigration into Texas with a view toward ultimately annexing the area. Repeated overtures by the United States to purchase Mexico in the 1820s and 1830s seemed to support the Mexican contention that Texas had been the object of an expansionist plot directed from the United States. Houston's long friendship with President Andrew Jackson was well known and added to these suspicions. In fact, the Texas rebels encountered little opposition from U.S. officials in soliciting donations, floating loans, purchasing supplies, or recruiting volunteers in the United States.

The eagerness displayed by an independent Texas for annexation was sufficient confirmation for most Mexicans of a U.S. plot. However, incorporation did not come immediately. While the United States recognized the independence of Texas in March 1837, there were both domestic and foreign problems associated with annexation. Some U.S. opponents of annexation shared the Mexican view that the developments in Texas were part of a U.S. plot, in this case a conspiracy by Southern slave owners to expand the area of slavery. This linkage aggravated growing sectional disagreements between North and South. Mexico's refusal to recognize Texas independence also posed major problems. Annexation, therefore, would constitute territorial aggression and an act of war, in the view of Mexican leaders. As early as 1836 Mexico was assembling a force in Matamoros with the official purpose of reconquering Texas. A political reorganization of the Mexican republic in December 1836 included the establishment of a "department of Texas." Even if Mexico had been prepared to recognize Texas independence, there was still disagreement over its southern boundary. Texas claimed the Rio Grande as its border, a position for which there was scant historical precedent or support; Mexico insisted on the Nueces River, considerably farther to the north.

An independent Republic of Texas therefore posed major diplomatic problems for all parties involved. As the spurned suitor, Texas officially withdrew its offer for annexation in October 1838 and began to entertain its own ideas of an empire stretching to the Pacific. Texas—which had once been unfinished business for the United States—now became unfinished business for Mexico. The recovery of Texas became deeply enmeshed in Mexico's volatile factional politics; Mexican leaders felt compelled to take a hard line on Texas or risk being thrown out of office. Mexican forces briefly retook San Antonio on two different occasions in 1842 but soon withdrew. These forays only served to provoke an equally unsuccessful counterattack by the Texans on the Mexican town of Mier, in Tamaulipas state.

An independent Texas also posed problems for the United States. The unsettled differences between Texas and Mexico might lead to a major conflict which would ultimately involve the United States. An independent Texas was also an invitation to meddling by European powers. Rebuffed by the United States, Texas leaders turned to Europe, in particular Britain and France, for diplomatic recognition and commercial ties. Expansionists in the United States had warned for decades that another American republic on the North American continent would lead to European intervention. Worse, the problems in annexing Texas might interfere with expansionist plans in other areas such as Oregon or Cuba.

Manifest Destiny

When the Texas question was raised again a few years later, it was in a broader
concept of expansionism known as Manifest Destiny and with a revived Monroe Doctrine for support. Although the former term was not used until 1845,
the concept itself had been evolving since the earliest years of colonization.
The thinking behind it was similar to that which had produced the Monroe
Doctrine. The people of the United States believed that they had developed
a new and better society and that God had singled them out to spread the benefits of republicanism and economic opportunity to undeveloped or more
backward areas. Thus U.S. expansionism was not simply a variant of European imperialism; rather, it enjoyed divine sanction because it involved extending the geographical area of freedom. The revival of the Monroe Doctrine
complemented the growing spirit of Manifest Destiny. The United States had
largely ignored the Doctrine despite interventions by Spain (1829) and France
(1838) in Mexico and ongoing interference in the La Plata region by France
and Britain in the late 1830s and early 1840s. European involvement in Texas
and U.S. designs on territory extending to the Pacific Coast revived interest in
the doctrine.

Manifest Destiny and the annexation of Texas came to the forefront in 1844.
The reaction in Texas over the initial rejection of annexation had run its
course, and the ongoing financial and military problems of the republic encouraged new efforts at union. On the U.S. side there was still strong opposition because of the slavery issue. When connected with the acquisition of
territories on the Pacific, however, acquiring Texas became increasingly attractive. Still, this new effort stumbled badly at the start; the U.S. Senate overwhelmingly rejected an annexation treaty in April 1844. Resistance from
northern states to the expansion of slavery figured prominently in the defeat,
but election year politics in 1844 were the most important reason for the lop-
sided rejection.

The presidential campaign that undid the treaty would soon produce a situation that would culminate in the annexation of Texas. The Whig Party candidate, Henry Clay, had opposed annexation on the grounds that it would
mean war with Mexico. James K. Polk, the Democratic candidate, campaigned
on an expansionist platform calling for the "reoccupation of Oregon and the
reannexation of Texas." When Polk narrowly won the election, the outgoing

president, John Tyler, generously interpreted the results as a mandate. Tyler had long supported annexation but recognized the difficulty of trying to get two-thirds of the Senate to approve an annexation treaty. He circumvented this problem by supporting a joint resolution in Congress which required only a simple majority in both houses; even so, it narrowly passed the Senate by a vote of twenty-seven to twenty-five. Tyler dispatched the resolution to the Republic of Texas on 3 March 1845, his last day in office.

Despite last minute efforts by Mexican officials to mollify Texans through belated recognition, the Texans and Polk were intent on incorporation into the Union. On 4 July 1845, Texas voted for annexation. Although the United States had wished to pursue a diplomatic solution, the Texas question had become part of a broader expansionist plan being pursued by Polk. The president was moving toward a resolution — or showdown — with Britain over the Oregon boundary and was determined to acquire California as well. In November 1845, he ordered John Slidell, a Democratic congressman from Louisiana who spoke Spanish, to negotiate a comprehensive settlement of borderlands problems. Polk instructed his emissary to get satisfaction for financial claims by U.S. citizens against the Mexican government, to obtain recognition of the Rio Grande boundary, and to purchase as much of the Mexican provinces of New Mexico and California as possible. Slidell arrived in Mexico when the administration of President Herrera was in its final days; Herrera's forced resignation on December 29 brought to the presidency the hardliner General Mariano Paredes, who made it clear that there would be no negotiations.

The failure of the Slidell mission represented the last chance to settle peacefully the outstanding issues between the United States and Mexico. The United States had begun its military preparations even before Texas acted on the offer of annexation. In June 1845, Polk had ordered General Zachary Taylor to move his troops into Texas to repel any Mexican invasion attempt. Taylor marched to the Nueces River but did not cross into the disputed area to the south. After the failure of the Slidell mission, however, Taylor moved his forces south to the Rio Grande, where Mexico was also concentrating its troops. In late April, Mexican troops moved north of the Rio Grande and attacked a detachment of U.S. dragoons, leaving several Americans dead. Polk was already working on the outline of a war message when news of the attack reached Washington. On 13 May 1846, the United States officially declared war on Mexico.

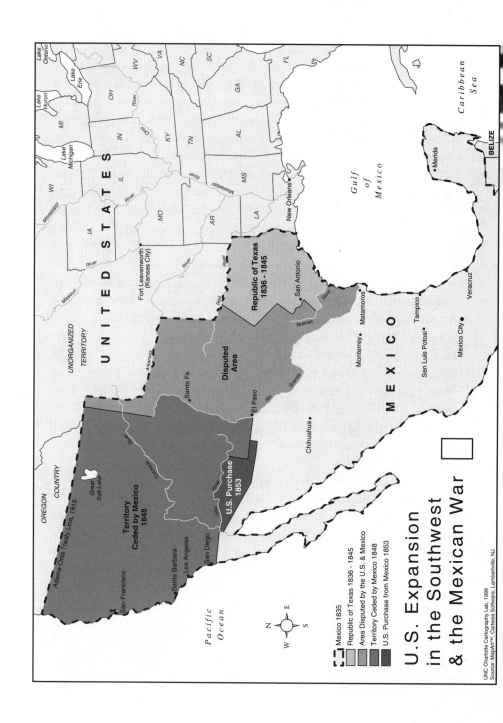

U.S. Expansion in the Southwest & the Mexican War

Mexico 1835
Republic of Texas 1836 - 1845
Area Disputed by the U.S. & Mexico
Territory Ceded by Mexico 1848
U.S. Purchase from Mexico 1853

UNC Charlotte Cartography Lab, 1999
Source: MapArt™, Cartesia Software, Lambertville, NJ.

Neither the United States nor Mexico was well prepared for the conflict. The United States greatly underestimated the logistical difficulties of waging an offensive struggle at a great distance from its principal resource centers. The United States had done virtually nothing to increase the size of its armed forces despite the fact that it was pursuing an aggressive foreign policy that courted confrontation, not only with Mexico but also with Britain. Mexico was counting on the advantages of fighting a defensive war and believed—incorrectly—that Britain and France would provide support. Mexico could not exploit its initial numerical advantage and suffered major supply problems despite fighting on its home soil. U.S. forces under Taylor successfully attacked into northern Mexico, but did not put sufficient pressure on the Mexican heartland to compel Mexico to negotiate. The United States then opened a second front by landing at Veracruz and attacking overland to Mexico City, which fell to U.S. forces under General Winfield Scott in September 1847.

Polk had hoped for a brief war and had been seeking negotiations from the beginning of the conflict. To facilitate negotiations Polk had sent a special representative, Nicholas Trist, to accompany the Veracruz expedition. Trist feuded with General Scott, found it difficult to get Mexican officials to negotiate, and received a recall notice from Polk in October 1847. A change in government in Mexico City, however, led to an offer to resume discussions, so Trist ignored his recall and dealt with the new officials. The result was the Treaty of Guadalupe Hidalgo, signed in February 1848. It provided for recognition of the Rio Grande boundary and the transfer of the Mexican provinces of California and New Mexico in exchange for U.S. payment of $15 million and assumption of claims by U.S. citizens against the Mexican government up to a total of $3.25 million. Polk was outraged that Trist had ignored his recall, but could not afford politically to reject a treaty that incorporated his own goals. Polk submitted it to the Senate, where it won easy approval in March 1848.

Point-Counterpoint: The Mexican War

"It was a premeditated and predetermined affair, the war of the United States on Mexico; it was the result of a deliberately calculated scheme of robbery on the part of the superior power. There were at Washington enough unprincipled men high in office . . . who were willing to lay aside all notions of right and wrong in the matter, and unblushingly to take whatever could be secured solely upon the principle of might. Mex-

ico, poor, weak, struggling to secure for herself a place among the nations, is now to be humiliated, kicked, cuffed, and beaten by the bully on
her northern border, whose greatest pride is christian liberty with pu-
ritan antecedents, whose greatest principle at this time finds exercise in
hunting about for plausible pretexts to steal from a weaker neighbor a
fine slice of lands suitable for slave labor."

—*Hubert Howe Bancroft,* History of Mexico, 1824–1861 *(San Francisco:
The History Company Publishers, 1883–1888), vol. 5, 307–08.*

"If our statesmen had been perceptive enough to see things as they were
and if they had recognized the legitimacy of the secession of Texas, both
the war with Texas—with its shameful and ruinous consequences—and
the struggle with the United States—which was its inevitable result—
would have been avoided. . . . If blind and foolish patriotism—or rather,
the contending factions in Mexico—had not converted the Texas question into a political weapon to discredit each other with mutual accusations of treason, great calamities could have been avoided. . . . The
treaty [of Guadalupe Hidalgo] was finally signed on February 2 [1848].
We gave up what was, in fact, already lost: California, New Mexico, Texas
and the part of Tamaulipas beyond the Bravo [Rio Grande]. The rest was
returned to us shortly and with an indemnity of fifteen million pesos.
This was not the price of the territory given up; that was not possible,
because nothing was given up to the Americans which they did not already possess. . . . It was a painful but not an ignominious agreement."

—*Justo Sierra,* Evolución política del pueblo mexicano *(Mexico: Consejo
Nacional para La Cultura y Las Artes, 1993), 222, 239, 255.*

In the afterglow of these successes, the supporters of Manifest Destiny could
not foresee that their optimism about the territorial expansion of the country would soon give way to anxiety about incorporating the new areas into the
union. The growing sectional controversy would soon bring an end to expansionist plans targeting the Caribbean and Central America. Most U.S. citizens could little appreciate the long-term negative impact that the war with
Mexico would have on U.S.-Latin American relations. On the contrary, they
saw it as a glorious and relatively easy victory, vindication for their belief that

unique U.S. political institutions justified a special role in the Americas. For Mexico the war was a national trauma that would embitter relations with the United States for generations. For the rest of Latin America, it was a preview of the U.S. feelings of superiority and of the disparity in power between the United States and Latin America that would characterize future relations.

CHAPTER 2

REGIONAL POWER AND
EMERGING IMPERIALISM, 1848-1898

Vignette: The Water Witch Incident

While U.S. interests in South America were primarily commercial, the United States almost wound up in a military conflict with an unlikely foe, Paraguay's long-time dictator [1841–1862], Carlos Antonio López. The United States signed a treaty of commerce and navigation with Paraguay in 1853, but problems developed in its final ratification. As the United States grew increasingly impatient about treaty implementation, an incident occurred which precipitated U.S. action. In February 1855 Paraguayan forces fired on the U.S. naval exploration and survey vessel, *Water Witch*, which López had ordered out of Paraguayan waters. The United States government had dispatched the lightly-armed vessel in early 1853 to explore the Paraná River, which made up part of the boundary between Paraguay and Brazil. The commander of the *Water Witch*, Lieutenant Thomas Jefferson Page, had received permission from the López government to ascend the Paraná, but exceeded his authorization by entering into Brazilian territory. Page had also become involved in the dispute between López and the U.S. Consul in Asunción, Edward Hopkins, who were feuding over Hopkins' personal business activities. López was also distracted by a potential war with Brazil. When the *Water Witch* began a second ascent of the Paraná in February 1855, it was fired on by Paraguayan gunners at the Itapiru fortress, near the confluence of the Paraná and Paraguay Rivers. The Paraguayans fired several warning shots before directing their fire at the U.S. vessel.

An outraged Lieutenant Page—who was not on the *Water Witch* at the time of the attack—went to Montevideo, Uruguay, to consult with the commander of U.S. naval forces in the region, Commodore William Salter, who declined to take action. In fact the U.S. government did not respond until the spring of 1858 when the Congress authorized President James Buchanan to use force to obtain redress from the Paraguayan government. The United States demanded an apology, an indemnity for the one U.S. sailor killed, and ratification of the 1853 treaty or a new commercial treaty. To back up its demands, the United States assembled a fleet of eighteen vessels—the largest flotilla ever assembled by the U.S. Navy to that date—with instructions to blockade Paraguay and occupy its capital of Asunción if negotiations failed. This unexpected show of force alarmed not only López but also Paraguay's neighbors. Argentina, Brazil, and Uruguay offered to mediate, an offer promptly rejected by the United States. The United States did accept mediation by the leader of the Argentine confederation, Justo José de Urquiza. López gave into all U.S. demands, paying a $10,000 indemnity and ratifying a new commercial treaty in 1859. The incident reflected the nonexpansionist interests of the United States in Latin America as well as its growing willingness—and ability—to project its power in the hemisphere.

Based on Robert D. Wood, The Voyage of the Water Witch *(Labyrinthos, 1985).*

The war against Mexico had resulted in the acquisition of more than 500,000 square miles of territory. The desire for further territorial expansion continued, both as a part of U.S. official policy and as a result of private ambition, but the major task for the United States in the second half of the nineteenth century involved the consolidation of its enormous territory into a coherent nation. While attempts to add yet more land continued, the unification of the nation—especially through improved communications and transportation— was the driving force for much of its Latin American policy.

The success of U.S. expansionism in the 1840s both encouraged additional expansion in the 1850s and complicated efforts to acquire new territory. The emergence of the United States as a Pacific Coast power followed by the discovery of gold in California highlighted the need for improved transportation and communications. U.S. interest in new transit routes focused attention on Central America and the Isthmus of Tehuantepec in southern Mexico. Overland transportation dictated the construction of a transcontinental railroad; the projected southern route for such a railroad convinced many Americans of the importance of acquiring additional territory in northern Mexico. However, any effort toward territorial expansion became engulfed immediately in the larger controversy over extending the area of slavery. The Compromise of 1850 and the doctrine of "popular sovereignty" encouraged many supporters of Manifest Destiny to believe that the sectional controversy over slavery would not be a major obstacle to continued expansion; this optimistic assessment soon had to yield to the growing threat of national disunity.

Further Attempts at Expansion in Mexico

Problems with defining the boundary established by the Treaty of Guadalupe Hidalgo opened the door to the acquisition of yet another bit of Mexican territory: the Mesilla Valley north of El Paso. General Santa Anna had returned to the presidency, and his need for money was so great that he was prepared to take the highly unpopular action of selling national territory. The Gadsden Purchase, as it became known, added almost 30,000 square miles to the United States at a cost of $10,000,000. This potential route for a railroad to the Pacific Coast was the only territory added to the United States in the period between the U.S.-Mexican War and the U.S. Civil War.

President James Buchanan offered to purchase the border states of Baja California, Sonora, and part of Chihuahua for $12,000,000, but the United States was unable to acquire any more land. However, the McLane-Ocampo Treaty of 1859 did provide the United States with perpetual transit rights across the Isthmus of Tehuantepec as well as two routes across northern Mexico. The Treaty, which included favorable agreements on trade as well, was nevertheless rejected by the U.S. Senate, with voting along sectional lines.

Filibusters

With the sectional controversy restricting official efforts at expansion, unofficial and unauthorized efforts achieved greater prominence. Filibustering expeditions were launched against targets long sought by the supporters of Manifest Destiny: Cuba, Mexico, and Central America. The principal figure in filibustering activities against Cuba was General Narciso López. Born in Venezuela, López had accumulated extensive political and military experience in the wars for independence and later in Cuba and Spain. As an exile in the United States, López organized three expeditions aimed at liberating Cuba from Spanish control. Opposed by both U.S. and Spanish officials, all failed and López himself was executed in 1851 by Spanish authorities.

Chaotic conditions in Mexico and Central America in the 1850s attracted filibusters as well as official U.S. attempts at expansion. California in the Gold Rush era offered a prime recruiting ground for filibusters; the new arrivals were typically young, male, eager for adventure, and looking for quick wealth. Filibustering activities — often under the guise of "colonization" schemes — were directed at Baja California and Sonora. The leading figure in these activities was William Walker, who would gain even greater notoriety for his filibustering in Central America. Walker first attempted a colonization scheme in Sonora in June 1853, but Mexican officials forced his return to California. In October 1853 Walker led an expedition to conquer Baja California and Sonora and to establish an independent republic. After occupying the undefended capital of Baja California, La Paz, Walker overreached himself by invading Sonora with a force of approximately 100 men. After his "army" disintegrated, Walker returned to the United States in May 1854. Indicted for violating the neutrality laws, Walker went to trial in October 1854; after deliberating for eight minutes, the jury returned a verdict of not guilty. Walker then turned his attention to Nicaragua, an area of heightened interest as a result of its use as a transit point to California during the Gold Rush. In May 1855 Walker departed San Francisco with fifty-eight men to intervene in the political conflict between liberals and conservatives in Nicaragua. After helping to install a liberal president and securing his own appointment as commander-in-chief of the liberal forces, Walker deposed the liberal president and had himself elected president in June 1856. He was quickly confronted with a military coalition comprised of the four other Central American countries. He was also opposed by the powerful U.S. entrepreneur, Cornelius Vanderbilt, whose transportation monopoly in Nicaragua was threatened by Walker's actions. Thrown out of the country, he launched additional expeditions against Nicaragua in 1857 and 1860, finally surrendering to the British, who were themselves still involved in Central America. The British delivered Walker to Honduran officials, who executed him in September 1860.

Official U.S. Interest in Cuba and Central America

Much of the official opposition to filibustering was based on a concern that it interfered with official efforts at expansion and promotion of commerce, especially in regard to Cuba and Central America. Expansionists had coveted Cuba throughout the nineteenth century, differing only on whether aggressive measures should be taken to acquire it or whether a passive approach of letting Cuba "gravitate" to the United States would succeed. Cubans themselves first raised the possibility of annexation by the United States with the Monroe administration in 1822, but the United States—fearing opposition from Great Britain—did not pursue the initiative. For southerners, Cuba represented fertile ground for the expansion of a plantation system and slavery. For northerners, Cuba offered growing trade possibilities. By the 1850s, U.S. trade with the island substantially exceeded that of the leading European commercial power, Great Britain, and that of Spain, which still controlled Cuba, its "ever faithful isle." Spanish efforts to mobilize British and French support for its control of Cuba also worried the U.S. government.

Cubans and North Americans envisioned the terms of annexation very differently. Cubans anticipated the admission of Cuba as a state in a process similar to that of Texas in 1845. U. S. policymakers, however, were thinking in terms of replacing Spain in a colonial relationship to the island. Racism and disdain for the abilities of the Cubans to govern themselves precluded the equality of status within the Union to which the Cubans aspired.

While Spain had rejected a U.S. offer in 1848 to purchase Cuba for $100 million, President Pierce's administration was greatly interested in acquiring the island. In 1854, U.S. ambassadors to Spain, England, and France met in Ostend, Belgium, and recommended that the United States attempt to purchase Cuba from Spain; if Spain again refused to sell, the ambassadors advised that the United States seize the island. When the secret recommendation became public, it caused a political uproar in the United States, particularly among those who opposed the expansion of slavery.

James Buchanan, who had been U.S. ambassador to England at the time of the Ostend meeting, became the Democratic candidate for the presidency in the election of 1856. His platform, unsurprisingly, called for the annexation of Cuba. He had long emphasized its strategic significance, referring to it as the "Gibraltar" of the Gulf of Mexico. During his campaign, he asserted dramatically that "if I can be instrumental in settling the slavery question . . . , and then add Cuba to the Union, I shall be willing to give up the ghost."[1] However, as president, he failed several times to interest Congress in buying the island. Questions of the potential extension of slavery continued to be troubling in sectional terms. Moreover, in both the northern and southern United States, there was widespread concern that the population of Cuba, so different in both cultural and racial terms, would prove highly difficult to assimilate.

The United States government also maintained an active interest in Central America as a transit route, market, and arena for competition with Great Britain. That European power had been expanding its presence in the region since the colonial period, controlling Belize (British Honduras) and the Mosquito Coast of Nicaragua. The United States had generally ignored this disregard for the Monroe Doctrine until the Gold Rush increased traffic across the isthmus. Renewed concern led to negotiations with Britain in the 1840s. A treaty guaranteeing the United States right of transit across the Isthmus of Panama, the neutrality of the isthmus, and Colombia's sovereignty over the territory was negotiated in 1846 and approved by the Senate in 1848.

Secretary of State John Clayton became personally involved in continuing negotiations in 1850, which led to the Clayton-Bulwer Treaty. This agreement was a laundry list of what the two countries promised not to do. Both pledged not to try to gain exclusive control over an isthmian canal and not to fortify such a canal. Both agreed to guarantee the canal's neutrality. In addition, they agreed not to "occupy, colonize, or exercise dominion" over any part of Central America. Although the United States interpreted the provision on colonization as retroactive and assumed that the British would relinquish their protectorate over the Mosquito Coast, the British bluntly insisted on remaining there as well as in British Honduras. This difference of interpretation led to several incidents, the most serious being the 1854 shelling of Greytown, Nicaragua, by a U.S. warship. Greytown, which had been occupied by the British in 1848, was located at the mouth of San Juan River and controlled an important potential transisthmian canal route. Although the British did withdraw from Nicaragua in 1856, President Buchanan called for the abrogation of the Clayton-Bulwer Treaty in 1857. Terms could not be agreed on, however, and the Treaty remained at the center of Anglo-U.S. affairs in Central America.

Relations with South America

While U.S.-Latin American relations primarily revolved around Cuba, Mexico, and Central America, there were growing connections with countries farther south. The filibusters did not completely ignore South America, although the distances involved made such political buccaneering difficult. A group of about forty Californians set out in 1851 to try to restore exiled president, Juan José Flores, to power in the Andean nation of Ecuador; the effort failed, with fifteen to twenty of the Americans killed. In 1855, Flores attempted to organize a second expedition in the United States but could not attract recruits or financing.

Few major issues troubled U.S.-Brazilian relations in the three decades leading up to the U.S. Civil War despite the political instability that disturbed both countries. U.S. trade with Brazil increased despite problems with Brazilian maritime regulations and unsuccessful efforts to negotiate a new commercial treaty.

The slavery issue which figured so prominently in U.S. domestic politics also affected U.S.-Brazilian relations and injected Britain—the principal rival of the United States in Brazil—into the relationship. Britain had assumed world leadership in suppression of the international slave trade and had pressured Brazil into agreeing to abolish the trade by 1830 as part of the price demanded for recognition. When the agreement expired in 1845, Brazil refused an extension; Britain responded by passing legislation unilaterally extending the ban on the slave trade and requiring that all alleged violations be tried in British naval courts. In 1850 Britain began entering Brazilian territorial waters to search for violators. The profitability of this slave trade had attracted U.S. shippers, particularly from New England, who had become major suppliers for Brazil. Although U.S. diplomatic and naval officials sought to stop American involvement, British insistence on broad powers to search and seize vessels and cargos revived a longstanding problem between the two countries that had never been resolved. U.S.-British rivalry in Brazil also lessened U.S. enthusiasm for strict enforcement since many claimed that Britain was exploiting the issue to promote its commercial position. The issue declined in diplomatic significance after Brazil passed a tough new law in 1850 declaring the slave trade to be piracy.

U.S. involvement with the nations of the Rio de la Plata revolved almost exclusively around trade. The great distance between the United States and the region exempted the area from the pressures of U.S. expansion. The United States did not even exhibit concern about applying the Monroe Doctrine in the Rio de la Plata. The region's internal and external problems led to military interventions by both France and England in the 1830s and 1840s, with the British seizing the Malvinas [Falkland] Islands—claimed by Argentina—in 1833 without action by the United States. Regional rivalries, European intervention, and internal strife in Argentina between the port of Buenos Aires and the interior complicated U.S. efforts to promote trade. In 1853, the United States signed a treaty of commerce and navigation with the confederation comprised of Argentina's interior provinces. U.S. representatives also attempted unsuccessfully to mediate between the confederation and Buenos Aires, but Argentine unification would finally come through military action. The United States also signed a treaty of commerce and navigation with Paraguay in 1853, but problems developed in its final ratification. After a brief military altercation between the United States and Paraguay, the two countries approved a new commercial treaty in 1859. By the late 1850s the United States had commercial treaties in force with Argentina, Paraguay, and Uruguay. The United States and the nations of the Rio de la Plata had avoided a military conflict in the 1850s; all would find themselves involved in major regional military struggles or civil wars in the next decade which interrupted the normal development of relations.

The U.S. Civil War

Secession and civil war in the United States interrupted the process of territorial acquisition and commercial expansion that had characterized U.S. ambitions in Latin America since the 1820s. Both the United States and the recently established Confederate States of America put primary emphasis on their relations with Europe. Both were little interested in Latin American affairs except for Mexico and the Caribbean-Central American region. Mexico in particular figured prominently in the diplomatic activities of both the Confederacy and the United States. Texas, a Confederate state, shared about half of the northern Mexican border. The Confederacy also had western designs on the U.S. territories of New Mexico and Arizona and parts of northern Mexico, especially Baja California. Moreover, the Texas-Mexico border offered the most promising way for the Confederacy to circumvent the Union naval blockade.

The Confederate diplomatic commissioner to Mexico, John T. Pickett, had served as U.S. consul at Veracruz. He had personal ties to Mexican president Benito Juárez, leader of the winning liberal faction in Mexico's recent civil war. Pickett believed that the Confederacy could purchase diplomatic recognition from Mexico for about $1 million. However, when Pickett arrived in Mexico City, he found strong pro-Union sentiment. This sentiment reflected the widely held view that U.S. expansionism had historically been driven by southern slave owners and that the Confederacy was plotting to seize additional Mexican territory. Pickett tried to ease these fears by assuring the Juárez government that the Confederacy had no such ambitions and by hinting that part of the territory lost by Mexico in 1848 might be returned in the event of a Confederate victory. Officials of the Juárez government, however, had been routinely intercepting Pickett's diplomatic correspondence and knew that talk of retrocession was simply a political maneuver. In addition, the U.S. minister in Mexico City, Thomas Corwin, had been attempting to block Confederate inroads and had been working with the financially strapped Juárez administration on a loan from the U.S. government. Pickett, frustrated, was eventually expelled by the Juárez government after a fight with a Union sympathizer led to his arrest.

Confederate diplomacy in the key northern border area enjoyed considerably more success in the capable hands of José A. Quintero, born in Cuba but a Confederate citizen. Quintero developed good relations with Santiago Vidaurri who controlled much of the region immediately south of the Rio Grande. Vidaurri actively promoted Confederate trade between Mexico and Texas for political as well as personal financial benefit. The trade flourished throughout the war despite bandit attacks and the efforts of both the U.S. and Mexican governments to suppress it. However, U.S. and Confederate relations with Mexico underwent a major change in 1862 as a result of the French intervention discussed later in the chapter.

The Caribbean–Central American region was of significance to both the Union and the Confederacy as a destination or way station for ships running the Union blockade of Confederate ports and also as a target for future expansion. Havana was a particularly popular port of call. The rise in cotton prices caused by the war encouraged greater production and export of the crop in Guatemala, El Salvador, and Nicaragua, often financed with northern money. Citizens of both the Union and the Confederacy viewed Central America as a target for expansion; southerners considered it a superior area for plantation agriculture while northerners thought it would make an excellent place for establishing colonies of freed slaves from the United States. A limited number of Confederate privateers also operated out of Central American ports.

The end of the Civil War in 1865 did not immediately end Confederate involvement in Latin America; even before the war was officially over, Confederate exiles began to move south. A number of factors led to the Confederate exodus. The political and legal treatment that would be given ex-Confederates was uncertain; so-called "general" amnesties issued in 1863 and 1865 made important exceptions for those who had held civil office under the Confederacy or who had taxable property in excess of $20,000. Moreover, the economic devastation of the war had left many with little economic future in the southern United States. Some exiles even dreamed of continuing what they regarded as the war for southern independence from exile.

Mexico and Brazil were the principal destinations of most Confederate exiles, some of whom began their exodus even before the war concluded in 1865. Mexico attracted the greatest number of former Confederates despite a civil war there between the liberals led by Juárez and the French-supported "empire" of Maximilian. Although various colonization schemes developed, most who sought exile in Mexico came individually or in small groups. Both the liberal government of Juárez and the imperial government of Maximilian would permit former Confederates to enter the country as long as they were unarmed and conducted themselves in a peaceful manner.

The exile movement to Brazil, where slavery was still legal, was more organized. Companies or associations in the southern states facilitated resettlement. The Brazilian government provided loans for the passage to Brazil, temporary housing for exiles in Rio, and free transportation to their final destinations. Brazilian authorities also provided tax breaks, inexpensive land, exemption from military service, and easy access to citizenship. Although the Brazilian government generally had a good record for carrying out its promises, most of the colonists did not want to become Brazilian citizens and found it difficult to adjust to the hardships of frontier life in a foreign country. In both Mexico and in Brazil, most of the Confederate colonists soon grew disenchanted with their new countries and returned to the United States.

The Civil War encouraged the major European powers to increase their level of involvement in Latin America. The Spanish moved back into the Dominican Republic in 1861, but were forced out again by a combination of guerrilla warfare and disease in 1865. In 1864, Spain also intervened in Peru, whose independence it had never recognized, by seizing the guano-rich Chincha Islands. In the fighting that followed, Chile, Ecuador, and Bolivia came to Peru's aid. The incident lingered on after the end of the U.S. Civil War, with the United States mediating a settlement in 1871. Interestingly, all participants except the United States referred to the Monroe Doctrine during the struggle.

The most dramatic intervention brought together Britain, France, Spain, and Mexico. The victory of the Mexican liberals under Juárez in the civil war of 1858–1861 did not bring peace but only another civil war and foreign intervention. The accumulation of four decades of financial problems finally forced Juárez in July 1861 to impose a two-year suspension of payments on Mexico's domestic and foreign debts. Napoleon III, the French emperor, saw an opportunity to revive imperial plans in the Americas. Although France, Great Britain, and Spain responded jointly by occupying Veracruz in late 1861 and early 1862, by April, the British and Spanish had realized that the French were interested in more than payment of the Mexican debt. A French army went on to drive Juárez from the Mexican capital; Austrian archduke Ferdinand Maximilian of Hapsburg was installed as emperor in mid-1864. However, Maximilian made the error of implementing liberal policies which quickly alienated his conservative supporters. The new Mexican Empire was soon at a stalemate. Imperial forces controlled the major urban areas but could not inflict a decisive defeat on liberal forces. Faced with the expense of the expedition and with the rising power of neighboring Prussia, Napoleon III began to withdraw French forces in late 1866.

Meanwhile, the end of the U.S. Civil War meant that the United States could abandon the passive position it had taken earlier and reassert the Monroe Doctrine. Following the defeat of the Confederacy in the spring of 1865, the United States monitored affairs in Mexico more closely. With 900,000 troops under arms and 100,000 troops on the U.S.-Mexican border, the United States was in a good position to intervene militarily. While key military figures such as Ulysses Grant and Philip Sheridan called for military action, Secretary of State Seward used diplomatic pressure to get the French and Maximilian out of Mexico. Meanwhile, Sheridan, in command of the U.S. border contingent, kept the military threat alive by putting his troops through public maneuvers. Maximilian's Belgian wife Charlotte, who had taken the name Carlota in her role as Mexican empress, traveled through Europe desperately seeking aid for her husband's cause, but the French had decided to cut their losses. Seward extracted a promise from Napoleon III to withdraw all French troops from Mexico by November 1867, a withdrawal which was completed almost eight months ahead of schedule. Maximilian himself took charge of the battle against Juárez, leading his few Mexican imperial troops north to Querétaro. There he was defeated, taken into custody, tried for various offenses against the Mexican people, and executed. Carlota, whose desperate journey had driven her mad, refused to acknowledge his death. She survived until 1927, a pathetic victim of France's failed imperial designs.

The Post–Civil War Period

In the years immediately following the Civil War, a number of factors distracted U.S. attention from Latin America. The political reconstruction of the country lasted over a decade. The Homestead Act opened up the Great Plains to settlement, providing an internal focus for the frontier movement. The construction of transcontinental railroads reduced the importance of establishing a transit route in Central America. The rapid industrialization of the country required major inputs of human and material resources.

The United States also lacked the military and naval power to support an aggressive foreign policy. The mighty army that had threatened Maximilian in 1865 quickly demobilized. The U.S. Navy went into a similar decline and lagged far behind the navies of the major European powers in making the transition to a "steel-and-steam" force. Between 1867 and 1890, there was little in the way of a foreign threat to the hemisphere that would arouse U.S. concern about the Monroe Doctrine. Britain—the major rival of the United States before 1860—for some time had been more interested in commercial expansion than in territorial expansion. Memories of Maximilian's failed empire and the threat of a unified Germany deterred French action. Germany's political unification and military build-up would ultimately cause concern for the United States, but was not viewed as a problem until the 1890s.

The Civil War did not end U.S. territorial designs. An interest in acquiring parts of northern Mexico produced no positive results but continued into the twentieth century. William Seward, a committed expansionist, continued as secretary of state until 1869. His efforts in Latin America were largely confined, however, to continuing negotiations for a canal route. These came to fruition in 1867 with a Nicaraguan treaty giving the United States a nonexclusive right of transit, and with an 1869 agreement with Colombia providing the United States exclusive rights to construct a canal in Panama. The latter treaty was a clear violation of the Clayton-Bulwer agreement, but the Colombian Senate rejected it in any case. Despite Seward's interest in acquiring islands in the Caribbean, his efforts in this regard were unsuccessful.

The administration of Ulysses Grant continued Seward's interest in the Caribbean. In 1870 Grant submitted a treaty for the annexation of the Dominican Republic, where the Spanish had once again been driven out only five years before, but the Senate decisively rejected it. The outbreak of civil war in Cuba in 1868 offered an opportunity for territorial acquisition, but the United States did not exploit the situation even though the war continued until 1878. Racial attitudes played an important role in rejecting the annexation of the Dominican Republic and refraining from intervention in Cuba; there was strong public opposition to acquiring areas with significant non-white populations.

The Quest for a Canal

The declining interest in territorial expansion was offset by a growing interest in commercial expansion in Latin America. Rapid industrialization and the opening of the Great Plains to commercial agriculture encouraged U.S. producers to place greater emphasis on exports. Periodic downturns in the economy—especially in 1873 and 1893—led many farmers, industrialists, and government officials to conclude that the U.S. domestic market had been saturated. It was therefore essential to economic recovery and growth to develop overseas markets where the surplus could be sold. This goal conflicted with the high tariff policies followed by the United States in the postwar years.

The drive for U.S. commercial expansion again focused attention on Central America as a market, but more importantly as a transit route to the west coast of South America and to Asian markets. The Clayton-Bulwer Treaty of 1850 calling for a joint U.S.-British involvement in any Central American canal had never been popular with the American people, and U.S. officials often acted as if the treaty did not exist. In 1872 President Grant appointed an Interoceanic Canal Commission to study potential sites for a canal. The Commission in 1876 recommended the Nicaraguan route, which could take advantage of natural waterways for most of its course; this recommendation would influence U.S. canal planning for the rest of the century.

U.S. interest and anxiety both quickened when a French company headed by the builder of the Suez Canal, Ferdinand de Lesseps, announced in 1879 that it had received a concession from the Colombian government to construct a canal in Panama. The United States implied that the agreement violated the Monroe Doctrine, although the French government assured the United States that the De Lesseps operation was strictly a private venture. In March 1880, President Rutherford B. Hayes committed the United States to a policy of unilateral U.S. control of any isthmian canal and exerted pressure on Britain to modify or abrogate the Clayton-Bulwer Treaty. When Great Britain rejected any changes, the United States signed a new treaty with Nicaragua in 1884 granting the United States exclusive rights to build a canal in return for a U.S. promise to guarantee Nicaragua's territorial integrity. Although the U.S. Senate refused to ratify the treaty in early 1885, it was prepared to reconsider it when it was withdrawn by the administration of the newly elected president Grover Cleveland. The bankruptcy of the De Lesseps company in 1889 ended the importance of immediate action on a Central American canal; the events of the 1880s, however, had made it clear that the United States was determined to act alone when a final decision on a canal was made.

Pan Americanism

U.S. commercial expansion was also closely connected with the rise of the Pan American movement in the 1880s and 1890s. The leading figure in promoting Pan Americanism was James G. Blaine, secretary of state briefly in 1881 and then again from 1889 to 1892. His call for a Pan American conference during his first period in office was not realized until November 1889. Blaine hoped that such a movement could be used to promote U.S. commercial activity in Latin America, undercut European economic and political involvement, and encourage peaceful settlement of inter-American disputes. Unfortunately, the meeting had little practical result. Although eleven nations, including the United States, signed a treaty for arbitrating international disputes, not a single nation subsequently ratified the agreement.

This inter-American conference demonstrated the difficulties involved in translating good will into concrete actions and institutions. Argentina—competing with the United States economically and politically for leadership in South America—boycotted the opening session, opposed Blaine's election as president of the conference, and refused to participate in a "grand tour" of the United States arranged for conference delegates. Chile, feuding with its neighbors Peru and Bolivia, bitterly opposed the arbitration agreement and refused to sign even the watered-down version passed by the conference. Mexico, despite its close political and economic ties to the United States, also refused to sign the arbitration treaty. All Latin American nations were worried about the prospects of Pan Americanism being used as a mechanism for translating the political and economic views of the United States into hemispheric policy.

The Growth of Imperialism

During the 1890s a number of forces converged to produce a new phase of U.S. expansionism and to complete the transformation of the United States into a world power. The late nineteenth century scramble for colonies by the European nations heightened U.S. nationalism and led many in the United States to equate national greatness with an overseas empire. The United States was on the verge of surpassing Britain as the world's leading industrial power, encouraging U.S. producers to look overseas for markets. There was growing support for a major build-up in U.S. naval forces to protect foreign commerce and project U.S. power overseas; these "navalists" emphasized the need for overseas naval bases, the construction of an isthmian canal, and expansion of the U.S. presence in the Caribbean and the Pacific. Even the intellectual currents of the day such as social Darwinism and geographic determinism supported a more aggressive international posture by the United States and provided rationales for a renewed expansionism that would soon be called the "New Manifest Destiny."

Indications of the changing role of the United States were present in two major incidents in the early 1890s. The first incident grew out of a civil war in Chile in 1891 provoked by a power struggle between the president and congress. U.S.-Chilean relations had deteriorated after the United States opposed Chile's territorial gains at the expense of Peru and Bolivia after the War of the Pacific [1879–1883]; relations suffered even further when the United States supported the Chilean president and the losing side in the civil war. Some hard-drinking U.S. sailors found themselves injected into this volatile situation when they were granted shore leave from the USS *Baltimore* docked at Valparaiso. During a night on the town on 16 October, a group of them became involved in a fight with some of the locals, resulting in two U.S. dead and seventeen injured. The official U.S. version of the event maintained that the sailors had been conducting themselves in an orderly manner when they were the victims of a premeditated attack by civilians who were later joined by Chilean police. While U.S. Secretary of State Blaine attempted to reach a diplomatic settlement, President Harrison and Secretary of the Navy Benjamin Tracy—a navalist and an expansionist—pursued a belligerent course. Harrison threatened to break diplomatic relations and to use military force if Chile did not apologize. Facing a possible war, Chile caved in to U.S. demands, rendering an apology and paying an indemnity of $75,000. While the "*Baltimore Affair*" could have been dealt with in a more low-key manner, the bellicose posture of the United States was a preview of the activist role it would soon take in the Venezuelan boundary controversy of 1895.

The boundary between Venezuela and British Guiana had been in dispute since the colonial period. In 1886, Britain unilaterally claimed territory that Venezuelans believed to be theirs, provoking a break in diplomatic relations. This "expansion" of a European colony attracted the attention of U.S. policymakers as a possible violation of the Monroe Doctrine. The United States initially recommended arbitration, but soon the matter became embroiled in U.S. domestic politics. Republicans and even some Democrats criticized the response of Democratic President Grover Cleveland as pro-British. Diplomatic notes failed to gain any concessions from the British, and for a time there was talk of war. The issue was finally submitted to an arbitration tribunal composed of two representatives from Britain, two from the United States, and one from a neutral country. The tribunal assigned about ninety percent of the disputed territory to Britain. As had been the case with Chile, U.S. actions in the Venezuelan boundary question had embittered relations with the Latin American country involved and had increased the general uneasiness of other countries in the hemisphere over U.S. pretensions to political hegemony.

The forces of the New Manifest Destiny soon focused on a familiar expansionist target: Cuba. The Spanish government had never carried out the reforms it had promised when bringing the ten-year civil war in Cuba to an end in 1878. The Cuban economy was also in decline in the 1890s. The United States had signed a reciprocity treaty in 1891 that led to a major increase in U.S.-Cuban trade and a corresponding rise in sugar production. In 1894, however, the United States imposed a new forty-percent tax on sugar imports; Spain retaliated by canceling the earlier tariff concessions on U.S. exports to the island. Sugar prices plummeted, and prices soared for necessary items from the United States — including foodstuffs.

A new independence movement developed in 1895, producing a bitter civil war which caused widespread death and destruction and threatened the extensive U.S. economic interests on the island. The Cuban elites were horrified at the prospect of the independence movement turning into a social revolution and viewed U.S. intervention as a way of rescuing them from the rebels. At the same time, U.S. policymakers feared that a completely independent Cuba might fall under the influence of some other European power. The sensationalist newspapers of William Randolph Hearst and Joseph Pulitzer dramatized the atrocities committed by the Spaniards who were determined to retain the shriveled remains of their empire; U.S. popular sentiment on behalf of the Cuban rebels was high. In the 1896 presidential election, the victorious Republican candidate, William McKinley, ran on a platform which professed a policy of noninterference in Cuba, consistent with the Monroe Doctrine's declaration that the United States would not interfere with "existing Colonies (sic)."[2] However, he also demanded Cuban independence.

Although Congress pressured McKinley for vigorous action, the new president initially hoped that diplomacy might achieve this goal. A new liberal government in Spain in October 1897 introduced a series of reforms that raised hopes for a peaceful solution to Cuban problems. Spain recalled the controversial commander of Spanish forces in Cuba, General Victoriano "Butcher" Weyler; ended the reconcentration program, under which Cuba's rural population was being relocated; and drew up a comprehensive plan for Cuban autonomy. However, the building diplomatic momentum suffered a major setback when an explosion sank the U.S. battleship *Maine,* prepositioned in Havana harbor for the possible evacuation of U.S. citizens, in February 1898. Although U.S. officials never blamed the sinking on Spanish authorities, the yellow press and U.S. public opinion quickly assigned them responsibility. With pressure for military action growing, McKinley briefly entertained the notion of buying Cuba, a move that almost certainly would have been opposed by the U.S. Congress and the Cuban rebels. In late March the United States made a series of general — at times, vague — demands on the Spanish government: the rapid restoration of peace, absolute autonomy for Cuba, an armistice, and U.S. arbitration if needed. The unstated bottom line of these demands was Cuban independence, a concession which no Spanish

Cuban dead in a trench burial during the Spanish-American–Cuban War.

Courtesy Center for Southwest Research, University of New Mexico [No. 996–019–0009]

government could make and survive. In a message to Congress on 11 April 1898, McKinley requested authorization to employ force to "secure a final termination of hostilities" and the "establishment of a stable government" in Cuba. Congress exceeded the president's request by passing a resolution calling for the independence of Cuba and directing—not authorizing—the president to use force to obtain it. The McKinley administration then issued an ultimatum to Spain to give up control of Cuba by 23 April or face U.S. military action. Spain rejected the ultimatum and broke diplomatic relations, prompting the U.S. Congress to declare war on 25 April. The war resolution contained one important restriction imposed by the anti-imperialists—the Teller Amendment. The amendment stated that the United States had no intention of exercising sovereignty or control over the island beyond that needed for "pacification"; the governing and control of the island would be left to the Cuban people.

The hulk of the U.S. *Maine* in Havana Harbor. Controversy continues to rage about whether the remains showed that the explosion that sank the ship was generated from within or from without.

Courtesy Center for Southwest Research, University of New Mexico [No. 000–244–0815]

One of the most enthusiastic volunteers was Assistant Secretary of the Navy Theodore Roosevelt. He quickly resigned his post to lead a contingent of volunteers, recruited largely from the U.S. West, called the Rough Riders. According to President McKinley's call, this First U.S. Volunteer Cavalry would be "composed exclusively of frontiersmen possessing special qualifications as horsemen and marksmen," but Roosevelt enlisted as well fifty "gentlemen rankers" from Harvard and other Ivy League schools to provide some tone.[3] The Cuban effort was extremely popular despite the loss of lives, which indeed were fewer than most other wars. Still, 5,462 U.S. citizens died in the short conflict, less than 400 of these in combat. The vast majority fell to the tropical diseases that had devastated the French in Haiti almost a century earlier: malaria and yellow fever.

Point-Counterpoint: The Spanish-American-Cuban War

"Once the United States is in Cuba, who will get her out?"

—*José Martí, in Philip S. Foner,* The Spanish-Cuban-American War and the Birth of American Imperialism *(New York: Monthly Review Press, 1972), p. 13.*

"In the face of the present proposal of intervention without previous recognition of independence, it is necessary for us to go a step farther and say we must and will regard such intervention as nothing less than a declaration of war by the United States against the Cuban Revolutionists. . . . Should the United States then declare a protectorate over the island, however provisional or tentative, and seek to extend its authority over the government of Cuba and the Army of Liberation, we would resist with the force of arms as bitterly and tenaciously as we have fought the armies of Spain."

—*Horacio S. Rubens, member of the Cuban military junta, quoted in the* Washington Post, *8 April 1898, in Foner, as above, 258–59.*

"It should be borne in mind from the start that it is far removed from the feelings of the American people and the mind of the President to propose any solution to which the slightest idea of humiliation to Spain could in any way be attached. But no possible intention or occasion to wound the just susceptibilities of the Castilian nation can be discerned in the altogether friendly suggestion that the good offices of the United States may now be lent to the advantage of Spain. . . . the President has no desire to embarrass the Government of Spain by formulating precise proposals. All that is asked or expected is that some safe way may be provided for action which the United States may undertake with justice and self-respect, and that the settlement shall be a lasting one, honorable and advantageous to Spain and to Cuba and equitable to the United States."

—*Instructions of U.S. Secretary of State John Sherman to U.S. Minister to
Spain Stewart L. Woodford, 16 July 1897,* Foreign Relations of the United States,
1898, 561.

Still, despite confusion and poor military preparation, the United States gained a quick and decisive victory. The modernized and expanded U.S. Navy gave a good account of itself, smashing Spanish naval forces in both Cuba and the Philippines. The need for an isthmian canal was demonstrated by the dash of the USS *Oregon,* stationed in San Francisco Bay at the time the *Maine* exploded. Ordered to the Caribbean in March, her voyage around Cape Horn took her 12,000 miles in 67 days, a voyage that would have been cut to 4,000 miles had a canal existed. U.S. land forces in Cuba encountered major logistical problems and considerable resistance from Spanish forces, but U.S. naval victories soon made the land campaign moot, drawing hostilities to a close. The rapid conclusion of the war, the U.S. intrusion in the Philippines, and the U.S. conquest of Puerto Rico as a sidelight to the campaign in Cuba all complicated the peace negotiations. As an indicator of the island's future status, the Cuban rebels were systematically excluded from negotiations to end the fighting as well as the postwar peace conference. The war for Cuban independence had been converted into the "Spanish-American War." The Treaty of Paris signed in December 1898 provided for Cuban independence but only after a military occupation of indefinite duration by the United States. The United States received Puerto Rico and purchased the Philippines for $20 million. The U.S. Senate approved the treaty by a vote of 57 to 27; while there was little disagreement over the provisions relating to Cuba and Puerto Rico, there was considerable opposition to the acquisition of the Philippines.

The war had broad, long-range implications for U.S.-Latin American relations. The United States had acquired a strategic Caribbean possession, Puerto Rico, and effectively controlled the future of Cuba. The two-ocean conflict demonstrated the critical importance of an isthmian canal, heightening U.S. interest in Central America. It also highlighted the significance of a strong navy, which in the future would become a high priority for soon-to-be president Theodore Roosevelt. However, even countries far removed from the fighting, such as Chile and Argentina, worried about the war's effect on the apparent U.S. drive for political and economic hegemony in the hemisphere. The United States had fought to liberate a colony, only to become an imperial power in its own right. The Monroe Doctrine—originally envisioned as a defensive policy—was being transformed into an offensive one. The war not only signaled the arrival of the United States as a world power; it was also the first phase in a more interventionist policy in its traditional region of concern.

CHAPTER 3

THE ERA OF INTERVENTION, 1898–1920

Vignette: The United States versus Mexico —
The Last Punitive Expedition

In February 1917 when the last troops of Pershing's Punitive Expedition marched out of Mexico and into World War I, it was not the end of U.S. military action in Mexico. Despite wartime personnel demands, the U.S. government kept approximately 30,000 troops on the border, and the U.S. Army retained its policy of "hot pursuit" of raiders across the international boundary. Once World War I ended in November 1918, the United States adopted a tougher policy toward the Mexican administration of President Venustiano Carranza whose policies regarding taxation, foreign owned property, and wartime neutrality angered the Wilson administration. The end of the war once again made the U.S.-Mexican border the principal focus of U.S. military activity; by the summer of 1919, there were twenty-four Army posts in Texas alone as well as a newly established border air patrol.

This tougher approach showed itself in June 1919 when forces loyal to Pancho Villa attacked the key border town of Ciudad Juárez, across from El Paso, Texas, causing casualties on the U.S. side. Unlike a similar incident in May 1911 when the United States made no military response, on this occasion the United States quickly reacted with military force. The U.S. commander of the El Paso military district, General James B. Erwin, informed the Mexican federal army commander at Juárez to get his troops out of the way because U.S. forces would be crossing into Juárez to attack Villa's troops. The Mexican commander promptly

Pancho Villa in a characteristically cheerful pose with close associates including one of his most respected generals, Toribio Ortega, on the left side of the photograph.

Courtesy El Paso Public Library

complied, and on the evening of 15 June 1919, approximately 3,600 U.S. troops—including cavalry, infantry, and artillery—crossed into Juárez and drove off Villa's troops, inflicting an estimated 100 casualties. U.S. forces returned to El Paso the following day, having suffered two killed and ten wounded.

The last of the punitive expeditions arising out of the disorder of the Mexican Revolution took place in August 1919. On 10 August two members of the newly instituted border air patrol disappeared on a reconnaissance flight from Marfa to El Paso, Texas. The two airmen were being held for a $15,000 ransom by Jesús Rentería, notorious border bandit and sometime officer for Villa. The U.S. War Department decided to pay the ransom and selected the commander of a border cavalry unit, Captain Leonard F. Matlack, to make the exchange. Matlack crossed alone into northern Mexico and retrieved one of the hostages, paying $7,500. When he returned for the second flyer, instead of paying the remaining ransom, Matlack produced one of the two Colt revolvers he always wore, took control of the hostage, and told the two bandits escorting him to return to Rentería and tell him to "go to hell." Matlack and the second flyer then safely returned to the U.S. side. The U.S. Army had been planning a military response once all American personnel were safe, and U.S. cavalry units soon crossed into Mexico at three points along the Rio Grande. The border air patrol—armed with machine guns and bombs—also joined in the chase. After six days below the border, this last of the punitive expeditions returned to U.S. soil, having killed five bandits and captured six others. Rentería escaped, and the $7,500 in ransom money was never recovered.

This last punitive expedition completed the connection between the border conflict and the world war. The Pershing Punitive Expedition of 1916–1917 had provided a training ground for World War I. In turn, air and cavalry veterans of the world war applied their wartime experience to the postwar conflicts along the Rio Grande. Although the Wilson administration was pursuing a more belligerent policy toward Mexico, it was simultaneously demobilizing the armed forces it would need for any major intervention.

Based on Don M. Coerver and Linda B. Hall, Texas and the Mexican Revolution: A Study in State and National Border Policy, 1910–1920 *(Trinity University Press, 1984).*

The United States emerged from its war to end Spanish imperial rule in Cuba with an empire of its own. Although this empire was small and scattered, it foreshadowed important commitments and foreign policy involvements for the coming decades. The purchase of the Philippines—coupled with the annexation of Hawaii in 1898—represented America's arrival as a two-ocean power and opened the way to the long-sought Asian market. U.S. occupation of Cuba and acquisition of Puerto Rico provided the naval bases needed to control the eastern approaches to an isthmian canal whose construction was given a greater urgency by the war. Although the United States now had colonies, it had no officials experienced in colonial administration, no structure for imperial control, and no coherent colonial policy. Indeed, it refused even to think of itself as a colonizer or an imperialist power. This increasingly interventionist foreign policy dictated a close connection with military policy, but there were no formal procedures or mechanisms for civil-military cooperation prior to World War I.

The most immediate "imperial" problem facing the United States was the military occupation of Cuba. The Treaty of Paris had not assigned a termination date for the occupation, but prolonging the military occupation increased the risk of repeating the Philippine experience where U.S. control had produced a bitter guerrilla war waged by the same rebels who had earlier opposed Spanish authority. In December 1899 Secretary of War Elihu Root set down a plan for Cuban independence. The plan called for a census and municipal elections which would be followed by the selection of representatives to a constituent assembly to draft a constitution. Once a government was in place under the new constitution, the U.S. military occupation would end. Matters proceeded smoothly until the constitutional convention met in November 1900. Convention delegates confronted demands by the United States that the new constitution contain certain provisions passed by the U.S. Congress in February 1901 which would effectively establish a protectorate over Cuba. Collectively known as the Platt Amendment, these provisions placed a number of restrictions on the conduct of the new Cuban government. Cuba would not be permitted to enter into treaties which the United States considered a threat to Cuban independence, nor could public debt be incurred unless it could be serviced out of ordinary revenues. Cuba would have to provide locations for U.S. naval bases and to continue public health programs started under the U.S. occupation. The most important provision gave the

United States the right to intervene in the internal affairs of Cuba to preserve the island's independence and to ensure a government that could meet its domestic and international obligations. The Cuban constitutional convention—forced to choose between the acceptance of the Platt Amendment or continued U.S. occupation—reluctantly incorporated these provisions into the new constitution, and in May 1902 the U.S. occupation officially came to an end.

Although the military occupation of Cuba had ended, the Platt Amendment ensured that the United States would continue to be deeply involved in the economic and political affairs of the island. The U.S. economic presence on the island, already substantial, expanded rapidly after the end of formal occupation. The United States and Cuba signed a reciprocity treaty in 1903 providing for a mutual lowering of tariffs. The new treaty facilitated the integration of Cuba into the U.S. economic system and heightened Cuba's dependence on sugar. U.S. capital played a prominent role in transportation, utilities, ranching, mining, and sugar production. Colonization schemes sponsored by U.S. land speculators and real estate agents attracted smallholders and colonists by the thousands. U.S. cultural influence spread throughout Cuban society, from education to religion; the ability to speak English became a key to advancement in business. The Cuban elite traveled regularly to the United States, with some obtaining dual citizenship.

Politically, the United States continued to be a strong presence in the internal affairs of Cuba. A disputed presidential election in 1906 led to a second U.S. occupation. President Theodore Roosevelt appointed a "governor" for Cuba, lawyer Charles Magoon, who introduced reforms in the army, the administration, and the electoral system. After new presidential elections, the second occupation came to an end in January 1909. Another disputed presidential election in 1917 produced a brief visit by U.S. troops. The United States had unwittingly helped to create what became known as the Platt Amendment mentality in which the United States became an arbiter of Cuban politics and aspiring Cuban politicians were forced into collaboration.[1] The results were increasingly characterized by cynicism, irresponsibility, corruption, electoral fraud, and the use of violence to settle political disputes. Far from being discouraged by this initial encounter with nation-building, the United States considered Cuba a model for its subsequent involvement in Latin American affairs.

As the United States was officially engaging and disengaging in Cuba, it was becoming more deeply involved in another part of the Caribbean. The War of 1898, with its two-ocean conflict, had demonstrated the strategic value of an isthmian canal. The conviction that the United States needed overseas markets — especially in Latin America and in Asia — for its surplus agricultural and industrial production provided the economic imperative for a canal. The major obstacle was the Clayton-Bulwer Treaty negotiated in 1850 which required that any isthmian canal be a joint U.S.-British project. While there was strong official and popular support in the United States for a canal, there was virtually no enthusiasm for a joint undertaking. U.S. interest peaked at a time when Britain was reassessing its foreign policy and redeploying its naval forces to meet the demands of a rapidly changing world. In the Hay-Pauncefote Treaty of 1901, Britain agreed to the abrogation of the Clayton-Bulwer Treaty; the United States was free to construct, operate, and fortify a canal on its own.

With the United States now able to act unilaterally, attention focused on possible locations. Throughout the second half of the nineteenth century, technical and political considerations seemed to favor the Nicaraguan route. In 1899 President McKinley appointed a special commission to make a definitive study and recommendations. The final report of the commission in November 1901 recommended the Nicaraguan route but also made a strong case for Panama. The commission concluded that Panama offered a superior route, but that the company which had inherited the old De Lesseps concession, the New Panama Canal Company, was demanding an exorbitant price for its concession ($109 million versus the commission's estimated value of $40 million). When the U.S. House of Representatives overwhelmingly passed a bill (308 to 2) in January 1902 appropriating $180 million for a Nicaraguan canal, the New Panama Canal Company reduced its asking price to $40 million. This new offer and heavy pressure from President Roosevelt led the commission to issue a revised report favoring the Panama route. In June, Congress brought these diverse strands together in the Spooner Act. The act authorized the president to purchase the concession and all other assets of the New Panama Canal Company for $40 million and to begin canal construction; the Congress also directed the president to acquire control over a six-mile wide "zone" in which the canal would be located. If the government of Colombia, of which Panama was a province, refused to sign a treaty "within a reasonable time" embodying these provisions, then construction on a Nicaraguan canal

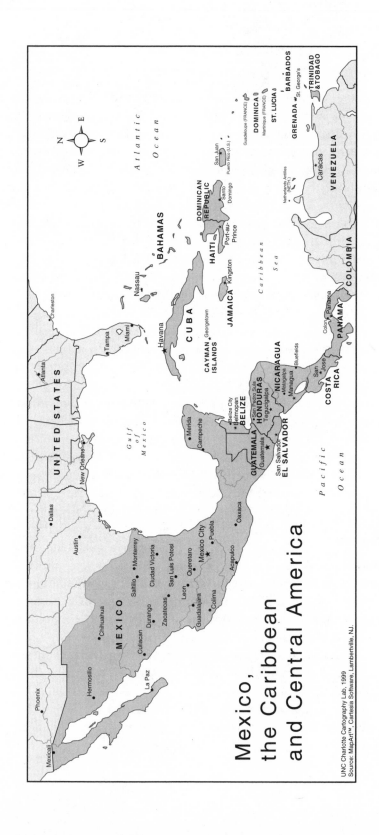

Mexico,
the Caribbean
and Central America

would begin. The Roosevelt administration immediately entered negotiations with the Colombian government, encountering major problems with the issues of financial compensation and U.S. control over the canal zone. In January 1903 the parties signed the Hay-Herrán Treaty which approved the transfer of the concession and provided a 100-year, renewable lease on a canal zone six miles in width. Colombia would retain sovereignty over the zone but would share judicial and police functions with the United States. The financial provisions of the treaty included $40 million for the concession, an initial payment of $10 million in gold to Colombia, and an annual fee of $250,000 to the Colombian government beginning after nine years.

The treaty still required the approval of both the U.S. and Colombian senates. The U.S. Senate overwhelmingly approved the treaty, 73 to 5. The Colombians in August 1903 unanimously rejected the treaty as a result of concerns about sovereignty in the zone and financial compensation. President Roosevelt, enraged by the actions of those he described as "contemptible creatures in Bogotá," was prepared to take more drastic measures to ensure the construction of a canal in Panama.[2]

Panama was no stranger either to revolution or to U.S. military intervention. The Colombian province had been averaging almost a revolution a year, often with the goal of independence. Despite this record, the Colombian government maintained a minimal force in the province, counting on its ability to move troops rapidly into the area by sea. U.S. forces had intervened briefly on several occasions prior to 1903, even during the negotiations for the Hay-Herrán Treaty.

In November 1903 local revolution and U.S. intervention converged. On 3 November a revolution financed and directed by an agent of the New Panama Canal Company began, with the rebels proclaiming Panamanian independence the following day. U.S. naval forces at Colón received orders too late to stop the landing of Colombian reinforcements, but the ranking U.S. naval officer did prevent Colombian troops from using the American-owned Panama Railroad, effectively blocking Colombian suppression of the revolt. The United States quickly recognized the new Panamanian government and concluded a new canal agreement. The treaty provided for an expanded canal zone ten miles in width and for perpetual U.S. control rather than a long-term lease. The financial provisions were the same as the earlier treaty with Colombia: $40 million to the New Panama Canal Company, $10 million to the new Panamanian government, and an annual fee of $250,000 beginning in nine

years. Most importantly, the United States guaranteed the independence of Panama, precluding future reconquest by Colombia. Both the Panamanian government and the U.S. Senate gave their rapid assent to the treaty.

Point-Counterpoint: Panama and the Canal

"It must be a matter of pride to every honest American, proud of the good name of his country, that the acquisition of the canal and the building of the canal, in all their details, were as free from scandal as the public acts of George Washington and Abraham Lincoln. . . . Every action taken was not merely proper, but was carried out in accordance with the highest, finest, and nicest standards of public and governmental ethics. . . . But the Colombian Government, for reasons which, I regret to say, were apparently very bad indeed, declined to consummate the treaty to which their representatives had agreed. . . . There is no more reason for giving Colombia money to soothe her feelings for the loss of what she forfeited by her misconduct in Panama in 1903 than for giving Great Britain money for what she lost in 1776. . . . Not only was the course followed as regards Panama right in every detail and at every point, but there could have been no variation from this course except for the worse. . . . We did harm to no one save as harm is done to a bandit by a policeman who deprives him of his chance for blackmail. . . . The United States has many honorable chapters in its history, but no more honorable chapter than that which tells of the way in which our right to dig the Panama Canal was secured."

—*Theodore Roosevelt, "How the United States Acquired the Right to Dig the Panama Canal,"* Outlook *99 (7 October 1911):314–18.*

"Nine years ago this [friendly attitude] was changed suddenly and unexpectedly when President Roosevelt denied to Colombia the right to land her troops upon her own soil to suppress a threatened revolt and maintain a sovereignty guaranteed by treaty stipulations. The breach came and it has been growing wider since that hour. By refusing to allow Colombia to uphold her sovereign rights over a territory where she had held dominion for eighty years, the friendship of nearly a century disappeared. The indignation of every Colombian, and millions of other Latin-Americans, was aroused and is still most intensively active. The confidence and trust in the justice and fairness of the United States, so long manifested, has completely vanished, and the maleficent influence of this condition is permeating public opinion in all Latin-American countries, a condition which, if remedial measures are not invoked, will work inestimable harm throughout the Western Hemisphere."

—*U.S. Minister to Colombia James T. Du Bois to Secretary of State Philander C. Knox, 30 December 1912, quoted in Howard C. Hill,* Roosevelt and the Caribbean *(Chicago: University of Chicago Press, 1927), p. 68.*

The U.S. role in Panama both reflected and accelerated broader U.S. involvement in the hemisphere, especially in the Caribbean and Central America. The Roosevelt administration became increasingly sensitive to perceived threats of European intervention in Latin America, especially in the circum-

Theodore Roosevelt took a great interest in the progress of canal building in Panama, including its technical aspects. Here he is seen at the controls of a 95-ton Bucyrus shovel at the south end of the Culebra Cut, the most difficult engineering feat of the project.

From David McCullough, The Path Between the Seas: The Creation of the Panama Canal, 1870–1914. *Simon and Schuster Touchstone, 1977*

Caribbean region. The Venezuelan crisis of 1902–1903 demonstrated this growing sensitivity. For some years the Venezuelan government had failed to meet
its international debt obligations or to address financial claims by foreigners
who had suffered from the country's recurrent civil strife. In December 1902
Britain and Germany initiated a naval blockade of the Venezuelan coast;
Venezuelan president Cipriano Castro tried to counteract European naval
power by requesting that the United States arbitrate the matter. Roosevelt
disliked Castro but was nervous about European intervention in the region,
particularly German involvement. He called upon Britain and Germany to
submit to arbitration. Britain — not wishing to be aligned with Germany
against the United States — agreed, leaving Germany with no alternative but
to agree as well. Britain and Germany terminated their blockade in February
1903. The United States transferred responsibility for arbitration to the Hague
Court, and Venezuela had paid off the major claims against it by 1907.

The Venezuelan crisis demonstrated a fundamental problem in U.S. Latin
American policy. The United States recognized European intervention to collect debts as long as there was no effort to acquire territory or exercise undue
influence. On the other hand heightened security concerns caused by the War
of 1898 and the construction of the isthmian canal made the United States
reluctant to sanction any form of European intervention. Roosevelt in particular did not want Latin American countries to think that the Monroe Doctrine could be used as a shield against European action when they did not
fulfill their international obligations. This consideration led Roosevelt to
formulate what became known as the Roosevelt Corollary to the Monroe
Doctrine. He set down his "corollary" in his annual message to Congress in
December 1904. Roosevelt divided the world into "civilized" and "uncivilized"
nations, maintaining that civilized nations ultimately had the responsibility
to ensure that the uncivilized lived up to minimum standards of international
conduct. Since the Monroe Doctrine limited outside intervention in the hemisphere, it became the responsibility of the United States in "cases of flagrant
wrongdoing" to exercise an "international police power." Roosevelt's pro-
nouncement represented the end point in the evolution of the Monroe Doctrine from a defensive policy opposing European intervention to an offensive
policy sanctioning U.S. intervention; it also implied a claim to regional hegemony in the name of security considerations.

While the Roosevelt administration was converting the lessons of the
Venezuelan crisis into the Roosevelt Corollary to the Monroe Doctrine, the

minister of foreign relations for Argentina, Luis M. Drago, was drawing far different conclusions from the same event. Drago brought together the issues of debts, intervention, and the Monroe Doctrine in what would later be called the Drago Doctrine. Drago set down his views in a formal note to the U.S. government in December 1902 when the Venezuelan crisis had been largely defused. Drago maintained that European intervention to collect debts implied territorial occupation to be effective, a violation of the Monroe Doctrine. He therefore asked the United States to recognize the principle that debt collection was not sufficient grounds for armed intervention nor the occupation of territory. Latin Americans subsequently embraced and expanded Drago's doctrine in hopes of curbing not only European intervention but U.S. intervention as well. Drago himself denied the existence of a "Drago doctrine," maintaining that he was simply expressing a "political viewpoint" and not a principle of international law.[3]

Despite Roosevelt's rhetoric, the United States was not eager to become the policeman for the Caribbean and Central America, a fact made clear by its actions in the Dominican Republic. In late 1903 France, Germany, and Italy threatened armed intervention to collect debts owed to their nationals. The Dominican government responded in early 1904 by encouraging the United States to establish a protectorate, complete with naval bases and a reciprocity treaty. Roosevelt—criticized for his actions in Panama and facing a presidential campaign—publicly rejected the protectorate but privately speculated that such an arrangement was inevitable for the Dominican Republic. Discussions then moved to the establishment of a U.S.-run customs receivership under which American officials would assume responsibility for the collection of customs revenue and the payment of creditors. After some haggling over how the customs receipts should be divided, the United States and the Dominican Republic signed a treaty on 7 February 1905 calling for a U.S.-managed receivership, with the Dominican government receiving forty-five percent of the revenue and the remainder divided among its creditors. The treaty also set a limit on spending by the Dominican government and provided for prior approval by the United States of any changes in the customs laws. At the request of the Dominicans, the treaty pledged the United States to guarantee the territorial integrity of the Dominican Republic.

When the U.S. Senate delayed approval, the Roosevelt administration and the Dominican government agreed to informally implement the treaty's provisions. The U.S. Senate finally approved a revised version in February 1907.

By the time it received official approval, the customs receivership had already proven itself a financial success; the Dominican government was actually receiving more money even though it was assigned only forty-five percent of total collections. A brief period of political stability followed between 1908 and 1911, leading the U.S. government to conclude that the Dominican receivership could serve as a model for other Caribbean countries.

Taft and Dollar Diplomacy

Roosevelt's successor, William Howard Taft, had firsthand experience with the problems of America's informal empire, serving as governor of the Philippines and as secretary of war during Roosevelt's second administration. Taft inherited a policy shaped by strategic emphasis on a large navy, insular possessions, an isthmian canal, and the models of the Dominican receivership and the Cuban occupations. While Roosevelt stressed strategic considerations, Taft shifted the emphasis to commercial advantage. In his annual message to Congress in 1912, Taft summarized his foreign policy by saying it was one of "substituting dollars for bullets." This "dollar diplomacy" was partially a continuation of the view that the government should help promote foreign trade as well as a reflection of the U.S. role as the world's premiere industrial power and a growing exporter of capital.

In applying dollar diplomacy to Latin America, Taft believed his main goal was to promote political stability, hopefully based on free elections. There was little prospect for political stability without financial stability. Therefore, American financial interests should be encouraged to make loans to Latin American governments. Dollar diplomacy was thus a logical outgrowth of Roosevelt's Corollary. If the United States was not going to permit European countries to intervene to collect debts in Latin America, then the United States would have to assume greater responsibility for the financial problems of the region. The Taft administration pressured Latin American governments to transfer their indebtedness from European to U.S. creditors while simultaneously urging U.S. financial institutions to expand their lending. Any debt collection problems would be kept within the hemispheric family, and new opportunities for U.S. trade and investment would develop. Taft and Knox recognized that the United States might have to intervene to protect U.S. economic and financial interests but hoped that such interventions could be kept to a minimum.

Although dollar diplomacy ultimately developed the negative image of an interventionist policy using public power to promote private profit, the reality of implementation was quite different. U.S. investors were not always eager to rush in to provide loans to politically and financially troubled Latin American nations. American financiers wanted a minimum level of political stability before they would invest. An acceptable alternative to political stability was a guarantee of protection by the U.S. government. However, such a guarantee had the undesired effect of placing the emphasis on intervention or the threat of intervention instead of deemphasizing it as Taft envisioned. While there were limited efforts to apply dollar diplomacy in Honduras and Haiti, its major test came in Nicaragua.

The United States had been experiencing periodic difficulties with Nicaragua since the 1890s, largely due to the unpredictable policies of its long-time ruler, José Santos Zelaya. When a revolution against Zelaya broke out in 1909, the U.S. government welcomed it but did not provide immediate financial or military support. When Zelaya ordered the execution of two Americans working for the rebels, Secretary of State Knox dismissed him as a "blot upon the history of Nicaragua."[4] The Taft administration expelled Nicaragua's representative in Washington and dispatched a naval force with 1,000 marines to Nicaraguan waters. Fearing U.S. intervention, Zelaya resigned in December 1909, hoping that the United States would accept his fellow Liberal, José Madriz, as his successor. Knox refused to deal with Madriz, and in May 1910 U.S. forces intervened to prevent Liberal forces from defeating the rebels. Madriz resigned in August, surrendering the government to Conservative control. In May 1911, the Conservative Adolfo Díaz assumed the presidency.

In June 1911 the new Nicaraguan administration signed the Knox-Castrillo Treaty which provided for the establishment of a customs receivership under U.S. supervision and for refinancing the national debt by floating new loans with U.S. banks. The Nicaraguan congress approved the treaty, but the U.S. Senate refused to ratify it. Taft then entered into an executive agreement—not requiring Senate approval—that contained provisions similar to the treaty. Nicaraguan customs collection improved, but political and financial stability still proved elusive. By July 1912 Díaz faced armed opposition from both Liberals and dissident Conservatives. When Díaz requested U.S. military assistance, the Taft administration was faced with the very problem that dollar diplomacy was supposed to avoid: military intervention to ensure political stability. Viewing the expanding revolution as a threat to American lives and property, the U.S. government ordered in the Marines in August 1912; the U.S. military presence soon exceeded 2,000 troops. By October the revolution had ended, and the United States exercised an uneasy and largely unofficial protectorate over Nicaragua.

The outbreak of revolution in Mexico in late 1910 posed an even graver problem for the Taft administration. General Porfirio Díaz had ruled Mexico almost without interruption since 1877. Díaz had pursued a policy of economic development primarily centered on attracting foreign capital and technology to accelerate the modernization of Mexico. As a result U.S. capital dominated such high-profile economic activities as mining and oil. Americans also figured prominently among foreign landowners, particularly in the politically sensitive area along the U.S.-Mexican border. Opponents of the old regime did most of their revolutionary plotting in the United States, and the heaviest fighting of the revolution took place in northern Mexico, near the U.S.-Mexican border.

During the first phase of the revolution from November 1910 to May 1911, revolutionary activity was concentrated along the Rio Grande boundary. Following a disputed presidential election in June 1910 which resulted in yet another electoral victory for Porfirio Díaz, the defeated candidate, Francisco Madero, went into exile in San Antonio, Texas, and immediately began plotting to overthrow Díaz. After the revolution began in November 1910, rebels in northern Mexico focused their attention on capturing Ciudad Juárez, Chihuahua, across the Rio Grande from El Paso, Texas. The capture of Juárez would give the rebels control of revenues from the customshouse, an entrepot for military supplies, and deal a major psychological blow to the Díaz regime. The Taft administration worried that a struggle for Juárez would spill over the border, causing casualties and property damage in El Paso. The United States began concentrating its forces along the border in November 1910, and in March 1911 Taft announced the creation of the "Maneuver Division" with headquarters at San Antonio, Texas. The official explanation for the division was that it was a training organization; in reality it represented a positioning of troops for possible intervention in Mexico. When rebel forces finally attacked Juárez in May 1911, stray shells killed six and wounded fifteen on the U.S. side. U.S. troops were present both in El Paso and at nearby Fort Bliss but operated under strict orders not to cross the border. In fact, the troops were in place principally to block Americans from crossing the border rather than to protect El Paso. The brevity of the fighting—two days—

prevented higher casualties and relieved the Taft administration of any need to reevaluate its policy of nonintervention. The successful rebel attack had the desired effect; Díaz resigned on 25 May 1911 and went into European exile.

Francisco Madero easily won the presidential elections held in October 1911, taking office the following month and quickly receiving diplomatic recognition by the United States. The revolutionaries soon began to struggle among themselves, and Madero was forced to put down a series of revolts by disgruntled revolutionaries as well as die-hard supporters of the old regime. The U.S. ambassador in Mexico City, Henry Lane Wilson, became convinced that Madero could not establish a stable government capable of protecting American lives and property. Although Madero's position continued to decline and Wilson's reports became increasingly strident, the Taft administration refused to depart from its Mexican policy which the president described as "patient nonintervention."[5]

Taft's policy of nonintervention received a major test in February 1913 when a coup directed against Madero led to significant fighting in Mexico City. The leaders of the coup were generals connected with the old regime: Bernardo Reyes and Félix Díaz, nephew of the former president. Troops loyal to Madero killed Reyes on the first day of the coup, leading to a military stalemate but continued fighting. Ambassador Wilson injected himself into the chaotic situation, demanding that Madero resign and threatening U.S. intervention. When Madero refused, Wilson worked secretly to bring together Félix Díaz with the leader of the troops defending Madero, General Victoriano Huerta. In what became known as the "Pact of the [U.S.] Embassy," Huerta and Díaz— with Wilson's approval—agreed to join forces, overthrow Madero, and install Huerta as provisional president. Huerta's forces arrested Madero and his vice president, José María Pino Suárez. Then, on 21 February, Madero and Pino Suárez were murdered while being transferred from the National Palace to a Mexico City prison. Huerta's official explanation was that the two deposed officials had been accidentally killed when their supporters attempted to free them; Ambassador Wilson quickly seconded the official version and strongly recommended U.S. recognition of Huerta. Taft refused to extend recognition to the Huerta regime and also declined to get the United States more deeply involved in Mexico; he would leave the presidency in March and was content to let his successor, Woodrow Wilson [no relation to Ambassador Wilson], deal with the latest crisis in U.S.-Latin American relations.

Woodrow Wilson and Missionary Diplomacy

Although Taft's dollar diplomacy had conjured up images of U.S. military force being indiscriminately used for private profit, there had in reality been very little direct military intervention, and in the most important case — Mexico — Taft had repeatedly rejected military action even when lives were lost on U.S. soil. By 1912 the image of dollar diplomacy had already become more important than the reality, and it was this image that came under attack by his Democratic successor, Woodrow Wilson, during the presidential campaign of 1912. The 1912 election had revolved primarily around domestic policy. Wilson demonstrated little knowledge of, or interest in, foreign affairs prior to becoming president in March 1913. Wilson was an idealist in international affairs, believing that foreign policy should be based on principles rather than pragmatism. He saw himself as the preeminent apostle of democracy. Wilson believed that democracy would some day be the political norm and that there would never be peace in the world until all nations had embraced democracy. As the definitive example of democracy, the United States had a special obligation to extend its benefits and to instruct "backward" peoples in its usages. This impulse to convert the political heathens gave rise to the phrase "missionary diplomacy" in describing Wilson's foreign policy.

Wilson's administration held out the promise of major changes in U.S.-Latin American relations. Wilson set down his vision of a new U.S. relationship with Latin America in a speech at Mobile, Alabama, in October 1913. He decried foreign — that is, European — economic exploitation of Latin America and promised that the United States would never again seek "one additional foot of territory by conquest." Wilson was ironically prophetic when he observed: "The future is going to be very different for this hemisphere from the past." While Latin Americans could interpret the Mobile Speech as a U.S. renunciation of expansion, intervention, and economic exploitation, it indicated at the same time a much greater U.S. involvement in Latin America, particularly within the traditional framework set down by the Monroe Doctrine of the Western Hemisphere versus Europe.[6]

While Wilson stressed the idealistic content of his foreign policy, he was also concerned with more mundane matters such as promoting trade and political stability. By 1912 the need to expand foreign trade as an outlet for domestic industrial and agricultural surpluses had become part of the conventional economic wisdom. Progressive sentiment also supported the pursuit of in-

ternational order but with the emphasis on a multilateral approach rather
than unilateral action by the United States. Wilson supported democratic
change through legal processes but had no sympathy for revolutions in an increasingly revolutionary world. His anti-military attitude led to bitter de-
nunciations of Republican interventionism, yet he supported the use of force
on behalf of world order, collective security, and democratic capitalism.

Wilson pursued his multilateral approach to international order through
the formulation of a Pan American Pact providing for collective security and
compulsory arbitration. The United States initially approached the ABC countries—Argentina, Brazil, and Chile—hoping that their acceptance of the pact
would lead to general hemispheric approval. Discussion of the pact continued for two years until it finally died quietly, primarily due to Chilean opposition and to the negative impact of U.S. military intervention in Mexico.

Woodrow Wilson's plans for a new hemispheric, and ultimately world,
order collided immediately with the reality of continuing revolution in Mexico. Wilson's first major policy decision involved the administration's attitude
toward the new regime of General Victoriano Huerta, which certainly did not
meet Wilson's new standard for recognition based on "constitutional legitimacy." The development of significant armed opposition to Huerta also discouraged U.S. recognition. Prominent leaders of the rebel factions were the
"Men of the North"—Venustiano Carranza in Coahuila, Pancho Villa in Chihuahua, and Alvaro Obregón in Sonora—and the rebel leader in the South,
Emiliano Zapata. The kaleidoscope of rebel factions and the uncertainty of
the military success of the rebellion precluded U.S. recognition of any rebel
group. The Wilson administration would not recognize any Mexican government between February 1913 and October 1915.

Wilson's refusal to recognize Huerta constituted a response to a specific situation rather than a comprehensive Mexican policy. The scale and location of
rebel activity, much of it near the U.S.-Mexican border, led to extreme pressure on Wilson to develop a plan for dealing with the Mexican struggle. Heavy
fighting in the North posed a threat to the extensive U.S. investments in the
mining and oil industries. Still, Wilson desperately sought to avoid military
intervention in Mexico, opting instead for a cautious approach similar to Taft's
"patient nonintervention." Wilson's Mexican policy came to be described as
"watchful waiting," a combination of two phrases used by the president in a
message to Congress in August 1913 in which he said that he would "wait" and
"vigilantly watch" revolutionary developments in Mexico.[7] Wilson tried to ne-

gotiate Huerta's resignation; when Huerta refused to leave voluntarily, Wilson embarked on a personal campaign to oust him. In February 1914 Wilson partially lifted the arms embargo imposed by Taft in March 1912. Under the new arrangement, anti-Huerta rebels—but not Huerta—would be permitted to import arms from the United States. This indirect approach to removing Huerta would soon give way to more direct methods.

In April 1914 a minor incident occurred in the Mexican oil port of Tampico when a small group of U.S. sailors was briefly detained by some of Huerta's soldiers for coming ashore in a restricted area. When the Mexican commander learned of the affair, he ordered the immediate release of the sailors and issued a formal apology. Rear Admiral Henry Mayo, commander of the U.S. naval squadron at Tampico, deemed the apology inadequate and demanded a twenty-one gun salute to the American flag. When the Wilson administration supported Mayo's demand, the minor incident escalated into a major confrontation. While the U.S. government haggled with a Mexican government it did not recognize over the terms of the salute, Wilson asked Congress for permission to use military force to obtain redress if necessary. As Congress was debating the request, the State Department received word that a German steamer was about to land at Veracruz with a shipment of arms for Huerta's government. Without waiting for congressional approval, Wilson decided to intervene.

Wilson's decision to intervene at Veracruz rather than Tampico reflected more than a desire to intercept an arms shipment; it provided an opportunity to tighten the screws on Huerta by interrupting his principal source of revenue, the customshouse at Veracruz. Wilson and his advisors were confident that there would be little if any opposition when U.S. forces landed at Veracruz on the morning of 21 April. The seizure of the customshouse went unopposed, but resistance mounted as the sailors and marines moved in to occupy the city. The local Mexican commander had mobilized the militia and had even released and armed convicts to resist the invasion; fighting was small scale but sharp. U.S. losses were 19 killed and 71 wounded; Mexican casualties were approximately 200 killed and 300 wounded, including a number of civilians. Wilson was shaken by the casualty reports as well as by the response of the various Mexican political factions. The leading rebel figures, with the exception of Pancho Villa, denounced the intervention and even talked of a temporary truce with Huerta in order to present a united front against the

American invaders. Nevertheless, Wilson's intervention hastened the downfall of Huerta who resigned in July 1914 and went into exile in Europe. U.S. forces continued to occupy Veracruz until 23 November 1914 without further military incident.

Huerta's downfall provided only a brief lull in the revolutionary confusion in Mexico. Forces under the leadership of Alvaro Obregón occupied Mexico City in August 1914 in the name of the Constitutionalist faction headed by Venustiano Carranza. When a convention at Aguascalientes in October 1914 failed to harmonize the disagreements among the different rebel groups, the Mexican Revolution entered its bloodiest phase. Troops loyal to Carranza and Obregón were aligned against the forces of Villa and Zapata. Wilson continued his efforts to guide the internal dynamics of the Revolution, initially tilting in favor of Villa who was considered the factional leader most likely to accept Wilson's tutoring in the ways of democracy. Villa, however, proved a mercurial student, and the military defeats he suffered at the hands of Obregón progressively reduced the area under his control.

Border security was a growing problem for Wilson as systematic raiding began along the Rio Grande in July 1915. These disturbances were connected with the "Plan of San Diego," an amorphous revolutionary manifesto issued in January 1915 calling for a combination revolution, race war, and separatist movement in South Texas. The Plan had murky connections to Carranza forces across the border, and there was a suspicion that Carranza himself was orchestrating the raids to pressure the United States into recognizing his government. In the end, however, Wilson's decision about recognition was essentially made for him on the battlefields of Mexico. By the fall of 1915 Obregón's military success had reduced Villa to his original status as a provincial leader, and, in October 1915, the United States extended de facto recognition to the Carranza government.

Although Villa could no longer contend for the Mexican presidency, he was still a major factor in determining U.S. relations with Mexico. Villa became increasingly anti-American in his pronouncements, denouncing his "betrayal" by the Wilson administration. The first major anti-American action by Villa's forces took place at Santa Ysabel, Chihuahua, on 10 January 1916. A group of American mining employees were returning to Chihuahua from El Paso to reopen mining activities suspended due to Villa's military operations; they were traveling by train with the encouragement and under the official protection of Carranza officials. A group of Villa's followers stopped the train and systematically executed sixteen of the Americans.

Although the Santa Ysabel massacre increased pressure for U.S. intervention, Wilson rejected a military response. Another attack by Villa's forces in March forced Wilson's hand. On 9 March 1916 Villa's troops attacked Columbus, New Mexico, killing seventeen Americans. Although U.S. forces were operating under longstanding orders not to cross the border, some of the 350 U.S. Army troops stationed at Columbus pursued the raiders into Mexico, engaging in a running battle that lasted almost eight hours and resulted in the deaths of between 75 and 100 raiders. This hot pursuit was the prelude to the much larger Punitive Expedition that would be launched under the command of General John J. Pershing.

Pershing received orders to enter Mexico, capture Villa, and disperse his forces so that they would no longer be a threat to the U.S. border. Although the expedition mobilized relatively quickly, the main force did not enter Mexico until 15 March, giving Villa almost a week's head start. U.S. hopes that Carranza would cooperate with the expedition also quickly disappeared when Carranza demanded immediate withdrawal of the expedition. By early April, Pershing's force had grown to almost 7,000 troops and had penetrated more than 300 miles into northern Mexico. On 12 April expedition forces clashed with Carranza's troops at Parral, Chihuahua, resulting in two American dead and Mexican casualties estimated at forty. Fearing another clash, Wilson approved an army recommendation for the expedition to concentrate its forces in the vicinity of Colonia Dublán, Chihuahua, and assume a defensive posture. War seemed likely after Carranza's forces and expedition troops engaged in a major firefight at Carrizal, Chihuahua, on 21 June. The U.S. patrol suffered twelve killed, ten wounded, and twenty-four captured; Mexican casualties numbered at least seventy-four. The possibility of war quickly dissipated when Carranza announced that the American prisoners would be returned and both sides agreed to submit their disagreements to a joint commission. The Pershing Expedition lingered on in northern Mexico until a phased withdrawal finally began on 27 January 1917; on 5 February the last of the expedition's forces left Mexican soil.

Although distracted by world war in Europe and civil war in Mexico, Wilson pressed forward with policies that would lead to greater U.S. involvement in Central America and the Caribbean. Wilson continued his predecessors' concern with political stability in the region and inherited the earlier inter-

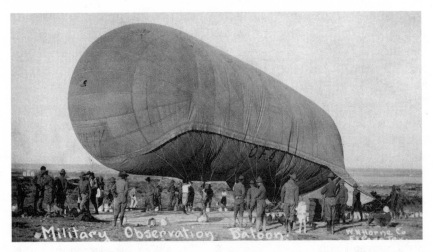

The U.S. Army used military observation balloons as spotters for artillery fire. The balloons were vulnerable to small arms, leaving the crew only fifteen seconds to get out in the event of a hit. This exigency led to the development of parachutes, which were denied to airplane pilots out of fear that they would use them too readily.

Courtesy Center for Southwest Research, University of New Mexico [No. 996–011–00233]

Carranzista officers and troops at the International Bridge in El Paso repatriating members of the black Tenth Calvary captured at Carrizal.

Courtesy Center for Southwest Research, University of New Mexico [No. 986–015–033]

vention in Nicaragua. In August 1914 World War I began, and the Panama Canal opened. These two events focused strategic attention on the traditionally turbulent island of Hispaniola, unhappy home of Haiti and the Dominican Republic. Located between the U.S. protectorate of Cuba and the U.S. possession of Puerto Rico, the island with its perennial financial and political problems assumed new significance after the outbreak of the European war. There was a long history of both European and U.S. intervention on the island in defense of foreign lives and property; what would be different about Wilsonian intervention would be the degree and the duration of U.S. presence. Intervention would be a way of reforming the two nations, not merely a method of restoring order.

Haiti had been a marginal consideration in U.S. Caribbean policy for most of the twentieth century. Haiti experienced growing political instability, enduring seven presidents between 1908 and 1915. One turnover in the presidency in July 1915 provided the occasion for U.S. intervention. A revolt against President Vilbrun Guillaume Sam ended when the wounded president was forcibly removed from the French legation where he had sought sanctuary and dismembered by an angry mob which later paraded through the streets of Port-au-Prince with various parts of the late president's body. Fearing a massacre of foreigners and unwilling to await orders from Washington, Admiral William Caperton—commander of U.S. naval forces in the area—ordered marines and sailors ashore to restore order. Caperton believed that this was merely the latest in a long line of brief interventions; it proved instead to be the beginning of a nineteen-year occupation.

The U.S. military presence in Haiti increased rapidly after the initial landing of 330 men on 28 July 1915. By the end of August there were over 2,000 marines in Haiti, and the U.S. occupation spread from the capital to other important coastal towns. At each location the marine commander took control of the customshouse; the cumulative effect of these customshouse seizures was to establish a de facto customs receivership. At the urging of Admiral Caperton, the Haitian National Assembly on 12 August 1915 selected as president Philippe Sudre Dartiguenave who proved amenable to suggestions from both Washington and Caperton. The State Department soon provided the new president with the draft of a treaty that would convert the U.S. occupation into a major reform effort. The treaty provided for U.S. administration of customs collection, U.S. supervision of the treasury, and the creation of a new national constabulary commanded by U.S. officers to replace both the army and the civil police. Using a combination of bribes, threats, and martial law, Caperton got the Haitian senate to approve the document in November 1915. In June 1918 the new Haitian constitution as revised in Washington received overwhelming approval in a national plebiscite held under Marine supervision. The Treaty of 1915 and the Constitution of 1918 provided the framework for an American protectorate that would last until 1934.

There had been a strong interaction between U.S. policies in Haiti and the Dominican Republic for some time. The Dominican receivership of 1907 influenced U.S. actions before and during the occupation of Haiti in 1915, which in turn would influence U.S. policy leading to intervention in the Dominican Republic in 1916. The new Wilson administration had to deal with the provisional government of President José Bordas who had been selected by the Dominican congress to serve for a maximum of one year and to preside over national elections in 1914. The U.S. government indicated that it would neither recognize nor turn over the customs collections to any revolutionary government. It did, however, promise to supervise the scheduled presidential elections if the various rebel groups disarmed. As the political situation deteriorated, the United States pressured Bordas to accept an American financial advisor who would control all Dominican governmental expenditures. A reluctant Bordas agreed, prompting further domestic opposition to the creeping American protectorate. Bordas's blatant rigging of the presidential election of June 1914 to secure his own election led President Wilson to set new demands: Bordas must resign and new elections must be held under U.S. supervision. The United States would intervene to maintain the democratically elected government. Threatened with U.S. intervention, the Dominican factions agreed to new elections; in December 1914 an ex-president, Juan Isidro Jiménez, became the new U.S.-guaranteed president.

The Jiménez presidency produced greater U.S. involvement but not political stability. The aging and sickly Jiménez soon came into conflict with his politically ambitious minister of defense, General Desiderio Arias, who was openly conspiring against the government. With revolutionary activity spreading, the Wilson administration in November 1915 issued an ultimatum to Jiménez: accept complete U.S. control of the treasury and abolition of the Dominican army or face U.S. military intervention. On 5 May 1916 the long-threatened U.S. intervention occurred, nominally to preserve the Jiménez government against new attacks by General Arias. Although the exasperated and exhausted president soon undercut the U.S. rationale for intervention by resigning, the U.S. minister, William Russell, pushed ahead by creating a "Council of Ministers" out of the remnants of the Jiménez cabinet and granting it official recognition. This move was immediately challenged by General Arias. The arrival on 12 May of Admiral Caperton broke the developing deadlock; Caperton ordered Arias to disband his forces or face U.S. attack. Although Arias commanded a larger force and already held Santo Domingo, he ordered a withdrawal from the capital. When U.S. officials could not find Dominican politicians willing to work under U.S. constraints, the State Department announced in November 1916 the creation of a military government. Unlike Haiti where the United States was operating through a protectorate, officers of the U.S. Army and Navy would rule directly in the Dominican Republic for the next eight years.

The U.S. military government carried out the reforms that the Wilson administration had been demanding from the beginning. The first priority was disbanding the army and disarming the citizenry. The U.S. occupation provoked small-scale but persistent military opposition. In April 1917 the military government created the Dominican National Guard to replace the old army; Marine officers commanded the Guard until Dominican officers could be recruited and trained. Tainted by the occupation, the Guard labored under a poor reputation from the start and drew criticism from its inception for abusing the local population. Control of national finances was now in U.S. hands.

World War I

Events in Haiti and the Dominican Republic had been overtaken by concerns with the continuing war in Europe. Fear of European — especially, German — involvement in the Caribbean had been a motive in both interventions. U.S.-Latin American relations in general experienced changes caused by the European war. These changes came in two phases: an initial phase from August 1914 to April 1917 when the United States and Latin American nations remained neutral, and a post-1917 phase after the United States entered the war.

The outbreak of war in August 1914 had led the United States and all the Latin American nations to declare their neutrality. Wilson's proposal for a Pan American Pact had been designed to present a united hemispheric front in the face of European war and to provide greater leverage in dealing with the belligerent powers. While discussions of the pact lingered on and ultimately failed, the economic impact of the war demanded more immediate and effective attention. The war produced an immediate disruption in the international flow of trade and capital. By late 1915 wartime dislocation was giving way to economic boom in many hemispheric countries, especially the United States. The opening of the Panama Canal within days after the outbreak of war promoted a greater role for U.S. business in Latin American economic affairs. Because the war cut Latin American countries off from their traditional European markets and suppliers, it opened the way to even greater U.S. economic penetration.

Changes in U.S. laws also facilitated the U.S. drive to dominate Latin American trade. The Tariff Act of 1913 dramatically lowered U.S. tariff rates, especially on such important Latin American exports as coffee, wool, and sugar; about ninety-five percent of South American raw materials could be imported duty free. In addition, the Federal Reserve Act of 1913 permitted U.S. banks to open foreign branches, helping to provide the credit needed to finance an expanded trade. U.S. direct investment increased substantially between August 1914 and April 1917, with most investment going to Latin America in such fields as agriculture, mining, and oil.

Entry of the United States into the war in April 1917 produced major political and economic changes in U.S.-Latin American relations. The changes began even before the formal U.S. declaration of war. When Germany resumed unrestricted submarine warfare on 1 February 1917, the United States responded by breaking diplomatic relations and urging Latin American nations to do the same. Most of the Latin American nations felt no direct threat from German submarines and did not take action until the United States officially entered the war in April. Within two weeks of U.S. entrance into the war, seven nations broke diplomatic relations with Germany. Panama and Cuba — figuring prominently in U.S. strategic planning — gave in to U.S. pressure and also declared war. By late 1917 six more Latin American nations had joined them. The United States was particularly interested in gaining the cooperation of Argentina, Brazil, Chile, and Mexico, but enjoyed limited success. Argentina was willing to cooperate economically but would not abandon its official neutrality. Chile felt no military threat from Germany, increasingly favored a Pan American movement without the United States, and had a German-trained army. The nationalistic regime of President Venustiano Carranza of Mexico continued its running feud with the Wilson administration, causing many U.S. officials to classify Carranza as "pro-German." Only Brazil faithfully followed the U.S. lead, breaking relations and then declaring war on Germany.

There were also substantial economic consequences in Latin America from the U.S. entry into war. U.S. involvement in the war brought an even greater demand for Latin American products as the United States mobilized and also assumed a greater responsibility for supplying the Allies. While the volume of trade increased, there was little change in the types of items being traded, with Latin American exports still being composed primarily of raw materials and agricultural products while manufactured items assumed a greater importance in U.S. exports. The United States Shipping Board promoted a major expansion in the U.S. merchant fleet, helping to alleviate the longstanding problem of Latin American dependence on European carriers. The U.S. Congress in 1918 passed legislation setting aside antitrust prohibitions by permitting U.S. firms to combine in the export trade, further hastening U.S. domination of Latin American markets. Investment followed trade, with U.S. direct investments expanding rapidly in such fields as Cuban sugar, Chilean nitrates, Argentine beef, and even Mexican oil. The U.S. government "blacklisted" or prohibited business dealings with firms or individuals connected with the Central Powers; when the first blacklist was published in December 1917, it had over 1,500 firms or individuals, all in Latin America.

Woodrow Wilson originally hoped that his proposed Pan American Pact would serve as a model for peace after World War I. By the time the Paris Peace Conference convened in early 1919, the Pan American Pact was long since dead, and Wilson was preoccupied with European affairs. The United States believed that the Latin American nations, with the exception of Brazil, had made no significant contribution to the war effort and, therefore, had no major role to play in the peace settlement. The United States eventually supported conference participation by any Latin American nation that had broken relations or declared war. The eleven Latin American nations that sent formal delegations to the conference were disappointed by the scant attention paid them and angered by the dominant roles played by the United States, Britain, France, and Italy.

The only prestigious position at the conference to go to a Latin American nation was Brazil's seat on the League of Nations commission, and even the Brazilians complained that they were cut out of the decision-making process.

There was little attention to Latin American issues except for the relationship of the Monroe Doctrine to the proposed League of Nations. While Wilson saw the creation of the League as simply making the Doctrine a multilateral policy, there were many even within the U.S. delegation who doubted that the League and the Doctrine could be harmonized. To appease these doubters, Wilson pushed through an amendment to the League Covenant recognizing the validity of any "regional understandings" promoting peace. While Wilson had saved the League at the Paris Peace Conference, he was not able to save the Treaty later in Washington; the U.S. Senate failed to approve the Treaty for a variety of reasons, including uneasiness about the status of the Monroe Doctrine.

The failure of the peace treaty left the Wilson administration on the defensive and Wilson himself physically incapacitated. Wilson's Latin American policy came under growing criticism, especially in regard to Mexico. In August 1919 a subcommittee of the Senate Committee on Foreign Relations began an investigation into Mexican affairs; under the leadership of Republican Senator Albert B. Fall, the subcommittee provided a partisan forum for critics of both Wilson and Carranza. In 1920 public pressure forced Secretary of the Navy Josephus Daniels to convene a special tribunal to investigate charges of brutality in the U.S. occupation of Haiti. While Wilson was not prepared to retreat from his interventionist policies, he was unwilling to get more deeply involved in such places as Mexico.

While the war had not produced the regional integration sought by Wilson, it had led to a dominant position for the United States in Latin American trade. The inability of the major European nations to maintain their normal trade and credit relations with Latin America had created a vacuum soon filled by U.S. traders and investors. The wartime expansion of U.S. shipping and banking in Latin America laid the foundation for long-term U.S. trade domination after the war. It was an established policy by 1920 for the U.S. government to promote U.S. business interests in Latin America. The period ended on a sour economic note with the depression of 1920 which crippled inter-American trade; the downturn, however, could not disguise the growing economic penetration of Latin America by the United States, a situation long feared by Latin American nations. While the United States was about to embark on a gradual retreat from interventionism, its drive for economic hegemony was to continue.

CHAPTER 4

WORLD POWER AND REGIONAL CONCERNS, 1920–1945

Vignette: Mediating the Peace in South America

During the 1920s and early 1930s the United States made several efforts to mediate complicated and often lengthy territorial disputes involving the South American nations of Bolivia, Chile, Colombia, Paraguay, and Peru. One of the longest running and most dangerous disputes involved the two provinces of Tacna and Arica.

The Tacna-Arica dispute represented unfinished business from the War of the Pacific which ended in 1884. Chile defeated Peru and Bolivia, forcing territorial concessions from both. The Treaty of Ancón ending the war provided that Peru would permanently transfer its province of Tarapacá to Chile and temporarily transfer the provinces of Tacna and Arica; after ten years a plebiscite was supposed to be held in Tacna and Arica to determine whether they would return to Peruvian control or remain under Chilean jurisdiction. Bolivia's loss of its coastal province of Antofagasta left it without access to the Pacific and with a continuing national interest in the Tacna-Arica dispute whose settlement might offer Bolivia a chance to regain a Pacific outlet. Chile would not permit the prescribed plebiscite to take place, and various efforts at mediation—including one by the queen of Spain—did not produce a settlement.

The issue was revived when Peru and Bolivia appealed to the League of Nations. Wishing to avoid "outside interference" in hemispheric affairs, the United States offered to mediate in January 1922, and talks started in Washington the following May. The Bolivian government sent an uninvited delegation which unsuccessfully sought admission to the

proceedings. When negotiations stalled, Peru and Chile signed a protocol in July calling for the disagreement to be arbitrated by President
Warren Harding. The death of Harding in August 1923 slowed the
process. Calvin Coolidge inherited the presidency and the role of arbi-
trator, rendering a decision in March 1925. As the original treaty provided, Coolidge called for a plebiscite presided over by a commission
composed of representatives from Peru and Chile, with a U.S. chairman.
To ensure the commission's prestige, Coolidge appointed as its chair
General John J. Pershing. As the recently retired "General of the Armies,"
Pershing had just completed an official diplomatic tour of South America in connection with the centennial of the Battle of Ayacucho during
the independence movement. In March 1925, Pershing received his appointment as chairman of the Tacna-Arica plebiscite commission.
     Thrust into a situation which had frustrated politicians and diplo-
mats in several countries for more than forty years, Pershing arrived at
Arica, headquarters for the commission, on 2 August 1925. While Pershing attempted to create what he called a "plebiscitary atmosphere," he
came under growing criticism from all sides, especially the Chileans.
Even U.S. Secretary of State Frank Kellogg urged Pershing to speed up
the process. Pershing's health also began to deteriorate. Pershing had
contracted amoebic dysentery on his earlier trip to South America; it
is also likely that Pershing suffered small heart attacks during the negotiations. Even Pershing's return to the United States in January 1926
brought claims from his critics that he was suffering from a "diplomatic
illness."
     Pershing's successor, U.S. General William Lassiter, later terminated
all proceedings, claiming that conditions created by Chile made it impossible to hold a fair plebiscite. Secretary of State Kellogg did get Peru
and Chile to renew diplomatic relations in October 1928. Two months
later during his goodwill tour as president-elect, Herbert Hoover discussed the dispute with the presidents of Chile and Peru and the foreign
minister of Bolivia. Drawing on these discussions, in May 1929 President
Hoover—acting as a neutral party, not a mediator—proposed the "final
bases" for a settlement which were incorporated into a treaty signed by
Peru and Chile in June 1929. After almost a half century of diplomatic
wrangling and threats of additional fighting, the treaty simply assigned
Tacna to Peru and Arica to Chile, with Chile paying Peru six million
dollars. The U.S. role in the proceedings drew almost universal praise

in Latin America—the notable exception being Bolivia which had been excluded from the proceedings and had lost its chance to regain a Pacific outlet.

Based on Frank E. Vandiver, Black Jack: The Life and Times of John J. Pershing *(College Station: Texas A & M Press, 1977), vol. 2, pp. 1064–84.*

U.S. disillusionment with intervention in Latin America and involvement in World War I led to a return to its traditional principle of isolationism after 1920. This isolationism, however, contained divergent and partially contradictory features. As the world's greatest industrial and financial power, the United States wanted to maximize its economic and financial involvement in the world while minimizing its political and military commitments.

In the aftermath of World War I, many in Latin America looked to the League of Nations as an instrument for influencing U.S.-Latin American relations. The Latin American nations hoped that this involvement in a more broadly-based organization would curb the interventionist tendencies of the United States and reduce the predominant economic and financial role played by the United States in the region. These hopes quickly unraveled when the League Covenant recognized the Monroe Doctrine, effectively leaving the United States with principal responsibility for hemispheric matters. The subsequent U.S. refusal to join the League further undercut Latin American hopes that the League could be an instrument for moderating U.S. influence. While all of the Latin American countries became members of the League, it never proved to be an effective instrument in pressuring the United States to accept the principles of nonintervention and the equality of all nations.

The Gradual Retreat from Intervention

As the United States and Latin America entered the postwar era, relations were at one of their lowest points. U.S. interventions in Nicaragua, Haiti, and the Dominican Republic continued after the war. Special treaty relations with Cuba and Panama involved the United States directly in the internal affairs of those two countries. The United States had no official relations with Mexico because of another revolutionary change in government in 1920. All Latin American nations were concerned about the Monroe Doctrine, the Roosevelt Corollary, and postwar economic relations.

Liquidating the interventions in Nicaragua, the Dominican Republic, and Haiti proved complicated. Presidents Harding, Coolidge, and Hoover opposed intervention not only on diplomatic grounds but also as an obstacle to achieving their major economic goals of expanding foreign trade and balancing the domestic budget. Efforts to end the interventions took place against a background of continuing political instability in Central America and the Caribbean.

The U.S. military presence in Nicaragua was small scale but high profile — an expanded Marine guard for the U.S. Embassy in Managua of approximately 100 men. Politics continued to revolve around the Liberal-Conservative feud although political loyalties were highly personalistic. U.S.-supervised elections held in October 1924 produced victory for a fusion ticket of a Conservative president, Carlos Solórzano, and a Liberal vice president, Juan B. Sacasa. The United States reluctantly recognized the new government after Solórzano promised truly free elections in 1928, acceptance of a U.S.-trained constabulary, and the resolution of Nicaragua's economic problems. After some delay in organizing the new constabulary known as the National Guard, the U.S. intervention in Nicaragua officially came to an end on 3 August 1925 with the withdrawal of the extra Marine force.

Peace and stability proved ephemeral as Conservative General Emiliano Chamorro used his military power to maneuver his way into the presidency in early 1926. His Liberal opponents revolted in May 1926. The conflict developed into a virtual civil war by August. Looking to the 1928 elections, Chamorro resigned from the presidency in October 1926, restoring to the presidency the Conservative Adolfo Díaz, the beneficiary of an earlier U.S. intervention in 1912. The United States recognized the Díaz government on 17 November 1926.

Worried about the deteriorating situation in Nicaragua, the United States embarked on a policy of "creeping intervention." Small-scale Marine landings started in May 1926 and escalated in January with the dispatch of an enlarged legation guard to Managua and the creation of U.S.-enforced "neutral zones" along Nicaragua's east coast where Liberal military activity was greatest. U.S. Marines disarmed Liberal forces in the neutral zones but permitted shipments of arms to the Conservative Díaz government. Creation of new zones soon brought all important points on the eastern coast under U.S. control. U.S. Marines later assumed responsibility for keeping open the rail line between Managua and the Pacific port of Corinto, establishing more neutral zones

along the route. By spring 1927, there were more than 3,000 U.S. Marines in
Nicaragua, including a squadron of aircraft.

The U.S. government hoped to avoid a greater military commitment by
mediating between Nicaragua's contending factions. In April 1927 the Coolidge administration dispatched a special mission headed by Henry L. Stimson, former secretary of war under Taft and future secretary of state under
Hoover. The Conservative president Díaz reluctantly agreed to plans for U.S.-
supervised elections in 1928 and the organization of a nonpartisan national
guard. Stimson achieved a breakthrough at his meeting with the Liberal minister of war, General José María Moncada, on the banks of the Tipitapa River
on 4 May 1927. In what became known as the Tipitapa accords, Moncada
agreed to disarmament, amnesty, supervised elections, and the continuation
of Díaz in the presidency.

After the Tipitapa meeting, U.S. policy focused on implementing the accords and supervising the elections of 1928. The only major Liberal military
leader who refused to observe the accords was Augusto Sandino, who began
a guerrilla struggle against both Nicaraguan and U.S. forces in July 1927. The
Marines started their withdrawal, reducing their forces to about 1,700 men by
the end of August 1927. Continued attacks by Sandino's forces soon forced a
reversal of policy; by March 1928 reinforcements brought the total number of
Marines in Nicaragua to 3,700, supported by five cruisers and 1,500 sailors off-
shore. Sandino did not try to disrupt the U.S.-supervised elections of November 1928 which led to a victory for Liberal General José María Moncada
who took office on 1 January 1929.

With Moncada in the presidency, the Tipitapa accords had basically been
fulfilled. Sandino, however, continued to engage in guerrilla warfare, making the United States reluctant to withdraw its forces quickly. The United
States wanted to turn the campaign against Sandino over to Nicaraguan
forces, permitting a gradual withdrawal. Marine forces declined from more
than 5,000 in January 1929 to about 1,400 in January 1931. The U.S. government also informed Moncada that complete control of the Guard would be
transferred to the Nicaraguans no later than 1 January 1933. U.S. officials and
Marines remained to supervise the elections held in November 1932. The win-
ner in the presidential contest was the Liberal Juan B. Sacasa, one of the targets of the earlier U.S. intervention. On 1 January 1933 Sacasa took office, and
the National Guard came under Nicaraguan control. The following day the
last of the Marines withdrew.

U.S. military involvement in the Dominican Republic dated from May 1916. Unlike other interventions of the period, the United States government did not operate through local officials; the refusal of Dominican politicians to cooperate had forced the United States to set up a military government run by a high-ranking U.S. naval officer. In June 1921 the new Harding administration announced its intention to make a "rapid withdrawal" from the Dominican Republic.[1] The withdrawal proposal put forward by the United States drew a quick rejection from Dominican politicians because of its numerous conditions, especially a required ratification of all acts by the occupation government. While negotiations proceeded, U.S. officials continued their training of a Dominican National Guard and reduced the military activities of the Marines. The arrangement of a loan to the Dominican government helped to pave the way for a withdrawal agreement in June 1922.

Harding dispatched Sumner Welles, chief of the Latin American Division of the State Department, to the Dominican Republic to oversee the with-

A mural of Augusto Sandino in a Jinotega, Nicaragua barrio, 1984. Sandino's struggle was an inspiration for Nicaraguan revolutionary forces in the 1970s and during the government of the FSLN in the 1980s. Acrylic, unknown artist.

Photograph by David Kunzle

drawal. The U.S. military government gave way to a provisional Dominican government in October 1922. At the same time command of the Guard, renamed the Dominican National Police, shifted to a Dominican general. Presidential elections held in March 1924 produced a victory for General Horacio Vásquez whose earlier political maneuverings had helped create the environment that led to U.S. intervention in 1916. Vásquez took office on 12 July 1924. The Marines began their withdrawal in June, completing it in late September.

Republican administrations were also interested in terminating the intervention in Haiti, another legacy of Wilsonian "missionary diplomacy." A treaty signed in 1915 officially recognized U.S. involvement in the internal affairs of Haiti. The Harding administration streamlined the occupation bureaucracy by placing it under the control of the State Department. The number of Marines in Haiti was reduced from 1,900 to 1,300 by July 1923; the remaining Marines withdrew from the interior and concentrated on the coast, transferring more of the police responsibilities to the Gendarmerie, later renamed the Garde d'Haiti. Harding reluctantly confined his actions to moderating, rather than abandoning, the intervention.

With improved technical services and a reduced military role, the Haitian occupation went on cruise control until 1929 when a series of strikes and riots took place as a result of efforts by President Louis Borno to perpetuate himself in office. The demonstrations had a pronounced anti-American tone as longstanding resentment against a foreign and white occupation came to the surface. The State Department rejected requests for Marine reinforcements, but martial law had to be declared in December 1929.

The disturbances prompted the Hoover administration to reevaluate its occupation policy and to appoint a special commission to investigate the Haitian situation. The commission was in Haiti from 28 February to 16 March 1930 and submitted its recommendations to the president on 26 March. The main recommendation was that the occupation continue until 1936 when the treaty of 1915 would expire. While the withdrawal would be gradual, the "Haitianization" of treaty services should be accelerated and presidential elections held quickly. Two days after receiving the commission's report, President Hoover announced that it would serve as the basis for future U.S. policy.

In November 1930 Dana Munro, chief of the Latin American Division of the State Department, became minister to Haiti and assumed overall supervision of the occupation. Plans for the Haitianization of treaty services were more formally defined in an agreement signed on 5 August 1931 which provided for the transfer of public works, health services, and educational programs to Haitian control effective 1 October 1931. U.S. control of finances was modified but not transferred completely. At the same time, the United States suspended martial law but did not set any date for the withdrawal of U.S. troops.

Although there were problems in implementing the Haitianization agreement, the way seemed clear to bringing an end to the long-running intervention in Haiti. The Haitian government survived political conflicts connected with the passage of a new constitution in July 1932, and in September 1932 Haitian and U.S. officials signed a new treaty which provided for the complete Haitianization of the Garde and the withdrawal of U.S. forces before the end of 1934. But, because it also called for reduced but continued U.S. control over Haitian finances, the Haitian congress unanimously rejected the treaty. The momentum for withdrawal, however, had been well established by the time Hoover left the presidency in March 1933. After a new agreement, the Marines withdrew ahead of schedule in 1934, although U.S. involvement in Haitian finances did not end completely until 1947.

Reappraising the Monroe Doctrine and the Roosevelt Corollary

The phasing out of interventions in Nicaragua, the Dominican Republic, and Haiti was part of a broader reappraisal of the Monroe Doctrine and particularly the Roosevelt Corollary to the Doctrine. Because the Doctrine had been used to justify military interventions, it had become unacceptable to Latin Americans, many of whom wanted the United States to renounce both the Monroe Doctrine and the right of intervention. Others, convinced that the United States would not do either of those things, worked to limit U.S. interventionism by multilateralizing the Monroe Doctrine. There was also talk of establishing a Pan American equivalent of the League of Nations. All of these factors came together at the Fifth Inter-American Conference at Santiago, Chile, from 25 March to 3 May 1923. The Uruguayan delegation at the conference initiated the discussion on an American League of Nations tied to a multilateralization of the Monroe Doctrine. While the United States was willing to study the question of a "closer association of the American republics," the U.S. delegation made it clear that it intended to maintain control. Despite this limited progress, the Latin American nations still made it clear that they would continue to press for an unequivocal renunciation of intervention by the United States in other hemispheric forums.[2]

By the time the Sixth Inter-American Conference met at Havana in January 1928, the United States had ended its intervention in the Dominican Republic, terminated but renewed its intervention in Nicaragua, and was watching the clock tick on its occupation of Haiti. Thirteen of the twenty-one nations at the conference favored some declaration against intervention, but the issue was referred to a subcommittee chaired by former U.S. Secretary of State Charles Evans Hughes. Drawing upon his extensive legal experience, Hughes ably defended the right of "interposition," as he called it. Faced with the unshakable U.S. opposition to a declaration on intervention, the Conference referred the matter to the next inter-American conference scheduled for Montevideo.[3]

Point-Counterpoint: The United States and the Right of Intervention

"What are we to do when government breaks down and American citizens are in danger of their lives? Are we to stand by and see them butchered in the jungle because a government in circumstances which it cannot control and for which it may not be responsible can no longer afford reasonable protection? . . . Now it is a principle of international law that in such a case a government is fully justified in taking action—I would call it interposition of a temporary character—for the purpose of protecting the lives and property of its nationals. I could say that that is not intervention. One can read in text books that that is not intervention. But if I should subscribe to a formula which others thought might prevent the action which a nation is entitled to take in these circumstances, there might come later the charge of bad faith because of acceptance of a formula with one interpretation in my mind, while another interpretation of it is in the mind of those proposing the formula. So it was necessary to have a fair understanding. Of course the United States cannot forgo its right to protect its citizens. . . ."

—*Former U.S. Secretary of State Charles Evans Hughes, head of the U.S. delegation to the Sixth Inter-American Conference, Havana, February 1928 quoted in Merlo J. Pusey,* Charles Evans Hughes, *vol. 2. (New York: Macmillan Company, 1951), pp. 559–60.*

"The policy and attitude of the United States Government toward every important phase of international relationships in this hemisphere could scarcely be made more clear and definite than they have been made by both word and action especially since March 4 [1933]. Every observing person must by this time thoroughly understand that under the Roosevelt Administration the United States Government is as much opposed as any other government to interference with the freedom, the sovereignty, or other internal affairs or processes of the governments of other nations. . . . I feel safe in undertaking to say that under our support of the general principle of nonintervention, as has been suggested, no government need fear any intervention on the part of the United States under the Roosevelt Administration."

—*U.S. Secretary of State Cordell Hull, head of the U.S. delegation to the Seventh Inter-American Conference, Montevideo, December 1933 in Cordell Hull,* The Memoirs of Cordell Hull, *vol. 1 (New York: Macmillan Company, 1948), p. 334.*

Although the United States was not prepared to renounce the right of intervention, it was rethinking the connection between intervention and the Monroe Doctrine established by the Roosevelt Corollary. The separation of the Doctrine from the Corollary took place with the drafting of what became known as the Clark Memorandum in December 1928. J. Ruben Clark was a prominent international lawyer and undersecretary of state during the Coolidge administration. His memorandum on the subject to Secretary of State Kellogg was not typical interoffice correspondence. In 236 pages and a seventeen-page cover letter, Clark examined the historical evolution of the Monroe Doctrine. He concluded that the Monroe Doctrine did not apply to purely inter-American relations and that the Roosevelt Corollary was not justified by its terms. Clark's memorandum did not constitute a rejection of the Monroe Doctrine nor a renunciation of intervention, but it did break the connection between the two and thus made the defense of intervention more difficult. Since Clark's conclusions did not coincide with the views of President Coolidge, the memorandum remained an internal communication until President Hoover had it published and publicly embraced its ideas in early 1930.

Hoover further circumscribed future interventions by implementing a new policy on the protection of American lives and property in April 1931. In response to the slaying of U.S. citizens in an attack by Sandino's guerrillas in Nicaragua, Secretary of State Henry L. Stimson stated that the U.S. government could not provide general protection for Americans in Nicaragua. Stimson also indicated that U.S. citizens conducting business in Latin America did so at their own risk and could not expect protection from the U.S. government. When a revolution broke out in Honduras that same month, the Hoover administration reiterated its policy of restraint.

U.S. Economic Activity in Latin America

While the United States gradually retreated from its interventionist policies, there was a growing interest in promoting U.S. economic penetration of Latin America during the 1920s. World War I had given the United States an economic and financial advantage over its European competitors, an advantage which the United States hoped to build on during the postwar years. It was accepted policy by 1920 for the U.S. government to promote American business interests in Latin America. The shift in emphasis from political/military matters to economic affairs led to an expansion of the State Department's Office of the Foreign Trade Advisor and greater attention to collecting foreign economic information. The State Department found a rising rival for control of international economic relations in the Commerce Department which was rapidly expanding under the leadership of Secretary Herbert Hoover. His vision was for the department to serve as a clearinghouse for international economic information.

There was extensive attention to the role that U.S. financiers would play in postwar Latin America. Both the Commerce and State Departments energetically promoted loans to Latin America in the early 1920s as a method of increasing trade and investment. Although the State Department often prescribed the terms of private loans to Latin American governments, it continued to maintain the official position that it did not render opinions on the financial soundness of loan projects. Hoover, in contrast, wanted the Commerce Department to pass judgment on the financial risk involved. In March 1922 the State Department made an official "statement on loans" which typified the country's ambiguous efforts to pursue both isolationism and greater economic involvement. The statement required U.S. lenders to inform the State Department of all details concerning potential loans to foreign governments while simultaneously disclaiming any responsibility for the foreign loans made by U.S. banks. Hoover wanted to get the U.S. government more actively involved in what he called "the preventive governmental supervision" of loans, restricting them to productive purposes that would generate the funds needed to repay the loans.[4]

Although bureaucrats wrangled over loan policy, most of the lending in the 1920s was done without the cooperation of the U.S. government. For most of the 1920s, bank funds available for foreign lending increased, leading to less cautious policies. Much of the lending took the form of the sale of dollar-denominated bonds by Latin American governments in the U.S. market. Argentina led all other Latin American nations in this regard, placing bonds worth almost $500 million in the United States between 1920 and 1930.

U.S. economic penetration of Latin America also took the form of increased direct investment in a variety of businesses, including the politically explosive area of resource extraction. The war had demonstrated conclusively both the strategic and economic importance of oil, and there was a widely shared fear in the years immediately after the war that domestic U.S. oil reserves might soon be exhausted. Latin America figured prominently in private and governmental plans for foreign oil development. Mexico was the second largest oil producer in the world in the early 1920s, after the United States, but its production declined when the Mexican government sought to restrict indiscriminate pumping from its fields and to control and tax what was produced. In response U.S. oil companies then shifted their attention to Venezuela where a major oil discovery in 1922 and a president more amenable to personal economic inducements proved attractive to U.S. investors. By 1929 thirty-nine U.S. companies had invested more than $200 million in Venezuelan oil operations.

During the 1920s U.S. investment in Latin America grew not only in scale but also in diversity. Mining continued to attract considerable U.S. investment. Led by such companies as Anaconda and Kennecott, U.S. investments flowed into Chile (nitrates and copper), Peru (copper, lead, and zinc), and Bolivia (tin); U.S. companies also searched for iron ore in Chile, manganese in Brazil, gold in Ecuador, and even platinum in Colombia. Ford Motor Company led the expansion of U.S. automakers into Latin America in the 1920s. Radio Corporation of America (RCA) was one of the leaders in expanding radio communications in Latin America while International Telephone and Telegraph (ITT) assumed a dominant role in telephone communications in the region. U.S. agricultural investments expanded in every part of Latin America; as in the past, these agricultural operations were devoted almost exclusively to the export trade. Total U.S. direct investment in Latin America almost doubled between 1919 and 1929. This growth was so pronounced and often in such high-profile activities that it aroused the concern of European competitors and Latin American governments.

The Great Depression

After 1929 U.S.-Latin American relations increasingly unfolded against the backdrop of a worsening international depression. Economic downturn caused major interruptions in inter-American trade and finance, led to a series of revolts in Latin America, and posed major problems regarding recognition of governments by Washington. The availability of U.S. loans in the 1920s had led many Latin American governments to contract excessive debts; compounding this problem was the fact that many of the loans had not been used to promote economic development directly or had been used to pay off earlier loans. By early 1933 Latin American governments were in default on approximately $1 billion in bonds. The Hoover administration made it clear to U.S. creditors that it would not play debt collector, but it also indicated to Latin American debtors that it would not work to implement a moratorium on Latin American debts as it had for European debts. These debt problems contributed to a dramatic decline in two-way trade between the United States and Latin America after 1929. Trade problems also partially reflected the increasingly nationalistic economic policies being followed by hemispheric countries. These policies involved restrictions on currency exchanges, prohibition of certain imports, and the raising of tariff barriers to protect local industries.

The drastic economic decline led to political instability and revolutions, forcing the United States to reevaluate its recognition policy. The Wilsonian policy of recognizing only those governments coming to power through constitutional means had been continued with diminishing enthusiasm by the Harding and Coolidge administrations. As many nations in Latin America experienced governmental upheavals in the early 1930s, this inherited policy came under review. There was also a growing feeling in Latin America that withholding recognition constituted a kind of indirect intervention, leading to pressures on the United States to abandon this tactic as well. The principles for recognition used by the Hoover administration represented a return to the traditional criteria used by the United States until the early twentieth century: (1) the new government must demonstrate effective control of the country; (2) there should be no substantial resistance to the authority of the new government; and (3) the new government must indicate its willingness to fulfill its international obligations. Implementation of these principles first came in September 1930 when the Hoover administration resumed normal diplomatic relations with governments in Argentina, Bolivia, and Peru. In February 1931 Secretary of State Henry Stimson officially stated that the United States had definitively abandoned the Wilsonian policy and was returning to its traditional stance.

By the end of the Hoover administration, the U.S. retreat from intervention was well established. The formal interventions in the Dominican Republic and Nicaragua had been terminated, and the groundwork laid for ending the Haitian intervention in the near future. The United States had also officially abandoned the use of recognition as a tool of intervention. Remnants of earlier involvements remained in the Platt Amendment with Cuba and the "special relationship" with Panama. The United States still had not publicly and formally renounced the right of intervention, a limitation that was the ultimate goal of the Latin American nations. It would be up to the new U.S. president taking office in March 1933, Franklin D. Roosevelt (FDR), to tie up these loose ends of empire.

Roosevelt and the Good Neighbor Policy

In the 1932 U.S. presidential campaign, Roosevelt had campaigned on a platform calling for an end to U.S. interference in the internal affairs of other nations and a cooperative approach to the Monroe Doctrine. With political attention focused on financial and economic problems, there was unspoken bipartisan agreement that intervention was expensive and ineffective. In his inaugural address Roosevelt described his foreign policy as the "policy of the good neighbor" who respected the rights of others. While many in Latin American looked favorably on the election of Roosevelt, there were still the specters of an idealistic Woodrow Wilson proclaiming a new day in U.S.-Latin American relations, not to mention a younger Franklin Roosevelt who as the Democratic vice presidential nominee in 1920 had bragged that he had written the Haitian constitution. FDR would soon have the opportunity to show if there was substance behind his statements at the Seventh Inter-American Conference at Montevideo in December 1933.

The Montevideo Conference had originally been scheduled for December 1932. The impact of the depression and subsequent political instability, however, led to its postponement for a year. The new U.S. Secretary of State,

Cordell Hull, headed the U.S. delegation; nine Latin American countries sent their ministers of foreign relations. With the depression near its worst point, economics figured prominently in the proceedings. Secretary Hull addressed the decline in trade by proposing a plan for reciprocal trade treaties, a suggestion that was passed unanimously. The debt question was deferred to a special economic conference to be held later at Santiago, Chile. The Latin American nations saw the issue of intervention as the true test of U.S. intentions. The problem was addressed in the proposed "Convention on the Rights and Duties of States." The Convention provided that all states were juridically equal and that no state had the right to intervene in the internal or external affairs of another state. Stressing the Roosevelt administration's commitment to a policy of nonintervention, Hull signed the convention, but made the condition that the renunciation of intervention was qualified by the "law of nations as generally recognized." The United States had taken one more step in its retreat from intervention, but it had still not provided the unequivocal assurances that most Latin American nations were seeking.[5]

For Roosevelt and Hull, reciprocity and reciprocal trade were key features of the Good Neighbor Policy. The Roosevelt administration saw the policy as a two-way street. The United States would respect the rights of its neighbors (nonintervention) for which Latin America would reciprocate by respecting the rights of its neighbor (fair treatment for U.S. citizens and property). Under the Reciprocal Trade Agreements Act of 12 June 1934, the U.S. Congress authorized President Roosevelt to raise or lower existing tariff rates by as much as fifty percent in response to actions by other countries. Hull saw Latin America as a testing ground for this program. Although many Latin Americans were worried about the economic consequences of binding themselves more closely to the United States, eleven countries signed agreements by 1 January 1940: Cuba, Brazil, Haiti, Colombia, Honduras, Nicaragua, Guatemala, Costa Rica, El Salvador, Ecuador, and Venezuela. Mexico was notable by its absence.

The first real test of the Good Neighbor Policy and nonintervention involved Cuba where the United States maintained a right to intervene under the Platt Amendment. The political situation there had been deteriorating steadily under the rule of Gerardo Machado, president since 1925. His corrupt and repressive regime generated growing political opposition and violence. The great depression hit the island especially hard, given the economy's heavy reliance on the production and export of sugar which experienced a rapid price decline.

By the time Roosevelt took office in March 1933, the growing opposition to Machado was about to reach a climax. The U.S. president did not want to intervene in Cuban affairs but was prepared to interfere in the unfolding political situation. He appointed veteran Latin American diplomat, Sumner Welles, as his new ambassador to Cuba. Welles arrived in Cuba in May 1933 with instructions to mediate among the different factions but to avoid any action that might force the United States to invoke the Platt Amendment. Although he was supposed to be an impartial negotiator, Welles operated on the assumption that Machado was finished and his departure should be facilitated. When a general strike occurred on 4 August 1933, Welles urged Machado to take a "leave of absence," hinting that the United States might intervene if he did not comply.[6] When top-ranking officers in the Cuban Army also indicated that Machado should depart, he requested a leave of absence and fled Cuba on 12 August 1933.

The interim regime of the respected civilian Carlos Manuel de Céspedes received support from the United States and leading officers of the Cuban army. Still, political violence continued as the economy deteriorated. On 5 September a combination revolt and mutiny took place. This "Sergeants' Revolt," led by Sergeant Fulgencio Batista, overthrew the Céspedes regime and the officer corps of the Cuban army. Batista—quickly promoted to colonel—struck an alliance with university students who had led the opposition to Machado and then Céspedes. Welles recommended intervention, but the Roosevelt administration declined to send in troops. The United States refused to recognize the regime of provisional president Ramón Grau San Martín, a popular university professor. After Welles departed the ambassadorship in December 1933, Batista—worried about possible U.S. intervention—forced Grau to step aside in January 1934 in favor of Carlos Mendieta, former army officer and opponent of Machado. The United States—convinced that Mendieta and Batista could restore order—recognized Mendieta on 23 January 1934, only five days after he took office. Batista would continue to be a force in Cuban politics until Fidel Castro came to power in 1959.

In May 1934 Cuba and the United States signed a treaty abrogating the Platt Amendment with the exception that the United States would retain its naval base at Guantanamo. Good Neighbor diplomacy in Cuba reached full development with the signing of a reciprocal trade agreement in August 1934, the first such trade treaty to be signed by the United States with any country.

At the inter-American Conference for the Maintenance of Peace held in Buenos Aires in December 1936, the evolution of the Good Neighbor Policy

from one emphasizing nonintervention to one stressing hemispheric solidarity began. The conference was a special meeting initiated by the United States
to prepare the hemisphere to deal with the deteriorating international situation in Europe and Asia. To emphasize the importance attached to the meeting by the United States, Secretary of State Hull headed the U.S. delegation,
and President Roosevelt participated in the opening ceremonies. On the issue
of intervention, the United States completed its postwar retreat from intervention by unconditionally renouncing the right of intervention: the nonintervention protocol declared that intervention was inadmissible either
"directly or indirectly, and for whatever reason, in the internal or external affairs" of American nations. The growing emphasis on solidarity was embod-
ied in the "Consultative Pact" in which the American republics agreed to
consult in the event that hemispheric peace was threatened by war between
American nations or in the event of an international war outside the hemisphere "which might menace the peace of the American republics." The Latin
Americans received the unconditional rejection of intervention by the United
States which they had long sought, while the United States received a promise of greater cooperation to meet the growing external threat to hemispheric
security.[7]

Still, events in such diverse places as Nicaragua and Bolivia provided severe
tests of the Roosevelt administration's commitment to its Good Neighbor Policy. There was strong Latin American pressure for Roosevelt to expand nonintervention to include noninterference, an approach that left Roosevelt with
the dilemma of how to deal with nondemocratic governments, on the increase
in the 1930s. The rise of Anastasio Somoza García in Nicaragua demonstrated
the quandary confronting the United States. When the United States terminated its Nicaraguan intervention in January 1933, it left the government in
the hands of the civilian Juan Sacasa and Sacasa at the mercy of the supposedly nonpartisan National Guard under the command of Somoza. While the
United States did not directly promote Somoza's rise, there was little the
United States could do to block the establishment of his dictatorship once it
accepted the policies of nonintervention and noninterference. Somoza forced
Sacasa to resign in June 1936, manipulated elections held in December 1936,
and assumed the presidency on 1 January 1937. The situation was made even
more acute for the Roosevelt administration by Somoza's blatant efforts to in-
gratiate himself with the United States and his willingness to support U.S. foreign policy. Somoza won recognition from the United States, deftly shifting

from an anti-communist to an anti-fascist stance as the international situation changed.

Developments in Bolivia presented a different kind of test for the Good Neighbor Policy by calling into question the willingness of Latin American nations to make the policy reciprocal as the Roosevelt administration insisted it should be. Actions by the Bolivian government raised the possibility that the Good Neighbor Policy might be used as a shield by Latin American nations to discriminate against U.S. investors. On 13 March 1937 the Bolivian government nullified the petroleum concession of the U.S.-owned Standard Oil Company of Bolivia and confiscated its properties, charging the company with tax fraud and illegal exportation of oil. The initial response of the U.S. government was to encourage a negotiated settlement. Direct negotiations between the Bolivian government and Standard Oil were not successful, even though the company was only seeking compensation for, not restoration of, its assets. In March 1938 Standard Oil initiated legal action, but a year later, the Bolivian Supreme Court, amid threats of violence against the justices, ruled that the company did not have the right to bring a lawsuit against the government. Although the State Department had promised the company to push for arbitration if there was a blatant denial of justice, it instead encouraged continuing direct and indirect negotiations. After September 1939 the position of the U.S. government was increasingly influenced by the war in Europe, with top priority given to maintaining close cooperation with hemispheric nations. In April 1942 the dispute was settled when Bolivia technically purchased the assets of the company for $2 million.

United States-Mexico Relations in the Inter-War Years

The unpredictable course of the Mexican Revolution continued to be the dominant force in shaping relations between the United States and Mexico. U.S. relations with the administration of Venustiano Carranza (1917–1920) became increasingly acrimonious over radical provisions in the new Mexican constitution of 1917 and Mexico's role in World War I. Constitutional restrictions on property rights and foreign business operations caused major problems, especially for the Mexican petroleum industry dominated by U.S. and British companies. Oil was a crucial source of revenue for the Carranza administration, and U.S. oil companies complained bitterly that they were the targets of discriminatory taxation. Article 27 of the new Constitution which assigned subsoil rights to the nation threatened the concessions held by American oil companies under the previous constitution. The Wilson administration also disapproved of the wartime conduct of Carranza; U.S. officials often interpreted Carranza's nationalistic policies and Mexico's continued neutrality as signs of a pro-German attitude. Carranza's efforts to dictate his successor in 1920 led to revolt by supporters of Alvaro Obregón and the overthrow and assassination of Carranza in May 1920, leaving Mexico with another revolutionary government unrecognized by the United States.

Mexican oil gusher brought in by the Texas Company.

Courtesy E. L. DeGolyer Sr. Collection [Mss 60 Box 214 Fd28], DeGolyer Library, Southern Methodist University

As Obregón—president from 1920 to 1924—labored to reconstruct exec-utive authority and to rebuild the economy, relations between the United States and Mexico centered on the closely related issues of oil, debt, agri-cultural lands, and recognition. The oil issue remained unsettled from the Carranza regime, especially the question of whether Article 27 would be retroactively applied. In rulings in 1921 and 1922, the Mexican Supreme Court dealt with the retroactivity issue by establishing the "doctrine of positive acts"; the doctrine stated that foreigners who had subsoil rights and who had en-gaged in the "positive act" of exploiting them prior to 1917 would not be sub-ject to retroactive application of Article 27. Both the U.S. government and U.S. oil companies were pleased with the principle established but wanted it put in the form of a treaty, a move politically impossible for Obregón in the highly charged post-revolutionary atmosphere.

Other issues were also on the table. The Revolution had interrupted pay-ment on Mexico's external debt; reaching agreement on this old debt was a prerequisite to receiving new loans which the Obregón administration des-perately needed to finance economic recovery. Mexico's major creditors (U.S., British, and French) formed the International Bankers' Committee to reach an agreement on the old debt. The agrarian reform program of Obregón led to the expropriation of properties owned by U.S. citizens. The U.S. govern-ment did not object to such expropriations as long as they were done in the public interest, did not discriminate against Americans, and compensation was prompt and adequate. Lacking the financial resources to provide cash pay-ment at once, Obregón offered to pay for the lands with government bonds. All of these factors fed into the problem of extending U.S. recognition. The new Mexican president wanted and needed recognition in order to carry out his political and economic policies but could not meet all U.S. demands be-cause of domestic political pressures.

While the International Bankers' Committee was able to reach a settlement with the Obregón administration in June 1922, the other issues were resolved in the Bucareli Agreements signed in August 1923. Both sides made conces-sions. On the issue of agricultural lands, the United States accepted govern-ment bonds as adequate compensation for properties up to 1,755 hectares (approximately 4,000 acres); for properties in excess of 1,755 hectares, the Mexican government agreed to pay cash, effectively eliminating such expro-priations since the government could not afford them. The Obregón regime also agreed to adhere to the doctrine of positive acts in dealing with subsoil resources but forced the United States to yield on its demand that this doctrine be part of a formal treaty. The only portion of the agreement that took treaty form was the establishment of two claims commissions: a general claims commission to handle cases arising between 1868 and 1910 and a special revolutionary claims commission to deal with claims from the 1910–1920 period. With these issues resolved, U.S. recognition quickly followed.

The basic weakness of the Bucareli agreements—the fact that most of them were not in treaty form—soon became evident after Obregón's successor, Plutarco Elías Calles, became president. Calles revived the dispute over the application of Article 27 by supporting the passage of the petroleum code of 1925 which called for a "modification" of the doctrine of positive acts. Under the code all oil companies had to have their concessions confirmed no later than 1 January 1927; no concession would be confirmed for more than a fifty-year term, effectively reducing the duration of many concessions. The major U.S. oil companies indicated that they would not comply with the new law, and a few even called for U.S. intervention. The appointment of a new U.S. ambassador, Dwight Morrow, helped promote a peaceful solution to the problem. Morrow—personal friend and former college classmate of President Coolidge —soon established a good working relationship with Calles who did not take action against the companies refusing to comply with the petroleum code. Calles came up with a way of backing down while still saving face. In November 1927 the Mexican Supreme Court reaffirmed the doctrine of positive acts, ruling the offensive portions of the code of 1925 unconstitutional. The following month the Mexican Congress passed a new petroleum code incorporating the doctrine of positive acts.

A period of relative calm settled over U.S.-Mexican relations until new controversy developed over the oil industry under Calles' successor, Lázaro Cárdenas, president from 1934 to 1940. In 1937 the oil workers went on strike, demanding higher wages, fringe benefits, and changes in working conditions. The dispute made its way to the Mexican Supreme Court which ruled on behalf of the workers. When the oil companies defied the court decision, Cárdenas retaliated by expropriating all foreign-owned oil companies on 18 March 1938. There was some pressure in the United States for intervention, but it was never seriously considered by the Roosevelt administration. As was the case with the Bolivian oil expropriations, the U.S. government was more concerned with promoting hemispheric solidarity than with the problems of U.S. investors. Unlike the Bolivian case, Cárdenas had indicated from the beginning that compensation would be paid; the only issue was the amount. It was not until November 1941 that there was an agreement on a method of valuing the properties. In the final settlement reached in April 1942, the Mexican government agreed to pay $23,995,991 for the U.S. properties plus three percent interest per annum since March 1938. Paying off this debt became an issue of national pride; Mexican schoolchildren were even encouraged to help pay the debt through their own small contributions. As for the United States, the evolving Good Neighbor Policy—and the international situation—had combined once again to promote compromise.

Mobilizing the Hemisphere

The attitude of the U.S. government in both the Bolivian and Mexican oil expropriations was a good indicator of the evolution of the Good Neighbor Policy from a policy of nonintervention and reciprocity to a hemispheric security policy. The early stages of this evolution were apparent at the Buenos Aires Conference in 1936. At the Eighth Inter-American Conference in Lima in December 1938, the United States tried to continue the process of converting the Good Neighbor Policy into a collective security arrangement. The Lima Conference provided a familiar scenario for inter-American meetings: the United States versus Argentina. With the United States and Argentina at odds over even holding the conference, Brazilian mediation produced the "Declaration of Lima," which was unanimously approved. The Declaration expanded on the Consultative Pact agreed to at Buenos Aires in 1936. In the event of a threat to the "peace, security, or territorial integrity of any American republic," any American nation could issue a call for consultation. The Declaration went beyond the Consultative Pact by prescribing that a meeting of foreign ministers would be used to implement the procedure, not simply representatives designated by the different countries.[8]

Events in Europe soon produced an opportunity to invoke the Declaration. On 1 September 1939, World War II began in Europe with the German invasion of Poland. Panama issued a call for consultation, and on 23 September 1939 representatives from all twenty-one republics met in Panama to formulate a hemispheric response. The conference issued a "General Declaration of Neutrality," indicating that it was the intention of all the American republics "not to become involved in the European conflict." More controversial was the "Declaration of Panama," which established a 300-mile wide "security zone" around the Americas. Belligerents were supposed to refrain from "hostile acts" in the zone, which would be patrolled by the American republics. Also created was the Inter-American Financial and Economic Advisory Committee to promote economic cooperation and suggest solutions to economic problems caused by the war.[9]

The Havana Conference had to be held ahead of schedule in July due to developments in the European war. Germany strung together an astonishing series of victories in spring 1940, culminating in the fall of France in June. The most compelling reason for advancing the conference was the status of the "orphaned" European colonies in the hemisphere. Germany had already defeated France and Holland and was making preparations for an invasion of Britain. Since the late eighteenth century, U.S. policy had supported the "no-transfer" principle, which opposed the transfer of a hemispheric colony from one European power to another. The Havana Conference converted this no-transfer principle into a hemispheric policy by passing the Act of Havana, which also provided for collective administration by the American republics of any colony threatened with transfer. The Conference also passed a "Declaration of Reciprocal Assistance," which stated that an act of aggression against an American state by any non-American state would be considered an act of aggression against all American states, requiring consultation to determine what measures to take. The responsibilities of the Financial and Economic Advisory Committee were expanded, particularly in the area of promoting an orderly marketing of Latin American commodities.[10]

Preparing for War

After the Havana Conference, U.S. policy revolved around providing aid to Britain and strengthening hemispheric defenses. While Latin American nations generally supported U.S. defense efforts, there were fears that the war might lead to even greater U.S. influence in the region. More pragmatically, there was a growing concern that Germany might win the war and doubts about the willingness and ability of the United States to defend Latin America, especially outside of the Caribbean/Central American area. U.S. strategic planning did not envision an important military role for the armed forces of Latin America beyond defense of their own countries. The United States wanted the Latin American nations to furnish bases for U.S. operations, increase the flow of strategic materials, and take action to curb Axis subversive and intelligence activities.

The United States negotiated with the Latin American nations concerning closer military cooperation and the acquisition of bases. The first phase was the signing of a series of bilateral "staff agreements" in which the United States promised to provide military assistance in return for the Latin American nation's promise to call for assistance if attacked, to combat subversive activities, to exchange intelligence, and to permit the transit of U.S. forces going to the aid of another Latin American country. The request for bases encountered Latin American concerns about jurisdiction and access as well as demands for additional arms. Discussions took place against the background of the "destroyers for bases" deal concluded by the United States with Britain in September 1940. In that agreement, the United States transferred fifty destroyers to Britain in return for ninety-nine-year leases on locations for bases in the Caribbean, with the United States exercising jurisdiction on the bases. The United States hoped to reach similar agreements with a number of Latin American countries. The Latin American nations, however, wanted to retain jurisdiction over any bases involved and to restrict leases to the duration of the war. In signing an agreement with Uruguay in November 1940, the United States agreed to a formula that would be followed elsewhere. The United States provided financing and technical assistance while the host country retained jurisdiction and administration. The bases would be open not only to the United States, but to all other Latin American nations as well. The United States eventually signed base agreements with sixteen countries.

The base agreements committed the United States to a program of providing arms to the Latin American nations, a commitment restricted by U.S. laws regulating the sale of arms, the ability of the Latin American nations to finance purchases, and the defensive role assigned to Latin America in general. The U.S. Lend-Lease Act, which went into effect in March 1941, authorized the president to lend, lease, or sell military items to any country whose defense was deemed vital to the defense of the United States. In April Roosevelt certified that Latin America came under the provisions of the act, and in October 1941 the U.S. Congress passed a lend-lease appropriations act providing funds for arms to Latin America. By the time the United States entered the war in December 1941, the United States had signed lend-lease agreements with seven Latin American nations, although little aid was immediately sent.

The Hemisphere at War

Although the United States had been trying for some time to prepare itself and the hemisphere for war, U.S. entry in December 1941 still had profound political, military, and economic repercussions on inter-American relations. All Latin American nations made some positive response to official U.S. entry into the conflict. Nine countries—the Central American nations, Panama, Cuba, Haiti, and the Dominican Republic—declared war on the Axis powers in December 1941 and signed the Declaration of the United Nations on 1 January 1942. Colombia and Mexico broke relations with the Axis powers while Brazil, Ecuador, Paraguay, and Peru declared their solidarity with the United States, and the remaining countries granted the United States nonbelligerent status, giving it greater freedom of action within their national territories.

In keeping with the Declaration of Reciprocal Assistance signed at the Havana Conference, Chile and the United States called for a consultative meeting of the American republics which convened in Rio de Janeiro on 15 January 1942. While there was some sentiment for a joint declaration of war, the United States did not support such a measure because of the military demands that would result. Instead, the United States supported a joint declaration calling for a break in relations with the Axis powers. This proposal drew opposition from both Argentina and Chile where pro-fascist sentiment was strong. The conference approved a milder resolution which merely recommended a break in diplomatic relations as well as in commercial and financial connections. Those countries which had not already broken diplomatic relations quickly did so except for Argentina and Chile. The conference also established an Inter-American Defense Board made up of military and naval representatives from each country to coordinate hemispheric defense. Also created was the "Emergency Advisory Committee for Political Defense" to develop measures against Axis espionage and subversion.

The holding of the consultative conference in Rio de Janeiro was indicative of the special role that the United States assigned to Brazil during the war. Brazil traditionally pursued close relations with the United States and figured prominently in U.S. strategic thinking as war approached. U.S. planners believed that the most likely scenario for an Axis attack on the hemisphere was a German move out of Africa against Brazil's northeastern "bulge." Once established in Brazil, the Germans could threaten the Panama Canal, the Caribbean region, and even the United States. The presence of a substantial

German community in Brazil also heightened U. S. concern and added to the urgency of improving Brazil's military capability. While the United States wanted to send U.S. troops to defend the bulge, the Brazilians were unwilling to accept U.S. ground forces and wanted U.S. arms, not personnel. Both sides eventually accepted a tradeoff. The United States demonstrated Brazil's importance in hemispheric defense by agreeing in March 1942 to increase Lend-Lease aid to $200 million from the $100 million specified a few months earlier. Brazil responded by permitting unrestricted U.S. air operations in the Brazilian northeast and even the stationing of U.S. troops. In August 1942 Brazil declared war on the Axis after German submarine attacks on its shipping. It also became the only Latin American country to provide a major military force for combat. The growing military ties between the two countries became evident with the signing of an aviation agreement in June 1944 permitting U.S. forces to remain in Brazil after the end of the war. The United States even tried, although not very hard, to get Brazil a permanent seat on the Security Council of the new United Nations organization.

While Brazil and the United States developed closer ties, Argentina found itself increasingly isolated in the hemisphere, largely as a result of U.S. efforts. The United States and Argentina had traditionally staked out divergent paths in international affairs; they were to grow even farther apart under the pressures of war. The two countries had frequently been at cross purposes in the period leading up to hemispheric involvement in the war. Following the Rio Conference in January 1942, relations went into an even more serious decline. Secretary of State Hull interpreted Argentina's traditional obstructionist tactics as being pro-fascist and orchestrated a campaign to bring Argentina into line with the hemispheric policy defined by the United States. In February 1942 the United States began what was effectively an economic boycott of Argentina by refusing to license the exportation of important supplies such as steel and oil for which Argentina had virtually no other supplier. The U.S. government also tried to interfere with Argentine trade with other Latin American countries. An army coup in June 1943 briefly held out the possibility of improved relations, but Hull's demand that Argentina immediately break relations with the Axis provoked more conflict. With no Lend-Lease aid available, Argentina turned to the Axis for arms, a move which further angered the United States. When Argentina finally broke relations with Germany and Japan in January 1944, Hull demanded more concessions from the Argentine government, contributing to another presidential turnover in March 1944. The United States refused to recognize the new government of General Edelmiro Farrell and pressured other Latin American countries to withhold recognition. Hull turned up the economic pressure by freezing Argentine assets in the United States. It was not until Hull resigned due to poor health in November 1944 that tensions between the two countries began to ease.

The Economic Consequences of War

The economic impact of World War II on U.S.-Latin American relations was similar in many ways to that of World War I. The conflict interrupted normal patterns of trade and finance, giving the United States a greater role in hemispheric economic affairs. As had been the case in World War I, the economic impact of World War came in two phases (1939–1941 and 1941–1945), divided by the U.S. entry into the war in December 1941. The United States attached considerably more significance to the economic contribution of Latin America to the war effort than to any military role. The economic mobilization of the hemisphere brought an unprecedented level of cooperation as well as U.S. involvement in Latin American economies.

The United States recognized early on that it had to address the economic as well as the military consequences of war. Even before the European war began, President Roosevelt indicated in April 1939 that the United States would provide economic support to any Latin American nation under economic pressure from European nations. The Panama Conference in September 1939 created the Inter-American Financial and Economic Advisory Committee to analyze and make recommendations concerning the problems resulting from the war. By the summer of 1940 the United States was thinking in terms of a hemispheric economic policy calling for much closer economic relations with Latin America. The United States had already begun a program of stockpiling strategic materials, which it expanded in 1940 with a greater emphasis on Latin American sources. Strategic metals were of particular interest to the United States; in November 1940 the U.S. government contracted to purchase virtually the entire Latin American production of copper and tin. The United States also developed a blacklist of firms and individuals operating in Latin America considered pro-Axis or anti-United States. U.S. firms were prohibited from dealing with any listed person or firm, and the Roosevelt Administration successfully pressured Latin American governments to enforce this blacklist. Another U.S. agency, the Export-Import Bank, dramatically increased its lending power in September 1940, largely to meet the needs of Latin America. By December 1941 the Bank had authorized approximately $229 million in loans to sixteen Latin American nations, mainly to finance the export of goods from the United States to Latin America.

The entry of the United States into the war led to even greater efforts at economic cooperation between the United States and Latin America. At the Rio Conference in January 1942 a resolution was approved recommending a break in commercial and financial relations with the Axis powers. The conference also called for a complete economic mobilization of the American republics to ensure an adequate supply of both military and civilian goods. The United States stepped up its purchase of strategic metals and entered into contracts with sixteen Latin American nations to promote the production of rubber. The Export-Import Bank expanded its lending activities; between December 1941 and September 1945, the Bank authorized loans for more than $271 million to thirteen Latin American nations. Actions were taken to improve transportation and communications within the hemisphere. The Financial and Economic Advisory Committee set up a technical commission to improve maritime transportation. The United States tried to improve land transportation by reviving construction on the Inter-American Highway, concentrating on the Central American section of the road. Axis-connected firms operating airlines in Bolivia, Brazil, Colombia, Ecuador, and Peru were replaced by U.S. firms or locally controlled operations or were forced out of business. Despite wartime problems, direct U.S. investment in Latin America increased by approximately ten percent. The net effect of all of these actions was to create an even greater economic interdependence between the United States and Latin America; between 1941 and 1945 the United States purchased more than fifty percent of Latin America's exports while providing more than sixty percent of Latin American imports.

Planning for Peace: The Chapultepec Conference

Wartime themes and postwar plans came together at the Inter-American Conference on Problems of War and Peace held in Mexico City at Chapultepec Castle in February and March 1945. There had been no inter-American conference since the Rio meeting in January 1942, and there was growing concern in Latin America about its postwar relationship with the United States. The Latin American nations were concerned that they were being cut out of the important wartime decisions that would shape the postwar world and that the United States might relegate the inter-American system to a lesser role once it had served its wartime purposes. The Latin American nations were also worried about the economic consequences of peace, hoping that the United States would aid in Latin America's postwar development. The U.S. policy of isolating Argentina was having a negative effect on U.S.-Latin American relations in general and needed to be resolved.

When the United States finally agreed to the Chapultepec Conference, it sent an impressive delegation including the new secretary of state, Edward Stettinius, who was en route from the Yalta Conference. One of the key issues addressed was the relationship between the inter-American system and the new United Nations organization. The Latin American nations wanted the United Nations to recognize the autonomous status of the inter-American system in dealing with regional problems, a position opposed by the United States. A compromise was reached providing that each nation should make "observations" on the issue to the United Nations conference scheduled for April 1945 in San Francisco. The Latin American nations wanted to put the inter-American system on a more formal basis, but the United States delayed action until the next regular conference when the Governing Board of the Pan American Union would present a draft charter. Latin American demands for a strengthening of the inter-American security system led to the "Act of Chapultepec," which classified an attack against any American state as an attack against all, requiring consultation on the measures to be taken which could include the use of force. Although the Act applied only for the duration of the war, it was to be incorporated in a permanent treaty once the war concluded. On the question of economic relations, the United States agreed to aid in the transition to a peacetime economy by gradually reducing its purchase of strategic raw materials. The United States indicated in general terms its support for economic development in Latin America but did not commit itself to any specific programs of assistance. The status of Argentina, not invited to the conference, was the last issue on the agenda. The United States and the Latin American nations agreed to restore Argentina to the inter-American system and to support its membership in the United Nations if it would adhere to the Act of Chapultepec and declare war on the Axis.

The complete effects of the Chapultepec Conference would not be felt until after the war, but an early test came at the United Nations conference in San Francisco in April 1945. In rapid succession Argentina declared war on the Axis on 27 March, adhered to the Act of Chapultepec on 4 April, and received diplomatic recognition from the United States on 19 April. To gain admission as a charter member of the United Nations, a nation technically had to declare war on the Axis by 1 March 1945, a deadline Argentina had not met. As the result of a U.S.-Soviet deal, Argentina was granted charter membership in the United Nations. The Latin American nations also enjoyed considerable success in having their view of regional arrangements incorporated into the United Nations organization. The UN charter recognized regional systems and assigned them primary responsibility for resolving disputes among their own members but gave the UN Security Council the right to intervene in regional disputes. The Latin American nations also failed in their renewed bid to get a permanent regional seat on the Security Council. The warm glow of the Chapultepec and UN conferences soon gave way to renewed feuding between the United States and Argentina, the postponement of the meeting scheduled for Rio in October 1945 to put the Act of Chapultepec into treaty form, and repeated delays in holding the technical conference to deal with inter-American economic problems. The war had put the Latin American nations in the role of principal supporter of the inter-American system at the very time that the United States was shifting its emphasis to global organization. Latin America wanted to enlist U.S. support in dealing with its growing social and economic difficulties. The United States, however, was preparing for another struggle: the "cold war" with the Soviet Union.

CHAPTER 5

COLD WAR AND SOCIAL REVOLUTION, 1945–1968

Vignette: The Cuban Missile Crisis

As President John F. Kennedy was having breakfast on Tuesday, 16 October 1962, his National Security Adviser, McGeorge Bundy, brought him word that U-2 flights over Cuba had revealed that the Soviets were installing nuclear missiles on the island. According to Robert Kennedy's account, only a few minutes later the President called him and summoned him to the White House. He also called for the attendance of key officials within the administration and men outside government whose intelligence and experience he admired and trusted. This group would meet regularly to advise the president on the crisis, but it was clear throughout that any decision on response rested with John Kennedy. By Thursday, the U.S. intelligence community provided the group with evidence that the missiles being installed were directed at particular U.S. cities. These weapons had the potential of killing 80 million Americans within a few minutes of firing.

On the first day, the president made clear that action to remove the missiles was imperative; to fail to respond was not an option. Several advisers argued for an immediate and massive air strike to take out the missile sites. The president said later that "If we had had to act . . . in the first twenty-four hours, I don't think probably we would have chosen as prudently as we finally did." Robert Kennedy's immediate response was reflected in a note passed to his brother, "I now know how Tojo felt when he was planning Pearl Harbor." He immediately called for further consideration and the development of more alternatives.

Wednesday, as U.S. forces gathered in the Caribbean, Secretary of Defense Robert McNamara proposed a naval blockade. This action would provide a response that was flexible and would give Soviet premier Nikita Khrushchev time to reflect on his options. The United States, for its part, could move up or down in its level of response as needed. During the course of the week, the U.S. military, particularly General Curtis LeMay, the Air Force chief of staff, strongly insisted on a massive air strike. By the time the president left Washington on Friday night to campaign in the mid-term elections, the decision in favor of a blockade had been made.

The following morning, however, the advisers left behind in the capital again raised the concern that a blockade was insufficient. McNamara continued to oppose a strike. Then, in a moment which participants later indicated was decisive, Robert Kennedy began to speak. Arguing that given the memory of Pearl Harbor and the responsibility the president would carry for an unannounced strike that would kill thousands of Cubans and perhaps hundreds of Russians as well, it was unthinkable for him to order such an attack. Such a strike would betray what the United States stood for in the world. The men broke into working groups to examine the two options, and by the time they met again at 4:00 p.m., opinion had once again swung in favor of a blockade—to be called a "quarantine," which would not technically be considered an act of war.

John Kennedy returned that afternoon to Washington, claiming a cold to avoid alarming the American people. He presided over his advisers in one final debate. While McNamara spoke forcefully for the blockade, the military—not without some civilian support—continued to insist on a strike. Although no formal vote was taken, the preponderance of opinion was for the quarantine. The president responded negatively to the idea that each member of the group write down his own opinion, to avoid second guessing and recriminations later. He ordered that preparations to put the blockade in place begin immediately. A final meeting with the military on Sunday morning further convinced him that a strike would be an error. His decision had been made.

Based on Robert F. Kennedy, Thirteen Days: A Memoir of the Cuban Missile Crisis *(New York: W.W. Norton & Co., 1969), pp. 23–52: Arthur M. Schlesinger, Jr.,* A Thousand Days: John F. Kennedy in the White House *(Boston: Houghton Mifflin, 1965), pp. 800–09; and Arthur M. Schlesinger, Jr., Robert Kennedy and his Times (Boston: Houghton Mifflin, 1978), pp. 506–11. When accounts differ, Robert Kennedy's has been used. Schlesinger is, of course, the source for Robert Kennedy's significance in the final decision.*

The United States emerged from World War II as the world's greatest military and economic power. It was the only major nation whose industrial base had remained undamaged; it had not only financed its own wartime efforts but had provided massive material and financial aid to nations throughout the world. Militarily, it had assembled a vast conventional armed force and was the world's only nuclear power. Politically, the United States was the leader of the alliance that had defeated the Axis powers and created the United Nations. Culturally, the war had accelerated the spread of U.S. popular culture throughout the world; this "coca-colazation" of the world would continue apace after 1945. The war had also brought an unprecedented degree of cooperation between the United States and Latin America in military, financial, and economic matters. However, the euphoria of the successful effort against the Axis powers lasted only briefly, yielding to the growing rivalry between the United States and the Soviet Union.

This superpower rivalry soon evolved into the Cold War with both powers trying to recruit or retain allies for their respective blocs. The United States was convinced of the expansionist designs of the Soviet Union and fashioned its postwar policy to meet what it saw as the communist threat. Such an approach emphasized strategic considerations; it also served to prioritize the geographical areas of concern for the United States. The U.S. focus was on Europe, Asia, and the Middle East, given the degree of potential threat from the USSR. The United States was prepared to provide extensive resources for the rebuilding of Europe, the maintenance of a pro-U.S. China, and the expansion of influence in the Middle East.

The whole direction of U.S. foreign policy in the immediate postwar years proved disappointing to Latin America. Few in Latin America believed that Soviet expansionism or international communism posed a significant threat to the region. Instead of strategic concerns, Latin American nations wanted the United States to stress economic development in the postwar era. The U.S. government believed that it needed to promote postwar economic development in Latin America but was unwilling to make any specific commitment for assistance. As a region Latin America ranked low on the U.S. priority list; other areas were seen as facing more immediate Soviet threats.

U.S. policy took concrete form with the implementation of the containment policy, the Truman Doctrine, and the Marshall Plan. The containment policy was based on the contention that the Soviet Union was inherently hostile to the United States and ideologically committed to expansion. According to this doctrine, the United States should respond by containing these expansionist designs, leading to a break-up or mellowing of Soviet power. President Harry Truman put forward his "doctrine" in March 1947 in response to communist pressures on Greece and Turkey. Truman committed the United States to a general program of providing military, financial, or economic aid to any free country threatened by internal subversion or external pressure. The Marshall Plan, named after Secretary of State George Marshall, promised billions of dollars in U.S. aid for the reconstruction of Europe. While these actions held out the possibility of U.S. assistance for Latin American development, more realistically they reflected priorities which would limit aid for the region. When the success of the Marshall Plan in Europe led to Latin American requests for a similar program, U.S. officials responded by soliciting Latin American contributions for European recovery.

The Rio Treaty and the Bogotá Conference

When the Truman administration turned its attention to Latin America, it was primarily to deal with the unfinished business of the Chapultepec Conference. The Conference had provided that the wartime collective security system under the Act of Chapultepec be put on a permanent basis once the war was over, and a meeting was scheduled for October 1945 in Rio de Janeiro to draft a treaty. The conference was postponed at the last minute when the United States balked at letting Argentina participate, accusing Argentina of not fulfilling its international obligations. After a failed effort in 1946 to block the election of Juan Perón as president, the United States agreed to a date for the conference. By the time it finally convened in August 1947, it had already been overtaken by global events. In March Truman enunciated his new policy, and in June Secretary of State Marshall put forward his program for European recovery. The Conference, attended by Truman and Marshall, produced the Inter-American Treaty of Reciprocal Assistance, generally referred to as the Rio Treaty. It provided for a collective response against aggression, whether originating within or outside of the Americas. A meeting of foreign ministers would determine what measures for reciprocal assistance would be taken, including armed force. These measures required a two-thirds vote of approval, and all parties were required to implement them. The only exception was that no state would be required to use armed force without its consent, even if two-thirds of the members approved military action. The Rio Treaty was the first in a series of postwar regional security arrangements entered into by the United States and was a model for later agreements, including the North Atlantic Treaty Organization. Although the drafting of the treaty had produced little rancor, it represented the increasingly divergent views held by the United States and Latin America on inter-American affairs. For the United States the treaty was part of a global policy of containing communism; for Latin America it was a means of strengthening a system of inter-American cooperation.

The Chapultepec Conference had also directed that the Governing Board of the Pan American Union prepare a draft charter for a formal inter-American system for consideration at the next conference scheduled for Bogotá in March 1948. Once again the United States and Latin America approached the meeting with different expectations. The United States hoped to use the meeting to rally Latin America behind its policy of anti-communism while Latin America viewed the conference as another opportunity to pressure the United States to make a commitment to economic development. The conference was interrupted by ten days of rioting in the Colombian capital, known as the *bogotazo*. When the conference reconvened, the main focus was on drafting the charter of the inter-American system, creating the Organization of American States (OAS).

The OAS Charter provided a constitutional basis and a bureaucratic structure and also set down the fundamental principles guiding inter-American relations. It included a sweeping prohibition on intervention: no state had the right to intervene directly or indirectly, for any reason, in the internal or external affairs of another state. The existing Pan American Union would serve as the secretariat for the new organization. The Governing Board of the Union would be transformed into the Council of the OAS, with the Council supervising daily operations. The "supreme organ" of the OAS was the Inter-American Conference, which was supposed to meet every five years to determine general policy.

While the bogotazo was an emphatic reminder of the growing unrest in Latin America due to social and economic problems, the conference did little to address these issues. When Latin American delegates pressured Secretary of State Marshall for a "Marshall Plan for Latin America," he made it clear that the United States was assigning top priority to European recovery and that there would not be a comparable program for Latin America. The Secretary indicated that Latin America would have to depend primarily on private capital for its postwar economic development. The conference did approve an economic agreement covering general principles of cooperation, but only three countries subsequently ratified it. The only specific promise of economic assistance by the United States was the announcement that the lending power of the U.S. Export-Import Bank would be increased by $500 million, with most of the money dedicated to Latin America.[1]

Dictators and Democrats

U.S. preoccupation with the communist threat and its relative inattention to social and economic issues translated into a policy of pursuing political stability. This search for stability in a threatening world forced the United States to make hard choices about dealing with undemocratic governments. While the Allied victory in World War II encouraged and briefly strengthened democratic forces in the region, the outcome of the war had not permanently weakened the traditional ruling groups in Latin America who were determined to reassert control. While the United States was trying to harmonize the pursuit of stability with the promotion of democracy, other Latin American nations seized the initiative. At the Chapultepec Conference, the Guatemalan delegation had proposed multilateral action against "antidemocratic regimes" in the Americas by refusing recognition, but the proposal died due to the vagueness of the concept and fears that such action threatened the broader principle of nonintervention. In November 1945 Uruguay proposed in a diplomatic note to the American republics that there be collective multilateral action to promote and protect democracy. The Uruguayan proposal won the quick support of the United States and a few Latin American nations, but the large majority of Latin American nations were understandably opposed to it. Opponents were nervous about any qualification attached to the principle of nonintervention and about the role the United States might play if the door were opened in this way.[2]

The question of how to deal with authoritarian regimes was not just a general issue; it also involved specific cases. Lacking hemispheric support for collective action, the United States attempted unilaterally—with notable lack of success—to prevent the 1946 election of Juan Perón in Argentina. Perón was viewed as a fascist by U.S. policymakers despite his popular base. The United States also considered the use of nonrecognition as a way of encouraging democracy and blocking dictatorships. In May 1947 Anastasio Somoza, Sr. deposed his hand-picked successor as president of Nicaragua. The United States initially withheld recognition but later recognized the new government when other Latin American nations did not support nonrecognition. When the military overthrew the government of Venezuela in November 1948, the United States first consulted the other Latin American governments which recommended recognition. A coup in Panama in November 1949 led the United States to consult once again on nonrecognition, with the same results. In the absence of hemispheric support for collective action, the U.S. government began a policy of not discriminating between democratic and undemocratic governments, leading to later criticism from Latin America that the United States was more comfortable dealing with dictators who were strongly anti-communist than with democratic elements with different political and economic views.

Containing Communism: The Korean War and Hemispheric Relations

The first major military challenge to the U.S. global policy of containment came in June 1950 when communist North Korea invaded U.S.-supported South Korea. Although the fighting was far from and posed no threat to the Western Hemisphere, the United States wished to maximize Latin American support for U.S. efforts to block communist expansion. The United States chose to respond through the United Nations in hopes of developing multilateral opposition to the invasion. The two Latin American members of the Security Council—Cuba and Ecuador—were crucial in getting the two-thirds vote needed to bring about collective military action. Although the OAS Council quickly approved the UN action, it was not until December 1950 that the United States requested a consultation of foreign ministers as provided for by the OAS Charter. The meeting took place in Washington in March 1951, with most of the Latin American nations insisting that economic matters as well as political and military matters be discussed. While the United States encountered little difficulty in enlisting Latin American support for military cooperation, there was continued wrangling over U.S. assistance for economic development. Unwilling to expand its economic aid program, the United States avoided any specific economic commitments. Once again the ministers agreed that a much delayed economic conference would be convened immediately after the Korean war.

While the United States stalled on the question of economic assistance, it did begin a program of military aid to Latin America under the Mutual Security Act of 1951. The act authorized military assistance to Latin American countries to "promote the defense of the Western Hemisphere." Under the Act the United States entered into bilateral military agreements with twelve Latin American nations. The United States provided arms, equipment, and services which the Latin American country promised to use only in carrying out specific defense plans agreed to by both governments. The agreements also provided that the Latin American nation would "facilitate the production and transfer of raw and semi-processed materials required by the United States" and "cooperate in measures designed to control trade with nations which threaten the security of the Western Hemisphere." Despite this aid, most of the Latin American nations were either unable or unwilling to provide troops for the multinational force ultimately assembled; only Colombia eventually furnished troops for service in Korea. The amount of aid provided was also a good indication of U.S. priorities on a global scale. Latin America was scheduled to receive less than one percent of all aid requested for the entire military assistance program in 1951.[3]

While foreign policy figured prominently in the U.S. presidential elections of 1952, the issues involved touched only indirectly on Latin America. The most prominent foreign policy issue was the stalemated war in Korea, with the Republicans heavily criticizing Truman's containment policy. The victorious Republicans — with Dwight Eisenhower as president and John Foster Dulles as secretary of state — called for a "new look" in foreign policy, with the United States assuming the offensive in the Cold War. Even if the new look were to materialize, it offered little prospect for a major change in U.S. relations with Latin America. Like their Democratic predecessors, Eisenhower and Dulles were primarily interested in European and Asian matters and initially demonstrated little interest in the problems of Latin America. However, revolutionary conditions in Bolivia and Guatemala offered two exceptions during Eisenhower's first term.

Containing Communism: Bolivia and Guatemala

Bolivia had intermittently concerned U.S. officials since a successful coup by young army officers in December 1943 placed Major Gualberto Villarroel in power. At the time Secretary of State Cordell Hull worried about Villarroel's connection with the Movimiento Nacionalista Revolucionario (MNR), a group of civilian reformers whom Hull suspected of being pro-Axis. As a result, the United States refused to grant recognition to Villarroel until he removed three MNR ministers from his cabinet.

One of the ministers removed, Victor Paz Estenssoro, later led a successful MNR revolt in April 1952. The Truman administration's response to this latest revolt was cautious. The MNR had both Marxist and fascist connections, and Paz had recently returned from a lengthy exile in Juan Perón's Argentina which was still suspect for its fascist sympathies. It was widely assumed that one of the earliest actions by the MNR would be to nationalize the tin mines in which U.S. citizens had substantial investments. Anticipating U.S. concerns, Paz adopted a conciliatory approach, saying that compensation would be paid for any expropriations and presenting the MNR as a counterbalance to the communists. The Truman administration, fearing the rise of a more extremist regime, extended recognition to Paz's government on 2 June 1952. The United States then attempted to prop up the new government in September by offering to purchase all available Bolivian tin. Dealing with the revolutionary government would be primarily the responsibility of the incoming Eisenhower administration.

Eisenhower and Dulles continued and expanded the program of aiding the Bolivian revolution, encouraged by the Bolivian government's progress in reaching an agreement on compensation for the expropriated mining interests. In July 1953 the United States offered a one-year contract to purchase Bolivian tin at prevailing world prices, even though the U.S. strategic stockpile of tin was adequate; the United States continued these purchases until 1957. In October 1953 President Eisenhower authorized the transfer of $5 million in agricultural commodities, the provision of another $4 million under the Mutual Security Act to purchase "essential commodities," and a doubling of the technical assistance program. Bolivia was one of only three Latin American countries to receive aid in the form of outright grants, rather than the loans which characterized the expanding U.S. foreign aid program. On a per capita basis, Bolivia received more U.S. economic aid than any other country in the world during the 1950s.

U.S. concern with Guatemala also dated back to World War II. In 1944 the longtime dictatorship of General Jorge Ubico was overthrown, leading to major reforms under the administrations of Juan José Arévalo, an educator, and Jacobo Arbenz, a reform-minded army colonel. Their nationalist, reformist programs — especially in the areas of labor and agrarian reform — quickly led to conflict between the government and foreign-owned companies. Most notable among these were the powerful United Fruit Company and its subsidiary, the International Railways of Central America. The U.S. government was concerned about the growing role played by communists, especially in the labor movement and agrarian reform program. When the Guatemalan government implemented a new pro-labor policy, the United Fruit Company pressured the U.S. government to impose economic sanctions, which the Truman administration declined to do. In June 1952 the Arbenz government introduced a new agrarian reform law calling for the expropriation of uncultivated lands with compensation in government bonds. When United Fruit properties were expropriated in early 1953, the Eisenhower administration protested the action as discriminatory and the compensation as inadequate.

The Eisenhower administration decided to follow a two-track policy under the Brothers Dulles: a diplomatic track under Secretary of State John Foster Dulles and a covert track under CIA Director Allen Dulles. At the public level, the United States prepared a diplomatic case against Guatemala which it hoped would produce multilateral action at the Tenth Inter-American Conference scheduled for Caracas in March 1954. At the same time the United States was preparing a covert military operation to overthrow Arbenz, using a force of Guatemalan exiles under the leadership of Colonel Carlos Castillo Armas. Further complicating the U.S. response was the Dulles connection to United Fruit. John Foster Dulles had previously been with a New York law firm which represented United Fruit while Allen Dulles had served on United Fruit's board of directors. Secretary of State Dulles headed the U.S. delegation to the Caracas conference. Dulles wanted the conference to focus on the "intervention of international communism in the American Republics," while Latin American delegations hoped that the emphasis would be on economic problems. Dulles spent two weeks getting the conference to pass a compro-

mise resolution classifying international communism as a "threat to the independence of American States," and calling for a consultation of foreign ministers to deal with specific cases.[4]

More important to the situation in Guatemala and inter-American relations in general was the second track being pursued by the United States.
While the Eisenhower administration pressured its NATO allies not to sell
arms to the Arbenz government, the CIA sponsored the arming of Guatemalan exiles. On 18 June 1954 a force of approximately 150 exiles under Castillo
Armas invaded Guatemala from Honduras. The invasion force had its own
three-plane air force flown by civilian pilots, most of whom were U.S. citizens.
The key to the situation was not the rebel force but the regular Guatemalan
army. When Arbenz tried to arm his civilian supporters, the army blocked the
move and forced Arbenz to resign on 27 June. A military junta appointed
Castillo Armas provisional president on 7 July, and the United States recognized the new regime on 13 July. Castillo Armas immediately began to roll back
a decade of revolution, including the return of United Fruit lands expropriated under Arbenz. The U.S. government reciprocated by providing support
for Castillo Armas, including military aid, development grants, and technical assistance.

International response to events in Guatemala was mixed. Two Latin American nations—Honduras and Nicaragua—directly assisted in the overthrow.
Honduras served as the launching point for the invasion while Nicaragua provided the base for the rebel air force. As soon as the rebels invaded, Guatemala
appealed to the UN Security Council to end the fighting, but this diplomatic
offensive fell victim to big power politics. The United States, chairing the
Council during June, supported a resolution referring the Guatemalan question to the OAS, a move vetoed by the Soviet Union. In the end, the only action taken by the Security Council was a vaguely worded resolution calling for
an end to any activities that might cause further bloodshed. A second effort
to get the Guatemalan issue onto the Security Council agenda failed, leaving
any international action by default to the OAS. On 28 June, the day after Arbenz resigned, the OAS Council voted to hold a meeting of foreign ministers
in Rio on 7 July to consider the Guatemalan crisis. However, the rapid consolidation of power by the Castillo Armas regime essentially brought the crisis to a conclusion, and the Rio meeting was never held.

Although the CIA had enjoyed considerable initial success in concealing its
role in the Guatemalan situation, it was correctly believed throughout Latin

America that the CIA had been deeply involved in the overthrow of Arbenz. Actions by the United States in the UN Security Council had kept the Guatemalan crisis a hemispheric issue to be handled by the OAS, but U.S. involvement in Arbenz's ouster struck at the heart of the OAS Charter's proscription on intervention. While the Eisenhower administration clearly saw the Guatemalan operation as a major "victory" in the Cold War, the United States continued to downplay the social and economic problems which figured so prominently in the priorities of Latin American countries. The success in Guatemala later encouraged the United States to adopt a similar approach in dealing with revolutionary Cuba, but with much different results.

Eisenhower, Social Revolution, and Economic Development

Although the United States had emphasized security concerns at the expense of social and economic problems throughout the postwar period, it was forced to reevaluate its approach during the second Eisenhower administration. Two major events brought home the danger of ignoring the "revolution of rising expectations" taking place in Latin America. First, in May 1958, Vice President Richard Nixon made a goodwill tour of South America en route to the inauguration of the new president of Argentina, Arturo Frondizi. Nixon was the target of hostile demonstrations throughout the tour, and his visits to Peru and Venezuela provoked major rioting which led to fears for the vice president's safety. This strong anti-U.S. feeling was widely seen as a response to postwar U.S. policy, especially neglect of Latin America and economic development. The second event was the rise to power of Fidel Castro in Cuba in January 1959. As Castro's revolution turned from nationalistic to anti-U.S. to pro-Soviet, U.S. officials concluded that new directions were needed in the Latin American policy of the United States.

U.S. attitudes about aid to Latin America had revolved around military and security concerns even when nonmilitary aid was involved. The emphasis had been on private investment and free trade as the keys to Latin American economic development. This trade-not-aid approach was particularly appealing to Eisenhower whose domestic program stressed a balanced budget. This U.S. formula for economic development was often in direct conflict with the postwar trend in Latin America toward greater government involvement in economic development with the emphasis on import substitution industrialization and protectionist measures.

As early as 1954 the Eisenhower administration was reconsidering its approach to third world economic problems, but this reevaluation was prompted primarily by concerns about Asia, not Latin America. In 1957 Eisenhower received reluctant congressional approval to establish the Development Loan Fund to make public loans for development purposes to third world countries, with loans repaid on easy terms in local currencies. Congress eventually approved this request but substantially reduced the appropriation requested from $750 million to $625 million, including the deletion of $20 million designated for Latin America. In August 1958 the United States indicated that it was dropping its longstanding opposition to a regional development bank and would support what later became known as the Inter-American Development Bank, officially established in October 1960. The Bank was capitalized at $1 billion, with the United States subscribing $450 million and the Latin American republics the remainder. Most lending would be on terms similar to those of regular commercial banks, but $150 million would be set aside for "soft" loans which could be repaid in local currencies for projects considered too risky for commercial banks. U.S. support for the Bank was part of a broader movement toward multilateralism and regionalism in Eisenhower's policy.

The shift in policy by the Eisenhower administration continued at Bogotá in September 1960 at a meeting of the "Committee of 21," a special committee set up by the OAS Council to study new measures for economic cooperation. In the "Act of Bogotá," the United States pledged $500 million to support a program of economic development and social improvement in Latin America. In return the Latin American nations agreed to follow sound economic policies and to eliminate obstacles to social and economic progress. Just as Herbert Hoover earlier laid the foundation for Franklin Roosevelt's Good Neighbor Policy, Eisenhower was laying the foundation for an even more ambitious program of social and economic development under his successor, John F. Kennedy.

The Advent of Fidel Castro

By far the most significant development in U.S.-Latin American relations during these years was the establishment of a revolutionary regime in Cuba, only 90 miles from the southernmost of the Florida keys. Although the first few years after the end of World War II had brought continued prosperity to the island, worse times were just around the corner. The economy remained dependent on sugar, a commodity in which competition from other producer nations was intense and market prices insecure. Fulgencio Batista returned to power in 1952 after a hiatus of several years, overthrowing the elected president. Resistance to Batista spread quickly, and political repression increased proportionately.

Among the revolutionary movements which were forming around the country, one was led by Fidel Castro, a young, charismatic lawyer and politician from the eastern (and traditionally more revolutionary) end of the island. On 26 July 1953, he and more than one hundred followers, including two women, attacked the Moncada barracks in Santiago, the capital of Oriente province in eastern Cuba. Although the attack failed and many of the surviving rebels were tortured and murdered by the dictator, Castro initially escaped and, when captured a few days later, was jailed along with other captured co-revolutionaries. In a mass trial in September, Castro himself led the defense. Rather than denying the attack, Castro defended its legitimacy, calmly declaring in the process of delivering his two-hour defense brief, that "History Will Absolve Me." Castro did not attack U.S. interests directly at this time, despite the later interpretation of anti-imperialism that his government would try to attribute to the speech. However, he did hint at the possible nationalization of the American-owned power and telephone companies. The date of the attack, 26 July, was taken as the name of his revolutionary movement.

Castro was, of course, convicted and put in prison on the Isle of Pines. He was later released, after the Cuban Congress passed an amnesty bill signed by Batista in May 1955. Castro made his way to Mexico. To raise funds, he undertook a trip to the United States, where he made contact with Cuban communities in cities such as Philadelphia and New York. He also received financial support in Cuba itself, including help from some American and Cuban officers of U.S. businesses. However, before leaving the United States, he began to target foreign interests in Cuba, attacking "foreign trusts" and protesting the quality and cost of electric and telephone services. By now, there could be no doubt about his general attitude toward U.S. business.

Castro returned to Cuba from Mexico in November 1956 in an aging yacht called the *Granma*. Significantly, Castro had added to his entourage a socially-minded Argentine physician, Ernesto "Che" Guevara, who had been present in Guatemala during the CIA-sponsored coup against Arbenz. Although this small force was almost wiped out after landing, Castro adopted guerrilla tactics and led his rebellion from the countryside in eastern Cuba. Allied groups of students and workers struggled against Batista in the cities. While Eisenhower, strongly backed by his ambassadors Arthur Gardner and Earl E. P. Smith, continued to support Batista, U.S. public opinion was divided. An interview by *New York Times* reporter Herbert Matthews with Castro in the mountains of Cuba in February 1957 attested that Castro and his young rebel army were alive and well, despite Batista's attempts to persuade the public that the rebellion was contained. Matthews' opinion of Castro was favorable; he saw him as a courageous and determined young leader, although he felt that his program was vague. He did not hold out much hope for Castro's success,

Poster of Che Guevara, "Until the Final Victory," announces a documentary film by Santiago Alvarez. Silkscreen, 1967–68, by Alfredo Rostgaard.

Photograph by David Kunzle

however, and referred to him as "a myth, a legend, a hope, but not a reality."[5] Matthews has been heavily criticized for not understanding the degree to which his observations of Castro's forces were orchestrated to give a false impression of the size of the movement, when only a handful of men and women were actually fighting with him. However, Matthews was correct in recognizing the power of Castro's personality. He painted a relatively romantic picture of the Cuban revolutionary, and this picture was not unappealing to significant portions of the U.S. public. Anti-Batista and pro-Castro sentiment in the U.S. began to increase.

The Eisenhower administration remained leery, concerned by the instability which might be caused by revolution. However, the U.S. government did not focus very clearly on Cuban issues. This lack of interest reflected the gen-

Poster of Che Guevara, "October 8: Day of the Heroic Guerrilla Warrior," commemorates Che's death in Bolivia in 1967. Silkscreen, 1973, by Olivio Martínez.

Photograph by David Kunzle

eral inattention to Latin America on the part of U.S. policymakers, given the cold war atmosphere in which other problems (Berlin, the Arab-Israeli conflict, nuclear issues) seemed more significant. Further, until the summer of 1958, policymakers failed to realize that Batista was losing control of the situation. The illness of John Foster Dulles, Eisenhower's secretary of state, and the less forceful leadership of assistant secretary of state Christian Herter, may have also contributed to producing this window of opportunity for Castro and other opponents of Batista.[6]

Although the U.S. government through the CIA and other channels sought to derail Castro's sweep to power, by the time concrete action was taken, Castro had become too strong. Attempts to replace Castro with a more acceptable leader, who might serve as a U.S. surrogate in the usual Caribbean style, came too late. Only in December 1958 did Eisenhower finally pay significant attention to the warnings of CIA Director Allen Dulles who advised that Batista was about to fall and that Castro's government was certain to contain communists. At that point, Eisenhower asked whether the Defense Department had a scenario for military action to prevent a Castro victory. The answer was no. Despite sentiment that something should be done to prevent Castro's taking power and thereby setting up a situation in which communists could come to dominate, the moment for effective action had passed. Batista left Cuba during the evening of 31 December, and Castro's forces began a triumphant march toward Havana the following day.

Castro in Power: The Early Years

Although Eisenhower quickly recognized Castro, he was in no mood to trust or help the new Cuban government. Chosen as ambassador was Philip W. Bonsal, a career Foreign Service officer. His appointment was an indication that the Eisenhower administration would watch the new regime very carefully. Bonsal had been ambassador to Bolivia since 1957, where he had worked with financial institutions and U.S. agencies to slow down the reform agenda of President Victor Paz Estenssoro. He would face a similar task, but less successfully, in Cuba.

Very quickly, the fears of the policymakers in Eisenhower's government began to be realized. Castro was determined to seek political independence from the United States and significant redistribution of resources within Cuba. Neither goal would be acceptable in Washington. Among the reforms that he put into place were several which directly affected U.S. interests: the rates of the U.S.-owned Cuban Telephone Company were cut, a series of wage and salary increases affecting U.S. employers were instituted, and agrarian reform affecting U.S. cattle and sugar interests was undertaken. Although the earliest reforms had limited impact on U.S. businesses, U.S. banks and corporations, and particularly companies and individuals involved in the sugar business, began to view the situation with alarm.

Castro's first cabinet selections were reassuring to the U.S. government. A former official of the International Monetary Fund and National Bank president, Felipe Pazos, again became the president of the Cuban National Bank. Of seventeen cabinet members, only six had participated in the urban struggle against Batista, and only three had been involved in the guerrilla movement. However, many of the more conservative members of the cabinet were soon replaced, and their counsel was not heeded in any case. Castro and Che Guevara were the principal authors of the agrarian reform law, and pushed its implementation despite opposition from a number of cabinet officers. By the end of 1959, few of the cabinet members who were truly acceptable to the Eisenhower administration continued in office. By that time, almost all ministries were occupied by former guerrillas or civilian supporters of Castro. Pazos himself was replaced by Che Guevara, who had no banking experience whatsoever.

Although Eisenhower kept his distance from Castro, at least one member of his administration was able to get a closer look. When the American Society of Newspaper Editors invited Castro to the United States, Eisenhower refused to meet with him. He shuffled him off to Vice President Richard Nixon, who met with him informally. Nixon's take was that Castro was "either incredibly naive about communism or under communist discipline—my guess is the former."[7] By the beginning of 1960, according to some sources, the CIA was considering Castro's physical elimination. The State Department urged caution, however, given the fact that no one reliable seemed ready to move into the vacuum which would be created. The idea of assassination, however, continued in play for years.[8] The concern with communism was brought to a peak at about the same time that Anastas Mikoyan, deputy premier of the Soviet Union and close associate of Chairman Nikita Khrushchev, visited Cuba and arranged a trade agreement between the two countries. The visit, of course, led to further U.S. concern that Cuba was moving into the Soviet orbit.

A covert plan began to be spun out at about the same time. In March 1960, Eisenhower directed the CIA to begin training Cuban exiles for a possible invasion. Raids were begun along the Cuban coast as well. Publicly, Christian

Herter—now secretary of state—presented legislation to Congress requesting discretionary authority for the president to reduce the sugar quota to any country, should "... it be necessary to do so in the national interest...."[9] This threat was extremely significant, as the entire Cuban economy depended on sugar revenue.

Castro, predictably, responded with defiance. Rather than conciliating in any way, he pushed the Soviet connection. Included in the February agreement was a commitment to import one-third to one-half of Cuba's oil needs from the Soviet Union. As payment would be made in sugar rather than hard currency and the price was lower than was currently being paid for imports of Venezuelan oil, the benefits to Cuba were clear. However, Cuba's refineries were owned by foreign oil companies, including Standard of New Jersey and Texaco. Given the green light from State Department officials, in June they refused to refine the Soviet crude and began to reduce their American personnel on the island. The Cubans then moved to take over the major refineries. Eisenhower's response was quick. In July, he exercised his authority and cut the Cuban sugar quota by a total of 856,000 tons. His rationale was that Castro's government had undertaken deliberately hostile policies toward the United States in its agreement to sell sugar to the Russians.

Castro continued to defy the U.S. administration in the next few months, nationalizing the banks and extending the agrarian reform in October 1960. Sugar properties amounting to almost 3 million acres were expropriated and put under government control. Further U.S. pressure on the sugar quota led quickly to a new sugar agreement between Cuba and the Soviet Union. In the same month, Eisenhower put into place an embargo on exports to Cuba. Use of his authority under the 1949 Export Control Act left open the possibility that foreign subsidiaries of U.S. companies could continue sales to Cuba, a loophole not closed until the 1990s. In January 1961, Castro demanded that the American Embassy staff in Cuba be drastically reduced. Eisenhower quickly broke relations.

The Bay of Pigs

Meanwhile, John F. Kennedy had been elected president in November 1960. During the presidential campaign, he, as well as his opponent Richard Nixon, had made a strong case for isolating and overthrowing Castro. Although he did not specifically call for an invasion of the island, he made it clear that as president he would take action. After his election, he met with Eisenhower, who briefed him on the exile operation and recommended that it proceed expeditiously. Although Kennedy was suspicious, his eagerness to act and his public commitment to do something about the communist threat led him to put aside his objections. During the presidential race, he had even called for support of a Cuban exile force to defeat Castro, making it politically difficult for him to stop an operation already in motion that he himself had seemed to support.

The Cuban situation quickly became a major problem after Kennedy's inauguration in early 1961. Dealing with a situation not of his making, he immediately blundered seriously and damaged his credibility with Latin Americans, the American people, and his cold war adversary, the Soviet Union. After the events, he queried a close adviser, "How could I have been so stupid to let them go ahead?"[10]

The answer seems to be that despite misgivings, Kennedy was obligated by his own campaign rhetoric and, more importantly, by his belief that Castro was in fact a communist and an ally of the Soviet Union. Communist penetration of the hemisphere had preoccupied Cold War American policymakers for years, but the success of the Guatemalan coup sponsored by the CIA six years earlier had provided the illusion that rapid, decisive, and especially relatively inexpensive clandestine action, could solve such problems. The planning for the Bay of Pigs invasion was carried out by many of the same CIA officers involved in the Guatemalan intervention. Allen Dulles had continued as director of the CIA at Kennedy's request. The major architect of the Bay of Pigs operation was the CIA's deputy director for plans, Richard Bissell, who had previously been in charge of the development of the U-2 spy plane. He had also been involved in the planning for Guatemala and had a reputation, both personal and professional, as an aggressive risk taker.

The ease of the Guatemala operation seems to have misled the CIA planners. It may have misled Kennedy and his advisers as well. Kennedy's initial briefing took place in November 1960, and was conducted by Dulles and Bissell of the CIA. Much of the flow of information to Kennedy, once he became president, continued to come through that agency. However, by February 1961, he was aware that the military was not entirely enthusiastic about the operation. Specifically, the Joint Chiefs of Staff evaluation of what was now being called "Operation Trinidad," sent to the State Department on 3 February, asked for further study to determine whether the exile force was combat ready and whether the logistics made sense. McGeorge Bundy, Kennedy's assistant for national security affairs, misrepresented Pentagon opinion somewhat when he told Kennedy that Defense and the CIA were enthusiastic, although he passed on that the State Department had doubts about the operation. In fact, the Joint Chiefs always believed that the exile invasion would fail beyond the short term unless it inspired widespread anti-Castro uprisings on the island.

The operation was weakened further as Kennedy and his advisers sought to conceal American involvement and avoid diplomatic repercussions. The changes made to conceal U.S. participation were unavailing, however. The operation itself was seriously compromised by repeated security breaches among Cuban exiles in the United States. Days before the operation began in April 1961, the *New York Times* ran a story uncovered by vacationing reporter Tad Szulc, who had been covering Latin America for years. Szulc, in Miami visiting friends, heard both that Cuban exiles were being trained and that there was increasing traffic to Guatemala, probable site of the training. Although his story, when it ran, had been altered to include denials that the United States was involved after Kennedy himself had put pressure on the publisher, it still indicated that an invasion was near. A similar story in the *New Republic* was killed at Kennedy's request, and other reporters were close on the trail.[11] Castro was similarly aware that something was about to happen, and as a result, thousands of Cubans on the island whose loyalties he questioned were rounded up immediately before the invasion. This action eliminated the possibility that any major uprising might occur.

When the invasion began, serious problems arose almost immediately. The CIA had ignored information from the Cubans they were training that the specified landing site led across coral reefs which would damage their boats. The exiles were too few and the beach where they landed was well known to Castro himself. His government was actually supervising the building of a recreational facility in the area, and the beach was lighted by tall arc lights.[12] Most serious, perhaps, was Kennedy's misunderstanding of the need for air strikes at the beginning of the invasion and continuing air support throughout. He clearly rejected any use of U.S. military aircraft, but he also canceled all but one of the air strikes associated with the exile operation itself. Although the one strike permitted was effective, damaging five of Castro's twelve planes, the Cubans were left with enough air power to combat the invasion successfully. By the time further strikes by the invasion force were authorized, it was too late for them to be effective. U.S. Navy pilots from the carrier *Essex* were permitted overflights of the island but were not permitted to engage Cuban aircraft or to take any other offensive action. Kennedy seems at one point to have authorized the Navy to provide cover for the Cuban Brigade's bombers, but this message was never clearly conveyed to the pilots. In fact, orders read, "Do not seek air combat," and "Do not attack ground targets." The Navy's code for the operation was appropriately, "Bumpy Road."[13]

Kennedy was enormously angered by this spectacular failure. He ordered increased pressures on the Cuban regime, including covert action along with economic, propagandistic, and diplomatic efforts. Covert activities included sabotage—ranging from burning sugarcane fields to attacks on mining and petroleum operations—and even assassination attempts on Cuban leaders including Castro.[14] Brought in to head the new operation was General Edward Lansdale, who would later help install the Diem regime in Vietnam. Lansdale described what the Kennedys wanted: "boom and bang" on the island.[15] The new operation was formalized in December 1961, when Bissell was replaced by Richard Helms in overseeing Cuban affairs and President Kennedy began a stepped-up covert project called "Operation Mongoose." Robert Kennedy, the attorney general, took a special interest in Mongoose. Lansdale later emphasized the emotional involvement of both Kennedys in the Cuban situation. "Bobby felt it even more strongly than Jack. He was protective of his brother, and he felt his brother had been insulted at the Bay of Pigs. He felt the insult needed to be redressed rather quickly."[16] In the more public aspects of Cuban policy, the Kennedy administration decided to focus on isolating Castro in the hemisphere. By February 1962, the United States had succeeded in having Cuba thrown out of the Organization of American States.

Castro, for his part, took Cuba even more rapidly toward a military alliance with the Soviet Union and a commitment to communism. In fact, on 16 April 1961, the day after the Brigade air strike, he first described the Cuban Revolution as "socialist." It has been reported that he intended to make such a declaration on May Day, only two weeks away, but it is impossible to know now if that were indeed the case.[17] Certainly, however, the attempted invasion pushed him, through anger and fear of U.S. power and intentions, to discuss with the Soviets the emplacement of nuclear missiles on the island. Negotiations probably began in May 1962.

Kennedy had made a costly error. In authorizing and supporting an exile invasion of the island in April 1961 and then trying to disavow it, he alienated Cubans on and off the island, both those who supported Castro and those bitterly opposed to him. Castro was able to accelerate the revolutionary changes he was making in Cuba, gathering support with extreme anti-U.S. rhetoric. He moved to strengthen ties with the Soviet Union, both militarily and ideologically, leading to the increased fortification of the island and increased U.S. embarrassment, almost hysteria, at what was seen as a terrible threat in its own hemisphere — and, indeed, so it became.

The Cuban Missile Crisis

When the Cubans and the Soviets finalized the agreement to install nuclear missiles on the island, both anticipated benefits. The Cubans firmly believed, and Kennedy and his administration gave them every reason to expect, that they might be invaded by U.S. forces at some time in the relatively near future. Nuclear missiles might be used at that point as a threat against the invading nation. Further, Castro's lack of both modern weapons and high technology equipment had been made vividly clear by the success of the one air strike that the Cuban Brigade had been able to carry out. Surely, the introduction into Cuba of nuclear weapons solidified the Soviet resolve to protect what was rapidly becoming its Caribbean client.

The Soviets gained as well. Lagging far behind the United States in the missile race, particularly in the number of available intercontinental ballistic missiles, they could improve their odds in a global confrontation with an island launch base just ninety miles from Key West. They would also be better able to defend their new ally against invasion. Moreover, and this point was apparently significant to Khrushchev, Cuban missiles would be payback for U.S. missiles poised just across the Black Sea in Turkey. Although Kennedy already intended to dismantle the Turkish missiles, no action had as yet been taken, and, ironically, they became operational on 22 October 1962, in the middle of the crisis.[18] Personality may also have played a role. Observers have noted Khrushchev's willingness to take "an audacious gamble," that he was "unpredictable . . . a loose cannon."[19]

Kennedy was forced to respond for both national and international reasons. In the domestic political realm, he was faced with challenges from the Republicans with just two months to go until the mid-term congressional elections. Republican Senator Kenneth Keating revealed publicly on 1 September 1962 that he had information that the Soviet Union was installing medium-range missiles in Cuba. A storm of demands that Kennedy take some action issued from both Republicans and Democrats in Congress. It culminated in

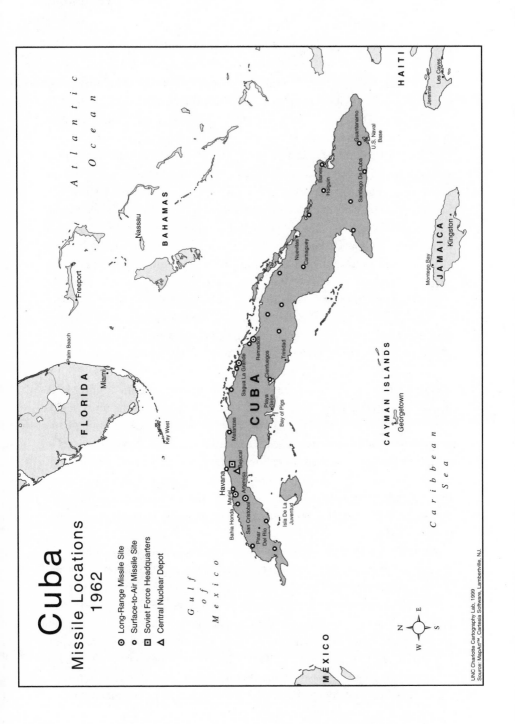

Cuba

Missile Locations 1962

- ◉ Long-Range Missile Site
- ◦ Surface-to-Air Missile Site
- ▣ Soviet Force Headquarters
- ▲ Central Nuclear Depot

UNC Charlotte Cartography Lab, 1999
Source • MapArt™, Cartesia Software, Lambertville, NJ.

late September with the approval of a resolution authorizing military intervention should it become necessary. On the international side, Kennedy was extremely unwilling to appear weak in the face of what he and his advisers felt was a deliberate Soviet provocation. Within two days of the discovery of the missiles by U-2 reconnaissance, Kennedy told his advisers resolutely, "We're going to take out these missiles."[20]

Only three options were seriously considered by EXCOM, the group of advisers gathered by Kennedy to work with him through the crisis: (1) a naval blockade; (2) an air strike, limited or otherwise; and (3) a military invasion. Various combinations and degrees of these possibilities were discussed, with most of those consulted favoring either a combined air strike and military intervention or a quarantine of the island based on a blockade. Initially, an air strike seemed to have the most support, with discussion centering only on its extent. Proponents of such a strike included Secretary of Defense Robert McNamara and the president's brother, Attorney General Robert F. Kennedy. The chairman of the Joint Chiefs of Staff, General Maxwell Taylor, also suggested a possible combination of naval blockade and air strike, but was leery of involving U.S. ground troops in "that deep Cuban mud."[21]

The decision clearly would be made by President Kennedy himself, but he was apparently much influenced by his brother. Robert Kennedy and McNamara soon came around to support for a naval blockade as the most flexible option. McNamara argued that should it fail, a more aggressive option could be chosen at that point. The president spoke to the American people on 22 October, confirming that there were Soviet missiles in Cuba and announcing a naval quarantine. From that date until 28 October, when Khrushchev agreed to withdraw the missiles in return for a verbal U.S. commitment to forego future military intervention on the island, the possibility of nuclear confrontation loomed.

Kennedy emerged from the crisis looking strong and secure in his presidency, having publicly defeated his Cold War adversary, the Soviet Union, and his personal adversary, Nikita Khrushchev. Still, it is evident that U.S. policy — designed to avert or roll back major economic and political change in Cuba — had failed. The reasons were several. Castro had been successful in overcoming and/or controlling Cuban elites with longstanding ties to the United States. His revolutionary movement had been able to establish its own military as the power on the island. That movement had further been able to acquire substantial aid from outside the hemisphere, specifically from the major cold war enemy of the United States, aid which would continue in one form or another for almost three decades.

Kennedy and the Alliance for Progress

Latin America, particularly Cuba, had received an unusual amount of attention in the U.S. presidential elections of 1960. The Democratic nominee, John F. Kennedy, had criticized the Eisenhower administration and the Republican candidate, Richard Nixon, for failing to identify U.S. policy with the rising aspirations of Latin Americans and for letting Cuba become a "communist satellite." After achieving a narrow victory, Kennedy in his inaugural address indicated that he intended to be a vigorous cold warrior and also called for an "alliance for progress" between the United States and Latin America. Thus, presumably, the communist revolutionary threat in the hemisphere would be confined to that island. A program of social and economic reforms would eliminate the need and the risk of violent revolutions which could be taken advantage of by the USSR.

In March 1961 Kennedy officially enunciated U.S. commitment to an Alliance for Progress with Latin America, a long-term program linking U.S. aid with structural reforms, economic development, and democratization. The program was given official form at a meeting of inter-American representatives at Punta del Este, Uruguay, in August 1961. The conference issued a "Declaration of the Peoples of America" which provided a lengthy list of objectives for the Alliance including democratization, acceleration of social and economic development, promotion of education, fair wages and working conditions, health programs, tax reforms, agrarian reform, fiscal stability, and the stimulation of private enterprise. The capital needed for the Alliance was projected at $100 billion during the next decade, with $20 billion coming from external sources, of which the United States would provide a major part. The remaining $80 billion would come from Latin American sources, both public and private. After years of calling for a Marshall Plan for Latin America, the region was the target for an even more ambitious program in the Alliance for Progress. The Marshall Plan had faced the difficult task of reconstructing Europe; the Alliance had the more daunting task of restructuring Latin America. For the United States, the Alliance was an effort to promote peaceful social revolution to head off violent social revolution; there must be no "second Cuba" in the hemisphere.

Despite its laudable objectives and advance publicity, the Alliance soon ran up against the harsh realities of domestic politics and international economics. In many cases the program depended on the willingness of traditional elites to support reforms that undercut their privileged positions. Such elites predictably were not interested in reforming themselves out of existence and did not believe that they had to choose between reform and violent revolution.

The high level of political instability in Latin America in the early 1960s created an unfavorable environment for the kind of structural changes envisioned under the Alliance. Latin American nations resented the restrictions placed by the United States on the use of aid funds, especially the requirement that they purchase U.S. products. In fact, much of the aid went to service earlier loans rather than to promote social and economic development. Improved growth rates in the absence of restructuring meant that the traditional elites reaped most of the benefits of economic development. U.S. officials were reluctant to press too hard for reforms for fear of exacerbating political instability in the area. The high rate of population growth in Latin America undermined potential advances in social and economic development.

Domestic politics in the United States also restricted the success of the Alliance. The death of Kennedy in 1963 removed the Alliance's most visible advocate. The difficulty of making long-range financial commitments under the U.S. political structure also hampered the operation of the Alliance; the long-term promises of a president could easily be undone by the annual congressional appropriations process. The Alliance also had to contend with the growing disenchantment in the United States with foreign aid programs in general. As the demands of the Vietnam War became greater, the United States diverted its attention and its resources to Southeast Asia. In the late 1960s the United States became less concerned with a "second Cuba" in the hemisphere, as Cuba curtailed its efforts to export revolution due to domestic economic problems and the death of Che Guevara in Bolivia in 1967.

The Alliance in Retreat and the Dominican Intervention

When Lyndon Johnson became president upon the assassination of Kennedy, it meant the replacement of a president who had given a high priority to Latin America by one who had little interest in the region despite his Texas background. Johnson was primarily interested in domestic issues, particularly the implementation of series of reforms which would eventually be known as the Great Society. In foreign affairs Johnson became increasingly preoccupied with the deteriorating situation in Vietnam. The overselling of the Alliance from the start made subsequent disillusionment with it predictable. Structural reforms stalled; the democratization process was in retreat; and the population explosion threatened to undo any social or economic advances. Faced with growing domestic demands and an escalating war in Vietnam, the U.S. Congress cut funding for the Alliance. As the Alliance lost its reform content, it evolved into a conventional aid program. The resurgence of more traditional concerns about security and anticommunism led Johnson to recognize military governments in the Dominican Republic, Honduras, and Brazil. Johnson's Latin American policy in particular was driven by the desire to avoid a "second Cuba" in the hemisphere, a predisposition that would result in the first direct military intervention in the postwar period.

By 1965 the United States had a long history of involvement in the internal affairs of the Dominican Republic. Earlier U.S. intervention had unwittingly laid the groundwork for the lengthy dictatorship of Rafael Trujillo who used his position as head of the national guard to take power in 1930. The United States also played a role in the old dictator's downfall when the CIA helped to stage Trujillo's assassination in 1961. Trujillo's death ushered in a period of extreme instability in Dominican politics which U.S. officials feared might be exploited by Cuba, then at the peak of its efforts to export revolution. The immediate occasion for U.S. intervention was an effort by a faction of the Dominican military in April 1965 to restore to the presidency the civilian reformer, Juan Bosch, who had served briefly as president in 1963. U.S. officials feared that the split within the military might lead to full-scale civil war and were alarmed by reports—later proven to be exaggerated—that communists were assuming a prominent role in the rebel ranks.

Point-Counterpoint: Lyndon Johnson and the Dominican Crisis

" ... The United States Government has been informed by military authorities in the Dominican Republic that American lives are in danger. These authorities are no longer able to guarantee their safety, and they have reported that the assistance of military personnel is now needed for that purpose.... Pursuant to my instructions, 400 Marines have already landed."

—*Statement by President Johnson, April 28, 1965,* The Department of State Bulletin, *Vol. LII, No. 1351, 17 May 1965, p. 738.*

"Meanwhile there are signs that people trained outside the Dominican Republic are seeking to gain control. Thus the legitimate aspirations of the Dominican people and most of their leaders for progress, democracy, and social justice are threatened and so are the principles of the inter-American system."

—*Statement by President Johnson, 30 April 1965, as above, p. 742.*

"Progress and justice do not flourish at the point of a gun."

—*Statement by President Johnson, 1 May 1965, as above, p. 743.*

"I want you to know that it is not a light or easy matter to send our American boys to another country, but I do not think that the American people expect their President to hesitate or to vacillate in the face of danger, just because the decision is hard when life is in peril.

"The revolutionary movement took a tragic turn. Communist leaders, many of them trained in Cuba, seeing a chance to increase disorder, to gain a foothold, joined the revolution. . . .

"This is what our beloved President John F. Kennedy meant, when, less than a week before his death, he told us: We in this hemisphere must also use every resource at our command to prevent the establishment of another Cuba in this hemisphere. . . ."

—*Statement by President Johnson, 2 May 1965, as above, pp. 744, 746.*

" . . . We cannot help but lament that the North American government has considered it necessary to order a measure that invokes such sad memories for many countries of the hemisphere.

"Mexico, faithful to the traditional principles which it has always sustained, states its sincere desire and puts forward its hope that the Dominican people can resolve their internal problems without any influence, direct or indirect, coming from outside its borders."

—*Statement from the Secretariat of Foreign Relations, Mexico, in* Excelsior, *30 April 1965.*

"Havana, April 29 — Premier Fidel Castro's Communist party newspaper called today for Cuban backing of the Dominican people, who it said were 'fighting the most brutal repression.'"

—*Paul Hoffman, "Cuba Assails Marine Landing; Other Latins Express Concern,"* New York Times, *30 April 1965.*

"Santiago, April 29 — Chile showed official criticism of the landing of American Marines in the Dominican Republic today, in instructions sent to . . . Chile's Ambassador to the Organization of American States.

Chile called for the 'immediate and collective action of the O.A.S. instead of unilateral measures.'"

"Lima, Peru, April 29 — Peru today termed the landing of United States Marines in the Dominican Republic 'lamentable' and a 'reverse' for the inter-American system."

"Buenos Aires, April 29 — A middle-aged man stopped at the edge of a crowd gathered round the Bulletin Board of the newspaper La Nación. . . . He sighed, turned to his wife and said: 'Now the North Americans are messing about in the Dominican Republic.'

"Even persons with pro-American views saw the landing of the Marines as intervention."

—*The three quotations above are from the* New York Times, *30 April 1965.*

The initial U.S. response came on 25 April 1965 with the dispatch of a small force of Marines to the Dominican capital to evacuate approximately 1,000 U.S. citizens. Fighting in the capital intensified, including rebel fire on the U.S. embassy on 29 April. The United States escalated its forces, eventually landing more than 20,000 troops. The Johnson administration attempted to deflect criticism by depicting the operation as a rescue turned peacekeeping mission. Instead of making a direct move to crush the rebels, U.S. forces worked with loyalist troops to wear down and isolate the pro-Bosch forces. The United States also moved to multilateralize the intervention by calling for a meeting of consultation under the OAS Charter. At the meeting held in Washington in May, the United States pushed for the creation of an inter-American force to take over in the Dominican Republic. There was considerable opposition to this proposal for collective intervention, as well as criticism of the U.S. intervention itself. The U.S. proposal barely passed, and the Inter-American Peace Force was created. Units from Brazil, Costa Rica, Honduras, Nicaragua, Paraguay, and the United States made up the force under a Brazilian commander. This approach permitted the first U.S. troop withdrawals in late May; by September 1965 all U.S. troops were out, although the rest of the Inter-American Peace Force remained until September 1966. The United States brokered an agreement between the contending Dominican factions, calling for new national elections in June 1966 which Bosch lost to the conservative Joaquín Balaguer.

While the Johnson administration viewed the Dominican intervention as a success, it was widely denounced throughout Latin America. The United States had blatantly disregarded the most sensitive principle of the inter-American system, that of nonintervention. It compounded its problems by trying to promote acceptance of the concept of multilateral intervention which had been rejected in the past. The Dominican intervention also conveyed the image of a United States allied with the forces of conservatism against the supporters of reform, an abandonment of the expectations aroused by the Alliance for Progress. Even though the United States ultimately turned the Dominican issue over to the OAS for resolution, it undermined the inter-American system by calling upon it only after acting unilaterally.

CHAPTER 6

FROM DETENTE TO
THE DEBT CRISIS, 1968–1988

Vignette: Eugene Hasenfus and the Unraveling of Iran-Contra

On 7 October 1986, careful readers of the *New York Times* might have discovered a story on the inside pages datelined Managua, Nicaragua. It reported that the Nicaraguan Defense Ministry had announced the downing of a plane being used to supply the Contras, the counter-revolutionary force battling Nicaragua's leftist Sandinista government. The only survivor claimed to be a U.S. military adviser in El Salvador.

The truth was stranger. Two days later, the family of the Wisconsin native had identified him as Eugene Hasenfus, an ex-Marine who had served in Vietnam. Marine Corps records, however, showed no overseas service. Classmates and other friends said he had told them that he had served for over a decade in Southeast Asia, part of that time with Air America, a company owned by the CIA. Recently, all sources agreed, he had been working in Florida for Southern Air Transport, yet another airline once owned by the CIA. On a recent visit, he had asked his brother William if he could borrow his parachute, perhaps the one that saved him. As his brother commented philosophically, "That's my parachute he used down there in Nicaragua. . . . So scratch one parachute."

President Ronald Reagan praised the crew of the supply plane, living and dead, comparing their efforts rather peculiarly to the Abraham Lincoln Brigade, which had fought in the Spanish Civil War. What Reagan did not point out, and was perhaps unaware of, was that the Brigade was a group of U.S. volunteers serving on the leftist side in that conflict.

While the Nicaraguans accused the Reagan administration of supplying their enemies, Reagan himself defended the rights of Americans to help the Contras. "We're in a free country where private citizens have a great many freedoms," he commented. Democrats complained that the Republicans seemed to be encouraging this help. Meanwhile, executives of Southern Air Transport denied that the C-123 was theirs, despite photographs that showed it parked in space owned by the company during the previous year. Retired General John Singlaub, head of a private group of Americans supporting the Contra insurgency, denied any connection with the plane, wondering publicly why U.S. government officials "would want to put out this misinformation. . . ." Hasenfus himself spoke at a news conference on 9 October, indicating that the supply flights were supervised by CIA agents in El Salvador. In another crew member's wallet, a card was found that belonged to Robert W. Owen, associated with Lt. Colonel Oliver North, currently on assignment to the National Security Council (NSC). North immediately began to shred documents. His comment to his supervisor, NSC adviser John Poindexter, was that "All this was going to result in somebody having to be offered up, as it were." Singlaub had the same thought. When asked by a reporter if he were being made a scapegoat, he commented, "Needless to say, the thought has crossed my mind."

At the same time, concerns were surfacing in the press and among members of the U.S. Congress about a rumored "arms for hostages" deal between the U.S. government and Iran. The connection between the two incidents was quickly exposed: investigators from Attorney General Edwin Meese's office, working through NSC documents provided by Oliver North, discovered a memorandum indicating that residual funds from the Iran arms arrangement had been used to purchase arms for the rebels. North, who had been shredding similar documents for several weeks, had provided materials to the investigators that he believed to be clean of incriminating information. In fact, he had been carrying documents past the attorney general's lawyers on his way to the shredder.

Meese, fearing that a coverup could potentially harm Reagan's presidency more seriously than revelation, quickly informed the president, who according to Meese seemed startled and puzzled by the whole affair. On 25 November 1986, the president and Meese went before the press to announce the discovery of the diversion of funds from arms sales to Iran to the Nicaraguan Contras. Meese's explanation focused largely on the unauthorized nature of the operation and the president's lack of involvement. Oliver North then resigned. The ability of the Reagan administration to aid the opposition to a Nicaraguan government it found seriously distasteful and believed to be communist was irredeemably damaged.

Based on Theodore Draper, A Very Thin Line (Touchstone, 1991), Chapters 17, 23, and 24, and the New York Times, 7, 11 October and 24 and 27 November 1986. The North quotation appears in Draper, p. 354. All other quotations are from the New York Times.

While **Johnson** was roundly criticized in Latin America for his handling of the Dominican crisis, it was his handling of another foreign policy issue — Vietnam — that led to his undoing. Faced with mounting opposition within his own party, Johnson decided not to seek reelection, thus opening the door for the political resurrection of Richard Nixon who won the Republican nomination and then the presidency in 1968. Nixon had an active interest in foreign affairs, as well as a predisposition to secret negotiations and diplomatic drama. He also had a well-established reputation for being anti-communist. The Nixon administration witnessed an important shift in power within the foreign policy bureaucracy; the position of national security adviser — increasingly important in the 1960s — eclipsed that of secretary of state as the dominant influence on foreign policy.

Nixon and his national security adviser, Henry Kissinger, distrusted the traditional foreign policy bureaucracy and sought a major redirection of U.S. policy. Both saw the Vietnam imbroglio as the symptom of a broader problem for U.S. foreign policy: the erosion of the dominant post–World War II position of the United States. The loss of this "hegemonic" position required dramatic new directions in U.S. policy. In pursuit of a more orderly world, the United States must seek new openings, particularly with the Soviet Union and China; this policy of "detente" reflected the Nixon-Kissinger view that national interests ultimately were more important than ideology in determining international relations. The whole thrust of this policy, however, still preserved the emphasis on East-West relations that had characterized earlier administrations. Nixon and Kissinger also retained the emphasis on political and strategic considerations, while downplaying economics. Both of these characteristics offered little prospect that either Latin America or economic development would figure prominently in U.S. foreign policy.

Although the Nixon-Kissinger world view assigned a low priority to Latin America, Nixon did turn his attention early in his administration to the region. Nixon appointed a fact-finding commission headed by Governor Nelson Rockefeller of New York to survey conditions in Latin America and make recommendations for policy. From May to July 1969, the commission made four often stormy trips to Latin America which must have reminded Nixon of his own reception there as vice president in 1958. Violent demonstrations greeted the commission in several countries; Chile and Venezuela asked that the commission "postpone" its visits, while the new military government of Peru rather undiplomatically said that a visit would be "inconvenient."

The commission submitted its report in August 1969 with some major recommendations. The commission called for a number of changes in the U.S. foreign policy bureaucracies dealing with Latin America, including the creation of a "secretary of western hemisphere affairs." The commission also addressed a number of long-time economic concerns of the Latin American nations. It described trade policy as "the central economic issue" in hemispheric relations and admitted that the United States imposed "formidable barriers" against imports from Latin America. The commission recommended preferential tariffs for Latin American products and a readjustment of import quotas where they existed. Development assistance should be on a long-term basis with the emphasis on low-interest loans and lenient repayment terms. The commission recognized the debt problems experienced by many countries in the region and advocated "a generous rescheduling of debt service requirements." The report also called for a major commitment by the United States to education in the hemisphere, "with financing in the magnitude of $100 million to start with." The United States should also provide loans and technical assistance to modernize agriculture, including "agrarian reform appropriate to the needs of the country." In a more traditional vein, the Rockefeller report emphasized the importance of private investment—both domestic and foreign—in Latin American development and urged an expansion of U.S.military assistance.[1]

At the same time that the United States was organizing the Rockefeller Commission, the Latin American nations were meeting on their own at Viña del Mar, Chile, to formulate their views on economic development. The conference took place amid growing disenchantment in Latin America with the Alliance for Progress as well as with trade relations with the United States. The conference issued what became known as the "Consensus of Viña del Mar," a virtual summary of Latin America's complaints about the U.S. role in economic development since World War II. The Consensus criticized both the aid and trade policies of the United States. The document stressed the need to tailor development efforts for each individual country. There was also strong criticism of the restrictions placed on U.S. aid, especially the practice of "additionality" which linked aid to the purchase of U.S. products. The Latin American nations again voiced their disapproval of U.S. trade policies which hindered access to U.S. markets. On 11 June 1969 a group of Latin American representatives formally presented the consensus to President Nixon.[2]

Nixon had time to absorb both the Rockefeller report and the Consensus of Viña del Mar by the time he set down his Latin American policy in detail in October 1969. The president called for a "new kind of partnership" between the United States and Latin America, indicating a larger voice in hemispheric affairs for the Latin American nations. While not indicating that the Alliance for Progress had ended, he talked instead about "Action for Progress." The United States would continue to provide development assistance for the hemisphere, but the president indicated that the emphasis would be on multilateral, not bilateral, aid. This approach would give the Latin American nations a greater voice in setting development priorities. Aid would no longer be linked to the purchase of U.S. products. Nixon also promised to address the longstanding problems of trade imbalance, debt service, economic integration, and sharing of technology. As one indication of the new partnership, Nixon called for the upgrading of the State Department position with primary responsibility for Latin American affairs from assistant secretary of state to undersecretary of state.

While Nixon responded to many of the Latin American concerns raised in the Rockefeller report and the Consensus of Viña del Mar, the general tenor of the policy was unsettling to many in Latin America. One interpretation of the new policy was that the United States was assuming a lower profile in the hemisphere and would devote less attention to Latin America than the last two administrations. Nixon's less-than-ringing support of the Alliance for Progress also called into question the commitment of the United States to major social and economic reforms. The test of this new policy was its implementation. Despite the supposed switch to multilateral aid, the Nixon administration delayed U.S. contributions to the Inter-American Development Bank and the World Bank. The trade issue raised by Latin American nations was largely ignored, with the United States even briefly adding a surcharge to all imports. Nixon's "untying" of aid proved to be only partial, since the United States required that its aid be used to purchase only U.S. or Latin American products.

There was also little action by his administration to deal with debt problems, technology transfers, or economic integration. Also discouraging to Latin American countries was Nixon's growing emphasis on protecting U.S. private investment in Latin America as a series of revolutionary and nationalist governments took power, threatening to nationalize U.S. properties.[3]

One Latin American country which attracted U.S. attention was Chile, one of the countries with a new nationalist, revolutionary government threatening U.S. investment. Chile—with one of the best-established democratic traditions in Latin America—posed a special problem for the United States. Throughout the 1960s U.S. administrations fretted over the possibility that the communists might achieve power legally, and tried to head off a communist electoral victory by making Chile one of the prime examples of the Alliance for Progress. In 1970 the United States worked without success to block the election victory of the Marxist candidate, Salvador Allende. Although Allende had received only thirty-six percent of the popular vote in the election, he embarked on a radical economic program, including expropriation of U.S.-owned properties. Allende completed the "Chileanization" of the copper industry started by his predecessor, Christian Democrat Eduardo Frei, but aroused the ire of the Nixon administration by announcing that there would be no additional compensation for the U.S. copper companies because they had taken illegal profits. As the nationalization program was extended to other U.S. firms, the United States doubted the ability of the Allende administration to pay compensation even if it had the will. The United States began a program of both public and covert activities to "save Chile." The Nixon administration drastically reduced U.S. aid to Chile which had been a major recipient of Alliance aid in the 1960s; the United States also used its influence with international agencies such as the World Bank and the Inter-American Development Bank to block new loans to Allende. Covertly, U.S. funding supported political groups, newspapers, business organizations, and unions opposing the Allende government. The United States continued military aid to Chile, monitored the various plots among military elements, and made no effort to discourage a coup. In September 1973, Allende was overthrown in a violent coup during which he was either assassinated or committed suicide.

While the United States was deeply involved in Chilean affairs, there was growing criticism in Latin America that detente had led to general neglect of the region. Responding to such criticism, Kissinger in October 1973 called for a "new dialogue" between the United States and Latin America. Kissinger further raised expectations when he personally attended an inter-American

A Chilean poster from the Allende period shows the hemisphere inverted. "The Art of Latin America is Revolution," silkscreen cover for a series published by the Latin American Art Institute, Chile, in 1973.

Photograph by David Kunzle

meeting in Mexico City in February 1974. In what was a hopeful sign for the Latin American delegations, most of the discussion at the meeting was on economic matters, with Kissinger promising U.S. cooperation on trade matters and maintenance of aid levels. In April 1974 Kissinger announced that the United States would be following the "policy of the good partner" in regards to Latin America. There was even optimistic talk that Kissinger intended to make 1974 "the Year of Latin America." The new dialogue and the new partnership soon came unglued in the face of international and domestic problems: the fallout from the Middle East war in 1973, the Arab oil embargo, an unresponsive U.S. economy, growing controversy over the "Watergate issue" coming out of Nixon's reelection, the resignation of Nixon in August 1974, and the weak political base of his successor, Gerald Ford.[4]

Carter, the Canal, and Human Rights

Kissinger continued as secretary of state under President Ford, and during the presidential campaign of 1976 indicated that Latin America was now the top priority of the Ford administration. The Ford-Kissinger team had little opportunity to implement this change in priorities, losing the election to the Washington outsider, Jimmy Carter. Domestic issues had dominated the election, and Carter had little foreign policy experience. The two principal figures on Carter's foreign policy team—Secretary of State Cyrus Vance and National Security Adviser Zbigniew Brzezinski—were primarily concerned with East-West relations. Although there was little in this background that indicated a major emphasis on Latin America, two issues did have a significant effect on U.S.-Latin American relations: the new Panama Canal treaties and human rights.

The Carter administration made the negotiation of new treaties with Panama its highest foreign policy priority. Treaty negotiations with Panama had a lengthy history. Treaties signed and ratified in 1939 and 1955 modified the original treaty of 1903, but did not address the basic issue of Panamanian sovereignty over the canal and the Canal Zone, the focus of dispute in the increasingly nationalistic years after World War II. The sovereignty issue provoked major riots in Panama in 1959 and 1964, leading the Johnson administration to enter into new negotiations which produced three new treaties in 1967. The most important provision of the new treaties was the transfer of control of the Canal Zone to Panama in the year 2000. These treaties were

Republic of Panama

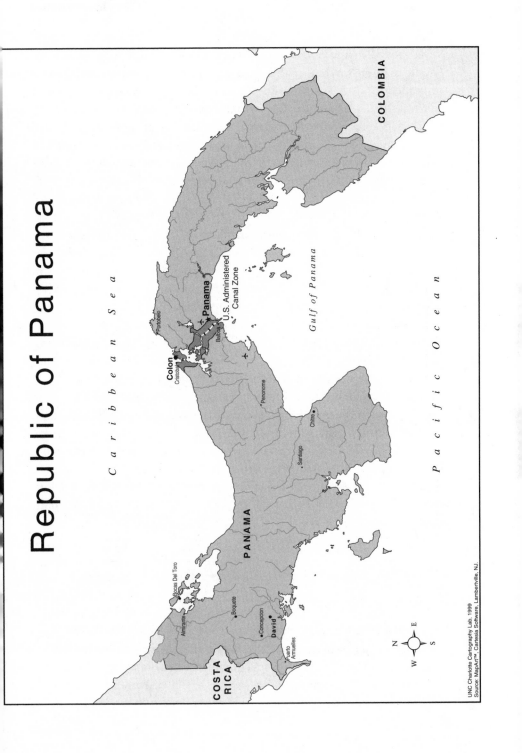

UNC Charlotte Cartography Lab, 1999
Source: MapArt™, Cartesia Software, Lambertville, NJ.

never ratified, falling victim to the bitterness of presidential elections in both countries in 1968. While neither Panama nor the proposed treaties figured prominently in the Nixon-Kissinger agenda, the rise to power in Panama of General Omar Torrijos forced them to reconsider the problem. Torrijos skillfully maneuvered on the international scene to bring pressure on the United States, leading to the renewal of bilateral negotiations in late 1973. These negotiations led to a "Joint Statement of Principles" in February 1974, which set the guidelines for the drafting of new treaties; the most important "principle" called for a treaty fixing a specific date for the transfer of control of the Canal Zone to Panama.[5]

There was little progress on formulating the treaties in the abbreviated administrations of Richard Nixon and Gerald Ford, but the Carter administration was able to quickly build on the negotiations of the 1960s and 1970s. In August 1977 Panama and the United States announced the conclusion of two new treaties. One treaty dealt with canal operations and transfer of the Canal Zone. This treaty called for the abolition of both the Panama Canal Company and the Canal Zone Government and the creation of the Panama Canal Commission with representatives from both the United States and Panama. After a three-year period, the Canal Zone would be integrated into Panama. The United States had the primary responsibility for operating the canal until the year 2000, when Panama would assume sole responsibility for administration. The second treaty dealt with the permanent neutrality of the canal and gave both Panama and the United States the right to defend the canal's neutrality beyond the year 2000. The new treaties aroused considerable opposition in both countries. In October 1977 a national plebiscite in Panama approved both treaties. In March and April 1978, the U.S. Senate narrowly ratified both treaties by a vote of 68–32.

Point-Counterpoint: Panama, Sovereignty, and the Canal

" . . . Let us take a look at some of the arguments being advanced against a new treaty and the most important questions which are being raised. *First, won't a new treaty mean surrender of U.S. sovereignty over the Panama Canal?* The simple answer is that the United States has never had sovereignty. The 1903 treaty specifically gave the United States certain rights and authority which it would have 'if it were the sovereign.' Obviously, these words would not have been necessary if the United States were in fact intended to be sovereign.

"Before the ink was dry on the 1903 treaty, Secretary of War William Taft wrote to President Theodore Roosevelt asserting that the treaty 'seems to preserve the titular sovereignty over the Canal Zone in the Republic of Panama.' A treaty of friendship entered into between the United States and Panama in March 1936 referred to the Canal Zone as 'territory of the Republic of Panama under the jurisdiction of the United States.' In 1946 John Foster Dulles, as U.S. Representative to the United Nations, acknowledged before the General Assembly that Panama had never ceased to be sovereign over the Canal Zone."

—*Address by Sol M. Linowitz, Senior Adviser to the Panama Canal Treaty Negotiations, 19 August 1977, reprinted in* Department of State Bulletin, *Vol. LXXVII, No. 1999, 17 October 1977, p. 522.*

"The United States acquired the use, occupation, and control of the Canal Zone under Article II of the 1903 treaty, but the rights of private property owners in the zone were specifically preserved. Subsequently, the United States constructed numerous facilities and installations, including the canal, and paid private property owners for the holdings taken from them, either through purchase or indemnification for damage in accordance with Article VI of the 1903 Treaty.

"In addition, the United States was given, by Article III of the 1903 treaty, the privilege of exercising the rights, powers, and authority over the area which the United States would exercise if it were sovereign of the territory.

"From 1904 to the present, however, the United States has consistently recognized that the Canal Zone remains Panamanian territory."

—*"Legal Basis for the Authority of the U.S. in the Canal Zone,"* Department of State Bulletin, *as above, p. 541.*

"When it comes to the Canal, we bought it, we paid for it, it's ours, and we should tell Torrijos and company that we are going to keep it."

—*Ronald Reagan, during the 1976 presidential primary campaign, quoted in John Dinges,* Our Man in Panama: The Shrewd Rise and Brutal Fall of Manuel Noriega *(New York: Times Books, 1991), p. 80.*

While the new canal treaties were well received in Latin America, the Carter administration's emphasis on human rights brought a mixed response. This emphasis was part of a broader effort to recast U.S. foreign policy in what was already being prematurely described as the post–Cold War period. In his inaugural address, Carter indicated that the U.S. commitment to human rights "must be absolute," but Carter found implementation of the policy difficult both on a global and regional basis.

Carter's Human Rights bureau within the State Department was led by dedicated individuals, but the bureaucratic situation, in which desk officers for particular countries were reluctant to see "their" countries stigmatized, made it difficult for action to be taken against violators. Moreover, although Carter was himself strongly concerned with human rights, his national security adviser, Zbigniew Brzezinski, was not. Brzezinski, born in Poland, was inclined to see Latin American policy within the usual Cold War framework. His influence, therefore, undermined to a degree Carter's own predilections.

Carter's principal tool in carrying out the policy was the manipulation of foreign aid. His administration reduced aid to Argentina, Bolivia, Chile, and Haiti over human rights abuses. The United States tried unsuccessfully to block loans by the Inter-American Development Bank to Argentina and Chile. Acting on annual "certifications" by the State Department of the status of human rights in each country, the Carter administration soon was caught up in the complexity and inconsistencies of its own policy. Even Latin Americans who supported greater attention to human rights often took exception to the unevenness in the application of the policy. Latin American nations were more frequently targeted for sanctions than repressive regimes in other parts of the world. Critics in Latin America accused the United States of "beating up on" easy targets such as Argentina and Chile while downplaying abuses in more strategically sensitive countries such as Iran, South Korea, and the Philippines. The pursuit of an active human rights policy invariably led to complaints that the United States was meddling in the internal affairs of the Latin American nations, a complaint which cut across the political spectrum. More to the point was whether the emphasis on human rights was producing the desired results; the State Department's annual report in 1979 found little improvement in human rights.

Central America, without question, was a reasonable area in which to test human rights policies, and in 1977, both El Salvador and Guatemala—along with Brazil, Argentina, and Uruguay in the western hemisphere—were cited for violations. The result was that El Salvador and Guatemala began purchasing weapons from Israel and Western Europe and did without U.S. aid for a time. No improvement in treatment of their citizens was forthcoming.

Nicaragua was somewhat different, although there is little evidence that the United States had much effect in occasioning Somoza's fall. The beginning of the end for that regime occurred in 1972, with a massive earthquake which destroyed much of Managua, the capital, and a number of smaller towns. President Nixon immediately sent $32 million to aid in reconstruction, and supplies poured in from around the world. However, Somoza officials and the National Guard, his own large and brutal internal security force, stole much of the money and sold relief supplies for a profit. Somoza and his friends then proceeded to make fortunes from reconstruction in a new area on the edge of Managua which they controlled. Business leaders were antagonized, and the poor, suffering terribly, were further alienated. In the wake of the devastation, a small radical group—the Frente Sandinista de Liberación Nacional (FSLN)—began to gain adherents.

When Carter came into office, the announcement of his human rights policy led Nicaraguan Archbishop Miguel Obando y Bravo to denounce National Guard atrocities in a pastoral letter. Democrats in the U.S. Congress also demanded improvements in human rights. Professional people in Nicaragua began to call for Somoza's resignation. Although Somoza and the National Guard eased the repression somewhat, disorder continued, accompanied by capital flight to foreign banks and guerrilla attacks on various targets including power plants. When, on 10 January 1978, the distinguished opposition leader Pedro Joaquín Chamorro was assassinated by Somoza gunmen, a mass uprising began, with people from urban slums joining the rebels. An increase in repression was the result.

As resistance to Somoza spread, the Carter administration began to get nervous. A spectacular strike by twenty-five FSLN guerrillas under the command of Edén Pastora (the famous Comandante Zero) captured the National Legislative Palace on 23 August. The guerrillas succeeded in obtaining a number of concessions from Somoza, including the release of Sandinista prisoners and a $500,000 ransom, before leaving via the Managua airport. The international press showed pictures of crowds lining the streets to cheer Pastora's men as they moved between the Palace and the airport through some of the capital's worst slums. "Operation Pigsty" (Operación Chancera) had been successful not only in obtaining actual concessions from Somoza but also in bringing international attention to the struggle.[6]

Nicaragua exploded, and Somoza retaliated with vicious repression by the Guard. As anti-Somoza uprisings occurred around the country, even without FSLN direction, other countries moved in to help. Costa Rica permitted the Sandinistas to establish a government-in-exile in its capital, San José, and in November broke relations with Somoza. Venezuela, Mexico, and Panama also moved supplies to the revolutionaries. Meanwhile, the United States vetoed a $20 million loan to Nicaragua from the International Monetary Fund and then called for Somoza's resignation on the grounds of his abysmal human rights record.

But the Carter administration was afraid to let events take their course. The FSLN was in no way beholden to the United States, and was viewed as too radical in any case. U.S. policymakers began to search for a moderate who would be more controllable, but their efforts were counterproductive. Between September 1978 and July 1979, when Somoza finally fled the country, U.S. vacillations confused the political picture and angered the Sandinistas. Even though Carter and Brzezinski called an emergency meeting of the OAS to arrange for an inter-American peacekeeping force, they received little support. Mexico fought Washington's initiative, and for the first time since the establishment of the OAS in 1948, a U.S. proposal to intervene was defeated. Although direct U.S. military intervention was never an option, the 1980 Republican presidential campaign would emphasize Carter's foreign policy failures, including the "loss" of Nicaragua.

Although the Cubans advised the Sandinistas to maintain a good relationship with the United States and particularly with U.S. business, and despite Carter's initial economic aid of $20 million, relations with the new Nicaraguan regime deteriorated quickly. When the Sandinistas delayed elections for five years, Washington's conclusion—within both the Congress and Carter's administration—was that the Sandinistas intended to impose a communist regime and were thus an ideological and national security threat to the United States. Even on the day of the FSLN triumph in July, the CIA began—in an effort that resonated with the covert attacks against Arbenz in Guatemala and the support for Cuban exiles in the disaster at the Bay of Pigs—to reorganize the National Guard. As pressure mounted, the Sandinistas responded by repressing the opposition. Moderates Violeta Chamorro and Alfonso Robelo resigned from the junta in May 1980.

Faced with this potential second Cuba, the Carter administration responded by setting aside its concern for human rights and returning to the earlier policy of support for dictatorships. It supported the repressive government of El Salvador despite extensive human rights violations, including the assassination of Archbishop Oscar Romero and 10,000 other political murders (by the count of the Roman Catholic Church) in 1980. Two highly publicized atrocities took place in late 1980. In November, six leaders of the opposition front were dragged from a meeting in a Jesuit high school and killed; in December, four U.S. churchwomen were murdered by the military. Still, U.S. military aid including advisers was resumed by Carter in January 1981, in the face of threats from the rebel movement FDR-FMLN (Revolutionary Democratic Front-Farabundo Martí Liberation Front). Guatemala, with probably the most repressive military regime in the hemisphere, remained beyond the pale.

The Cathedral in downtown Nicaragua in 1982, hung with banners. The most prominent banner depicts Augusto Sandino. The cathedral was heavily damaged by an earthquake in 1972 and remains unrepaired.

Photograph by David Craven

Reagan and the "Return" of the Cold War

Ronald Reagan's campaign against Jimmy Carter in 1980 focused vocally on
the decline of American power around the world. The Republican platform
vowed to end this decline in Latin America by doing away with Carter's "economic and diplomatic sanctions linked to undifferentiated charges of human
rights violations."[7] Reagan's election would lead directly back to support for
military repression of civilian populations in Central America.

In office, Reagan equated the Cold War struggle against communism with
the Monroe Doctrine's admonition against colonialism. Bringing to the fore
issues of American power, he viewed the Central American situation within a
national security perspective that emphasized the military and ideological
threat to the hemisphere. Rebel movements in Central America were characterized as Marxist and therefore extremely dangerous; the revolutionary
government in Nicaragua was a Soviet "beachhead in North America." Despite
its small size, Nicaragua was, in his view, "a privileged sanctuary for . . . struggle against the United States." It became, in his description, "a safe house, a
command post for international terror." As president, he described the forces
led by former Somoza officers — called "Contras" or counter-revolutionaries —
as "freedom fighters" and equated them with the French Resistance that had
fought the Nazis.[8]

Reagan's administration would signal the return to the idea by containment
policy author George Kennan that repression and military government would
be necessary to contain the poor and fractious Latin American masses.[9] In trying to impose such a policy and such a vision, Reagan inspired widespread dissent within the United States and a successful effort by Latin American
countries to work out a solution to their own problems, despite his opposition. He also wrote the last chapter in the history of the Monroe Doctrine as
the dominant paradigm in U.S.-Latin American interactions. With the end of
the Reagan administration, other issues — specific to the western hemisphere
and affecting U.S. domestic concerns and policy — came to dominate that relationship.

Reagan's choice of upper level officials quickly gave an indication of the direction of his policies. Many of his appointees were drawn from the military.
Secretary of State Alexander Haig was the former commander of NATO. In
developing foreign policy he looked to other former military officers such as
General Vernon Walters — a former deputy director of the CIA — and Robert

McFarlane, who would be intimately involved in covert action as well. Haig himself, however, would gain a reputation as favoring direct military intervention rather than secret operations. During the Vietnam War, he had been involved in ground operations in the Iron Triangle, an area of Vietcong strength near Saigon, and had come back a hero. He was an outspoken proponent of the idea that the U.S. had lost that war because of an unwillingness to use the force necessary to destroy the enemy, and a failure to recognize that it was a Cold War arena rather than a simple local conflict.[10] He would be a strong advocate of direct action to overthrow the Sandinistas in Nicaragua, although he later denied that he had supported "the landing of Marines in Central America."[11] However, he did oppose covert action in most cases, which may explain in part his replacement by George Schulz in the second year of the Reagan administration. McFarlane and Walters stayed, however.[12]

A top policy position in the Pentagon was given to Nestor Sánchez, a CIA operative who was deputy chief of the Agency in Guatemala at the time of Arbenz's overthrow. Thomas Enders, the new assistant secretary of state for Latin America, had helped direct the massive secret air attacks on Southeast Asia during Nixon's presidency. According to one scholar, control of Central American policy passed to the right wing as a payoff for their support in the election, and that view is undoubtedly correct.[13] However, given Reagan's strong anti-communist stance, it seems likely that he would have pursued the covert and overt use of force in Central America in any case.

One of the strongest voices for such policies was Jeane Kirkpatrick, Reagan's choice for ambassador to the United Nations. Rather surprisingly, given the neglect from U.S. policymakers in which the region had formerly languished, she stated clearly in early 1981 that "Central America is the most important place in the world for the United States today."[14] Kirkpatrick had come to Reagan's attention for her 1979 article, "Dictatorships and Double Standards," which distinguished between authoritarian and totalitarian regimes. Authoritarian regimes, which maintained traditional societies and open capitalist economic systems, were acceptable as they were usually anti-communist and friendly to the United States. Her selection of examples was ominous: Somoza in Nicaragua and the Shah of Iran (recently run out of his own country by militant Muslims). Totalitarian governments, however, sought to maintain complete control over their economies, using repression and terror; were not limited by the life of an individual, given their ideological nature; and were dedicated to expansion regardless of the means. Obviously, communist regimes were a particular target of her analysis. Carter's failure, in her opinion, was that he used power only against authoritarian regimes, when he should have been focusing on totalitarian ones, such as those recently established in Nicaragua (communist) and Iran (Islamic fundamentalist). A comment in her opening paragraph no doubt particularly pleased Reagan; she attacked Carter's Panama Canal treaties as laying "the groundwork for a transfer . . . to a swaggering Latin dictator of Castroite bent." She also voiced strong anti-revolutionary sentiments which would be resonant with Reagan's future policies, saying ". . . traditional autocrats tolerate social inequalities, brutality, and poverty, whereas revolutionary autocracies create them." Therefore, because traditional societies do not disturb the "habitual rhythms" of the culture, the people become accustomed to misery and do not flee. However, "revolutionary communist regimes," such as those in Vietnam and Cuba, so disrupt traditional patterns that they create millions of refugees who brave "walls, guns, fences and sharks" to escape, thereby becoming, apparently, a considerable inconvenience to the rest of the world.[15] She blithely ignored the Salvadorans who were already surging into the United States, forced out of their country by repression and civil war. Reagan, finding her arguments compelling, welcomed her into his administration.

The two major problems were Nicaragua and El Salvador. Approaches varied, given the circumstances in the two countries. In Nicaragua, an unacceptable regime—viewed as communist and tied to both Cuba and the Soviet Union—was in place. Therefore, despite the continued opposition of the American public, both covert and overt aid would be given to opponents of that regime. El Salvador, where the revolution was ongoing rather than victorious, aid was poured in to the strong and brutal military establishment. At the same time, a political process designed to support a moderate figurehead, José Napoleon Duarte of the Christian Democratic Party, was pursued. Kirkpatrick herself dismissed the murder of the American churchwomen mentioned above, claiming that they had been "political activists" for the FMLN, a charge which was inaccurate.[16]

It is instructive to look at the U.S. aid figures from 1980 to 1991.[17] (See Table 1.) During this time period, Costa Rica, bastion of democracy in the region, received a total of about $1.4 billion, with only a fraction for military aid. Interestingly, the two years in which it received significant military aid were 1984 and 1985, at the height of the civil war in Nicaragua. During the same period,

Table 1. U.S. Bilateral Aid to Central America　　　　　　(US$ millions)

	FY	Military	Total Aid
Costa Rica	1980	-	14.0
	1981	-	13.3
	1982	2.1	53.8
	1983	4.6	218.7
	1984	9.1	179.0
	1985	11.2	231.2
	1986	2.6	150.6
	1987	1.7	179.5
	1988	0.2	105.6
	1989	1.7	118.6
	1990	0.2	94.3
	1991	0.2	68.0
El Salvador	1980	5.9	63.7
	1981	35.5	149.1
	1982	82.0	264.2
	1983	81.1	326.7
	1984	196.6	412.5
	1985	136.3	570.2
	1986	121.7	437.1
	1987	111.5	507.8
	1988	81.5	401.6
	1989	81.4	382.7
	1990	86.0	328.7
	1991	91.4	375.4
Guatemala	1980	-	11.1
	1981	-	16.6
	1982	-	15.5
	1983	-	29.7
	1984	-	20.3
	1985	0.5	107.4
	1986	5.4	110.9
	1987	5.5	181.2
	1988	9.4	146.7
	1989	9.4	155.6
	1990	3.3	120.8
	1991	5.5	129.6

Table 1. (continued)

Honduras	1980	3.9	55.0
	1981	8.8	42.8
	1982	31.3	112.0
	1983	48.3	154.3
	1984	77.4	172.4
	1985	67.4	296.4
	1986	61.1	185.1
	1987	61.2	254.9
	1988	41.2	198.0
	1989	41.1	121.3
	1990	21.3	209.5
	1991	41.1	179.4
Nicaragua	1980	-	37.1
	1981	-	59.7
	1982	-	6.3
	1983	-	x
	1984	-	0.1
	1985	-	-
	1986	-	-
	1987	-	-
	1988	-	-
	1989	-	-
	1990	-	317.3
	1991	-	227.0

Source: Gabriel Aguilera et al., *Centroamerica de Reagan a Bush* (San José: FLACSO, 1991).

El Salvador received $1.1 billion for military support alone, although it is likely that the true figures were considerably higher. Total U.S. aid to tiny El Salvador amounted to an amazing $4.2 billion. With a population of approximately 5 million people, El Salvador was receiving the third highest level of U.S. aid in the world, behind only Israel and Egypt.[18] Aid also began to flow to Guatemala's military in 1985, with only $39 million of a total of over $1 billion designated for the military in the 1980–1991 period. Aid to Honduras likewise soared after 1982. It reached a total of $504 million in military aid out of almost $1.8 billion for the eleven years in question, with the high points between 1984 and 1987. Honduras was the primary base for Contra operations and was also

Table 2. Increase in Central American Armed Forces

	El Salvador	Guatemala	Honduras	Nicaragua
	Total	Total	Total	Total
1970–71	5,630	9,000	4,725	7,100
1979–80	6,930	17,960	11,300	8,300
1980–81	7,250	14,900	11,300	?
1981–82	9,850	15,050	11,200	6,700
1982–83	16,000	18,550	13,000	21,700
1983–84	24,650	21,560	15,200	48,800
1984–85	41,650	40,000	17,200	61,800
1985–86	41,650	31,700	16,600	62,850
1986–87	42,640	32,000	19,200	72,000
1987–88	47,000	40,200	16,950	72,000

Source: Gabriel Aguilera et al., *Centroamerica de Reagan a Bush* (San José: FLACSO, 1991

the site of major U.S.-Honduran military exercises several times during the 1980s, placing U.S. troops close to Salvadoran and Nicaraguan battlefields.[19] It is impossible to know exactly how much military aid actually went to each of these countries, however, because some was disguised in covert operations and still more was probably embedded in the total economic aid figures.

At the same time, the total size of the military increased in each country.[20] (See Table 2.) In El Salvador, the armed forces more than doubled in size between 1982–83 and 1984–85. Guatemala's military almost doubled in just one year, from 1983–84 to 1984–85. Honduran growth was much slower, but reached a high in 1986–87. Nicaragua, in the throes of civil war, saw an increase of more than tenfold in eight years, making its army the largest in Central America. Although Nicaragua was receiving aid from Cuba and the Soviet Union, the need to increase its expenditures on its military drew resources away from its program of reconstruction after the revolution against Somoza.

El Salvador in the 1980s

El Salvador—the focus of U.S. aid—became, in the 1980s, a textbook case of how U.S. support for a questionably democratic government would play out in its most extreme form. U.S. policymakers poured money into a country in which the most repressive forces of the military were beyond the control not only of any external restraints but also of the Salvadoran elites. It is highly ironic and tragic that this massive effort to resist Soviet penetration in the hemisphere occurred just as the Soviet Union was on the verge of collapse. It was, of course, closely tied to the fear of more Cubas and to the civil war which would be pursued with U.S. aid to overthrow the "communist" regime in Nicaragua.

The effort focused on El Salvador was devastating in both human and economic terms. According to one count, between 1979 and 1985 at least 50,000 civilians were killed or "disappeared," the term for actual or suspected members of the opposition to rightist regimes in Latin America who vanished during the 1970s and 1980s. Despite the input of U.S. funds during the 1983–1991 period of almost $500 million a year, the economy almost collapsed and the civil war continued. Only in 1992, during George Bush's presidency, would negotiations, which had been opposed by the Reagan administration, finally succeed in bringing a cease-fire.

Reagan policymakers pursued two tracks in their approach to El Salvador. On the one hand, they supported the Christian Democratic Party and its leader, José Napoleon Duarte, who was seen as a moderate in contrast to the hardline rightist alliance, the Alianza Republicana Nacionalista (ARENA), led by a former member of the military, Roberto D'Aubuisson, who had close ties to death squad activity. At the same time, aid to the military itself strengthened that sector at the expense of civilian political institutions. Duarte himself was successful in winning only one election in the 1980s—the presidency in 1984—with other elections favoring ARENA. Duarte, even during his four years as president, was completely unable to restrain the right, and U.S. military aid during this period was at its all-time high. The rule of law was not reestablished, death squad activity continued, and negotiations with the guerrillas were constrained by opposition from the Reagan administration and internal opponents. Duarte paid for such support as he actually received through helping the United States deliver aid to the Contras in Nicaragua. He fretted that disclosure of El Salvador's role might lead the U.S. congress to cut off funds to his own country.[21]

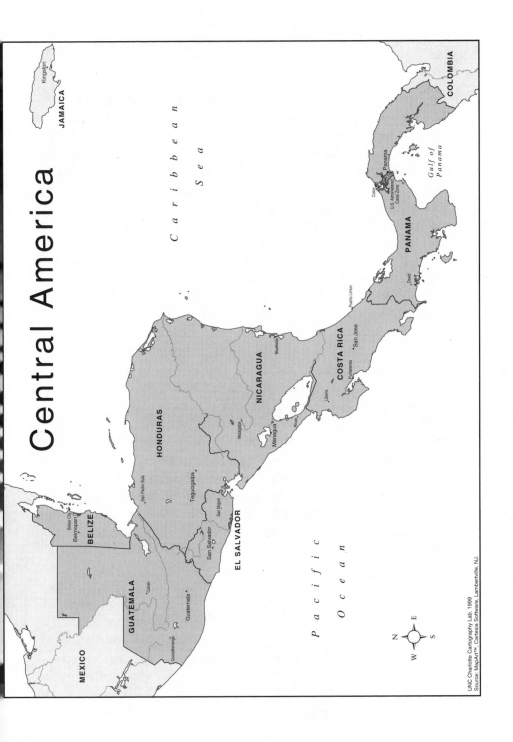

Central America

Kingston

JAMAICA

C a r i b b e a n

S e a

MEXICO

GUATEMALA

Quetzaltenango
Guatemala

BELIZE

Belize City
Belmopan

HONDURAS

San Pedro Sula

Tegucigalpa

San Salvador

San Miguel

EL SALVADOR

NICARAGUA

Matagalpa

Managua

Bluefields

Rivas

COSTA RICA

San José

Liberia

Puntarenas

Puerto Limon

PANAMA

David

Colón

Panama

U.S. Administered
Canal Zone

Gulf of
Panama

COLOMBIA

P a c i f i c

O c e a n

N
W   E
S

UNC Charlotte Cartography Lab. 1999
Source: MapArt™, Cartesia Software, Lambertville, NJ.

Not even a general settlement of Central American questions in 1987 could deter the U.S.-Salvadoran effort against the FMLN. By late 1987, the rebels were operating in all fourteen of the country's provinces, despite being outnumbered five to one by government troops.[22] Duarte, now dying of cancer, used the Arias plan (see below) to try to open discussions with the FMLN, but was unsuccessful. Then, in 1988 and 1989, ARENA won impressive election victories. The new candidate was not D'Aubuisson, but a moderate businessman, Alfredo Cristiani, who was more acceptable to the United States. Both aid and repression continued, along with the rebel struggle. After Cristiani won the presidential election in 1989, President George Bush congratulated his party for its commitment to democracy and D'Aubuisson was again welcomed at the U.S. embassy. Meanwhile, the FMLN, still viable, came into San Salvador itself, moving through residential neighborhoods and attacking the Defense Ministry. Perhaps in retaliation, in November 1989, members of the Salvadoran military dragged six priests and a housekeeper and her child from their residences at the Jesuit university in San Salvador, and executed them in cold blood.[23]

Meanwhile, Salvadorans were fleeing the country in large numbers. By the mid-1980s, half a million had sought refuge in the United States. As many as 1 million may have immigrated by the end of the decade. Even outside of El Salvador, they could not count on safety. Salvadoran death squads threatened and even kidnapped refugees who had fled to Los Angeles.[24] Meanwhile, the U.S. government began surveillance and harassment of American citizens opposed to U.S. policy toward El Salvador. Between 1981 and 1985, the FBI conducted secret investigations of the Committee in Solidarity with the People of El Salvador (CISPES), in an attempt to link the organization with terrorists. CISPES claimed that the investigations lasted until 1988 and had targeted 13,000 people and 11,000 organizations. The investigation cleared CISPES of any wrongdoing, and in 1988, FBI Director William Sessions publicly apologized.[25]

Despite years of U.S. aid, by the late 1980s El Salvador was devastated. Basic exports had dropped by almost half over the decade. Per capita income had dropped by a third, and the concentration of wealth had changed significantly in favor of the rich and the military. In fact, the military had profited so handsomely from U.S. aid (and were continuing to do so) that there was considerable question whether they actually wanted the civil war to end. They had moved far toward becoming not just enforcers for the oligarchy but also an independent class of entrepreneurs making profits off of the war effort and all kinds of associated corruption. Not a single officer had been convicted for death squad activities during the years of the Reagan administration. Any peace settlement would be dependent on bringing and keeping the military under control.[26]

The Reagan Administration and the Covert War in Nicaragua

Sandinista control of Nicaragua was the major Central American policy concern for Reagan and his advisers. Indeed, Nicaragua seemed to them to be another Cuba. When the United States invaded Grenada in the autumn of 1983 (see below), many observers believed that this action was only a prelude to an invasion of Nicaragua for the purpose of overthrowing the Sandinista government.[27] Reagan confronted, however, widespread domestic opposition. U.S. participation in the Vietnam War had ended in 1973, only seven years before Reagan's election. U.S. public opinion, the U.S. Congress, and even the U.S. military were unwilling to become embroiled again in a conflict in which the military goals were unclear. The administration was forced to back off and reassure the U.S. public that there were no plans to send U.S. combat troops into action.

This public stance was belied by a covert effort, beginning in November 1981, when Reagan signed the CIA plan, National Security Decision Directive 17, creating an anti-Sandinista force soon to be known as the "Contras." The CIA was already beginning training operations in Honduras. William Casey, a long-time cold warrior, was Reagan's choice to head the agency, and he lost little time in visiting Managua to see what steps could be taken to get rid of the Sandinistas. The ambassador, Lawrence Pezzullo, a career officer who had been sent in by Carter as Somoza was falling, preferred a negotiated settlement of some sort. Casey (and Reagan) were not interested. The Honduran camps provided space for training about one thousand men, with Argentines overseeing the training and the United States sending the money. The payoff for the Hondurans was money and weapons. Many joked that the "USS Honduras" was the largest aircraft carrier in the fleet.[28]

The Contras were promoted to the Congress and to the American public initially as an interdiction force against the movement of arms to rebel forces in El Salvador. However, the Reagan administration felt that much more was at stake. Reagan had pledged in his campaign to reassert American power throughout the world. As Robert McFarlane would later explain to Congress,

Demonstration in Masaya, Nicaragua, July 19, 1982, three years after the revolutionary triumph. Supporters carry a banner portraying martyred Nicaraguan revolutionaries Rigoberto López Pérez, Augusto Sandino, and Carlos Fonseca. Translated, the quotation reads "At whatever cost, we must persevere for the country."

Photograph by David Craven

Este hermoso mural estaba siendo pintado, en sus últimos toques por un artista de Masaya que quiso de ello en la celebración del Tercer Aniversario del Triunfo. Se encuentra en Las Siete Esquinas.

Murals in Masaya commemorate the third anniversary of the Sandinista victory. Taller de Gráfico Experimental, 1982.

From Barricada, *July 19, 1982*

FSLN Poster commemorates the July 19, 1979, victory of Sandinista forces against the dictatorship of Anastasio Somoza Debayle. The image, visible throughout Nicaragua after the victory, also appears in the Taller de Gráfico Experimental murals shown at left. Silkscreen, 1982, from the Taller de Gráfico Experimental.

Photograph by David Craven

"If we could not muster an effective counter to Cuban-Sandinista strategy in our own backyard, it was far less likely that we could do so in the years ahead in more distant locations. We had to win this one."[29]

It had been McFarlane himself who, in February 1981, had first developed extensive plans to undermine the Nicaraguan government for the administration. In a document called "Covert Action Proposal for Central America," he emphasized that prompt measures were essential on many fronts: "political, economic, diplomatic, propaganda, military, and covert. . . ." and that those activities had to be carefully coordinated. The strategy would have four main points: a paramilitary war, using the Contras and the CIA when necessary; economic destabilization; military psychological operations; and propaganda.[30]

The paramilitary force of exiles recalled the successful attack on the Arbenz government in Guatemala in 1954 and the unsuccessful effort against Castro at the Bay of Pigs in 1961. The CIA brought a number of different groups together, ranging from former Nicaraguan National Guard officers to civilians such as Adolfo Calero, who had formerly owned a Managuan Coca-Cola bottling plant. In late 1982, Calero became the new head of the Contra effort, at this point known as the Nicaragua Democratic Force (FDN). Enrique Bermúdez, who had been Somoza's military attaché in Washington, was the field commander, and his closest adviser was Ricardo Lau, a former Guardsman. The effort undertaken was almost completely ineffective militarily, but some Contra leaders became rich. By 1986, an American working to supply them clandestinely complained to Lt. Colonel Oliver North, head of the U.S. operation, that Contra leaders were "liars and greed and power motivated" and that "this war has become a business for them."

The CIA went beyond reliance on the exiles and began to launch its own attacks on Nicaraguan targets, sabotaging port facilities in September 1983; setting Nicaragua's largest oil storage installation on fire the following month; and mining Nicaragua's harbors in early 1984. North and others even suggested sinking a Mexican oil tanker in a Nicaraguan port in order to discourage insurers from covering ships scheduled into the country. Although this plan was never put into operation, paramilitary assaults continued, even after the U.S. Congress terminated direct and indirect aid to the Contras in October 1984 (see below). These included the bombing in March 1985 of a military complex near Managua undertaken by a British citizen who had been directly contracted by North.[31]

Economic destabilization included the immediate end to all economic aid programs as soon as Reagan took office. Nicaragua's sugar quota was soon cut, and two years later a full trade embargo was instituted. Pressure was exerted on U.S. allies in Latin America and Europe to cut down on their own trade and aid to the new Nicaraguan leadership; nevertheless, Mexico continued to help, and for that reason perhaps was the target of the planned but unfulfilled attack on the oil tanker. In particular, Nicaraguan credits from multilateral financial institutions where U.S. representatives had influence were blocked.

Military/psychological efforts centered on the war games that the U.S. repeatedly scheduled in the region. These caused major war scares among Nicaraguans, who felt that they needed to be ready at any time to meet a full-fledged attack. In this way, the Reagan administration forced the Nicaraguans to spend an inordinate amount of time, money, and effort in building defenses against such an attack, as well as creating an atmosphere of constant fear and tension.[32]

The propaganda war had two tracks. On the one hand, Reagan and members of his administration gave speeches and issued statements attacking the Sandinistas and praising their opponents, in particular the Contras. This effort was largely successful in convincing Congress, at least, of the evil nature of the Sandinista regime, although it did not convince that body that the policy of covert operations was warranted.[33] Jeane Kirkpatrick, Reagan's ambassador to the United Nations, was among the most vocal in attacking Nicaragua's leaders, emphasizing connections with Cuba and the Soviet Union and accusing them of seeking to subvert other hemispheric governments, especially El Salvador's.[34] Kirkpatrick constantly emphasized the similarity of the Nicaraguan situation to the Cuban one, most directly in an address that she gave to the Cuban American National Foundation in Miami in 1985. First accusing the Carter administration of a policy of "disarmament, passivity, and accommodation" which had led to the "establishment of new communist dictatorships in Grenada and Nicaragua," she then went on to defend the Reagan administration's help to the Nicaraguans "fighting against the establishment of another Marxist dictatorship" in the Western hemisphere. In heated rhetoric, she compared the Nicaraguan Revolution to the Cuban in eight basic points, including "intimate economic and political relations with the Soviet Union" and "consolidation of power by communists and . . . incorporation into the Soviet empire. . . ." She concluded, "Some say Nicaragua's freedom fighters cannot win. I say they cannot lose . . . if we provide half the assistance Moscow provides the FSLN. Some say it is not consistent to support rebels in Nicaragua and oppose them in El Salvador. But it is consistent to support a democratic government in El Salvador and democratic forces in Nicaragua."[35]

The second track involved the creation of the Office of Public Diplomacy for Latin America and the Caribbean, housed in the State Department but run out of the National Security Council within the White House. When the Office in fact operated publicly, it created and distributed pamphlets, briefing books, and white papers for the public, the press, and the Congress. However, it also engaged in covert propaganda, in planting articles favorable to the Contras in the U.S. press, in illegal lobbying, and other activities. The office was closed in December 1987 when a General Accounting Office investigation concluded that it was engaging in prohibited activities.

Congress Responds: Boland I and II

Congressional unease about Reagan's policy toward Nicaragua was growing in 1982. On the one hand, most believed that support for the Contras was not aimed at interdiction of supplies for Salvadoran rebels but rather at the overthrow of the government of Nicaragua. Contra leaders made clear that such an overthrow was their central purpose. Moderate opposition figures within Nicaragua itself, including private sector leaders and former Sandinista Edén Pastora, objected to the harsh economic measures the U.S. government was taking and to its support for the rightist former National Guardsmen in Honduras. Given that atmosphere, the House Intelligence Committee, in order to head off a move to cut off all funds for the Contras, adopted a measure which prohibited any U.S. effort to overthrow the Nicaraguan government or instigate military exchanges between Honduras and Nicaragua. The secret provision became law in September when the legislation authorizing intelligence activities for 1983 was approved. When congressional liberals led by Tom Harkin, Democrat of Iowa, tried later to prohibit all funds for military activities "in or against Nicaragua," Edward Boland, the head of the Intelligence Committee, noted that action had already been taken. He asked Harkin to withdraw his amendment which had been attached to Defense Department appropriations, and substituted the wording of the Intelligence Committee. It then passed, 411–0. Boland seems to have wanted to preserve some effort against the Sandinistas, which Harkin's measure would have prevented. Still, the Boland amendment legally established a prohibition against activities designed to oust the Sandinista government, and Senator Daniel Moynihan wrote to CIA Director Casey in late December that Congress meant for the CIA to observe the law, both in letter and spirit.

Reagan quickly initiated a public counteroffensive, and the Boland Amendment was permitted to lapse after one year. Reagan also established a bipartisan commission under former secretary of state Henry Kissinger, hoping that it would support his policies and arranging the membership to ensure that result. However, although the commission in its 1984 report recommended increased levels of military aid to El Salvador, it suggested that such aid be conditioned on progress on human rights. Its recommendations on Nicaragua, which indicated that continued Contra efforts would be an incentive to a negotiated settlement, thereby gave a lukewarm endorsement to administration aid. However, it was not the Kissinger report which would drive further congressional action. Rather, the election of Christian Democrat Duarte in El Salvador convinced Congress to greatly increase aid levels, while the revelation that the CIA had been involved in mining harbors in Nicaragua led to yet another congressional effort to stop aid to Contra forces.[36] The second Boland prohibition, known as Boland II, passed Congress, once again ordering an end to aid.

That Boland II passed, despite initial Senate opposition, was largely a result of the failure by the administration, and especially by CIA Director Casey, to keep the intelligence oversight committees in Congress informed. Although Casey claimed that he had let the committees know about the mining, even Republican Senator Barry Goldwater, Republican chair of the committee, believed that he had not done so or, at least, had been deliberately misleading. Although Casey apologized, Goldwater remained angry for years. In the meantime, in June 1984, Casey, Goldwater, and Moynihan worked out new operating guidelines for CIA reporting to the Senate committee. Basically, these mandated notification of activities requiring presidential approval prior to implementation. Moreover, the committee was to be provided with the text of any new presidential findings which concerned covert actions. These agreements were not honored by the administration.

The Reagan Doctrine and the Iran-Contra Affair

Despite the denial of aid to the Contras, congressional resolve did not last long. Although opinion polls showed consistently throughout the 1980s that the American public opposed providing military aid to El Salvador and to the Contras, Ronald Reagan's landslide in his reelection as president in 1984 gave members of Congress considerable pause. Reagan returned rapidly to the attack, announcing in his 1985 State of the Union address that anti-Soviet insurgents would be supported in order to restore freedom in areas in which communists supported by the Soviets had taken over, notably Afghanistan and Nicaragua. Such an effort, he claimed, was important to freedom and to U.S. self-defense. This stance would come to be known as the Reagan Doctrine.[37] At the same time, the Sandinistas took steps that made them less palatable to moderates and liberals in Congress, increasing press censorship and harassment of the opposition. Conferences, briefings, and publications from the Office of Public Diplomacy and the National Security Council, with names like "Central America: Resistance or Surrender" and "Central America: Freedom or Slavery," stepped up the pressure. Reagan was aided by an extraordinary miscalculation on the part of Sandinista President Daniel Ortega, who announced a visit to the Soviet Union the day after an April 1985 vote in Congress against renewed aid. He thereby completely undercut those in Congress who opposed funding the Contras. In June, Congress approved $27 million for humanitarian support to the Nicaraguan Contras.[38]

Similar pressures, including Reagan's insistence that failure to help the Contras would cause a flood of refugees into the southern United States, set the stage for renewed military assistance. After Reagan made concessions and courted Democrats, Congress approved $100 million for Contra military aid in June 1986. The struggle had been difficult, but the administration had for two years kept the Contra effort alive despite congressional prohibitions. However, the processes by which this goal was achieved had sown the seeds of the destruction of Reagan's Central American policies and would severely damage the president's own reputation and credibility.

Reagan's efforts began immediately after Boland II which prohibited military or paramilitary support for the Contras became law in October 1984. He ordered his National Security Adviser, Robert McFarlane, to keep the Contras together "body and soul." The excuse used was that the NSC was not a proscribed agency, although it was clear that continued activity violated at a minimum the spirit of the law. Certainly it was the intent of Congress that NSC be included in the prohibition.[39]

This move brought anti-Sandinista activities directly into the White House, where they were placed under the direction of Lt. Colonel Oliver North. North immediately began secret operations of various kinds. His top priority was funding. Approaches were made to U.S. citizens and to foreign governments requesting donations, even though Secretary of State George Shultz had warned that such an avoidance of a congressional mandate might be "an impeachable offense." Prospective donors were assured that President Reagan himself would be grateful for any assistance. Meetings were even arranged with the president, orchestrated to make it seem that donors were being thanked for their help. Strong allies of the United States contributed considerable sums, with Saudi Arabia alone contributing $32 million; private donors gave somewhat less. These sources were insufficient, however.[40]

It is ironic that the two countries which had given Jimmy Carter so much grief during the latter part of his presidency would now be strangely combined in the great scandal of Ronald Reagan's, as Iran and Nicaragua became entangled in the continuing supply effort. In 1985, the president was faced with a situation in which several American citizens were being held hostage in Lebanon. He deeply wanted to free them. He was also eager to fund the Contras. When an approach was made by highly questionable intermediaries from the Iranian government seeking arms for their war against Iraq, some members of the Reagan administration saw it as an opportunity to obtain the hostages' release by using Iran's influence. In September 1985, Israeli planes delivered the first U.S. missiles to Iran, and one hostage was freed. However, this exchange only opened up the opportunity for blackmail, as more hostages were taken in Lebanon when others were released in exchange for the arms deliveries. When the idea was initially introduced, secretaries of state and defense Shultz and Weinberger were both strongly opposed. From that point forward, they simply dropped out of the loop. McFarlane himself, dealing directly with the exchanges, became deeply troubled and resigned as national security adviser. His replacement was Admiral John Poindexter.

The arms deliveries were not free to the Iranians, however. In fact, the merchandise delivered was charged at an extremely high price and delivered through a company run by retired Air Force General Richard Secord. Much of the profit went directly to his company; another portion was diverted to pay for Contra arms, which were also delivered by Secord's company. Meanwhile, the General Accounting Office had reported in early 1986 that more than half of $12 million provided to the Contras at an earlier date had actually made its way to the Miami bank accounts of the leadership rather than into supplies, humanitarian or otherwise, for soldiers in the field.[41]

When congressionally authorized aid actually began to flow to the Contras again in October 1986, public opinion in the United States was running about 2 to 1 against renewed help. The sanctuary movement, in which undocumented Guatemalan and El Salvadoran refugees were sheltered by U.S. churches, was in full swing. Resistance to Central American policies was becoming stronger, despite Reagan's efforts. Suddenly, the whole affair began to unravel when on 5 October 1986, Sandinista troops shot down a supply plane loaded with 10,000 pounds of military supplies for the Contra forces. This incident led the U.S. press in November to the bigger story of the sale of arms for hostages. During its investigation, the Justice Department discovered the links between the sales and funding for the Contras.

Although the president was not targeted by the ensuing congressional investigation, Reagan's credibility and prestige took a nosedive. About half the American public believed that the president was lying when he claimed that he knew nothing of the diversion of funds. The final report of the Iran-Contra committees was a devastating indictment of administration policymaking, although several Republicans refused to sign it. At the time of the investigation, the U.S. public indicated by a 2 to 1 margin that it trusted Congress, rather than the president, on foreign policy questions.

The administration had not given up on funding, but events were being taken out of its hands. Central American leaders, spurred by President Oscar Arias of Costa Rica, were beginning to deal with the situation themselves.

The Arias Plan

In 1987, a new peace plan emerged from Central America itself. Oscar Arias Sánchez, a U.S.- and British-educated member of the National Liberation Party, had been elected president of Costa Rica in 1986. Faced with economic decline and political instability that were at least in part attributable to the terrible conditions in the region, he proposed to a meeting of all five Central American nations that immediate cease-fires be instigated throughout the region and negotiations begun between opposing forces. Other points provided for free elections throughout the area; an end to all outside military aid to "irregular insurrections and forces" including the Contras; and cease-fires, amnesties, and democratization throughout the region. In addition, no nation would permit its territory to be used as a base for attacks on other countries. The plan was signed by all five heads of state on 7 August 1987.[42]

These provisions were similar to those which had been put forward by the Contadora nations (Panama, Mexico, Venezuela, and Colombia) in 1983, but were considerably more specific and had come from within Central America itself. Moreover, the plan called for democratic reforms in both El Salvador and Nicaragua. Most important, all five nations concerned, including Nicaragua, had given formal approval to the accords. Reagan and his assistant secretary of state for inter-American affairs, Elliott Abrams, were reported to be furious.[43] Meanwhile, the U.S. Congress conducted hearings on the Iran-Contra affair, although investigators and members of Congress were reluctant to take any drastic action against the still-popular president. In the mid-term elections of November 1986, the Democrats had recovered control of the Senate and increased their majority in the House. Therefore, they were able to press forward, and Reagan at least seemed to be cooperating with the investigations. The scapegoats who emerged were the members of his National Security staff, particularly Robert McFarlane (now on the verge of a nervous collapse), his successor John Poindexter, and Oliver North. Poindexter and North were later convicted of a number of felony charges, in North's case including lying under oath and the destruction of government documents. Later, however, their convictions were set aside as violating the immunity granted them in their congressional testimony.

Aftermath

The movement toward peace in Central America was gradual but effective. Nicaragua held elections in February 1990, and to the surprise and dismay of the Sandinistas, they were defeated by Violeta Chamorro—widow of Pedro Joaquín Chamorro and former ally—and her National Opposition Union (UNO). She turned to the United States for economic aid to rebuild the country, but now that the Sandinistas were out of power, little help was forthcoming. George Bush, who had become president in 1989, managed to send a bit more than $300 million, but this sum was negligible, given the devastation of the civil war. The rebels in El Salvador and the ARENA government reached an agreement, as noted above, in the last few minutes of 1991. A cease-fire, monitored by the United Nations, began in early 1992. New elections brought yet another businessman from the ARENA party to the presidency in 1994.

In Guatemala and Honduras, human rights activists became presidents in the early 1990s, although violations continued and the militaries retained substantial power. In Costa Rica, Oscar Arias's PLN party was defeated in 1990 after the Republican Party's Institute for International Affairs had pumped in half a million dollars to aid the opposition. The PLN was returned to power, however, when José María Figueres Olsen, son of one of the country's most popular former presidents, was elected in 1994.

However, U.S. policy in the 1980s had left a significant and disturbing legacy. The economies of the region were devastated by more than a decade of civil war. Refugees—perhaps as many as 4 million—had scattered throughout the region, into Mexico, and frequently into the United States itself. The militaries of the region had gained in power and, at best, were difficult for civilian governments to control. They had extended their power into the economic realm, often aided by diverted U.S. funds, into both legal and illegal activities.

Central America, in the 1990s, has again slipped from the attention of U.S. policymakers. The collapse of the Soviet Union and of socialist regimes in Eastern Europe eliminated the Cold War as a rationale for U.S. interference in the region. From 1988 forward, the old reliance on an external threat as the basis for U.S. policy toward Latin America in general ceased to be persuasive, and the Monroe Doctrine, aimed at external threats, had lost much of its power.

Reagan and the Falklands War

The Falklands—or the Malvinas as the Argentines preferred to call them—were an unpromising collection of islands in the South Atlantic off the coast of Argentina. Although Britain had been in continuous possession of the Falklands since 1833, Argentina continued to claim them. Sporadic negotiations between Britain and Argentina in the 1970s yielded some progress but no substantive agreement on sovereignty. The United States never played a major role in the dispute, and its minimal influence declined even more with the Carter administration's criticism of and cut in aid to the Argentine military regime over human rights violations. The Argentine government was enthusiastic about the electoral victory of Ronald Reagan. Reagan had indicated a desire for improved relations with Argentina, and Argentine officials were hopeful that their support of U.S. policy in Central America would lead to U.S. support for Argentine claims to the Malvinas.

The dispute over the Falklands came to a head in early 1982 when Argentina became disenchanted with the pace of negotiations with Britain. The approach of the 150th anniversary of the British takeover also played a part in the Argentine decision to resort to force. Military action would also serve as a distraction from the dismal state of the Argentine economy. On 2 April 1982 Argentina invaded, quickly subduing the small British force. Britain responded diplomatically and militarily. In the diplomatic arena, Britain got the European Economic Community to impose economic sanctions on Argentina and the U.N. Security Council to condemn the use of force and call for Argentine withdrawal. Militarily, Britain dispatched a large task force to retake the islands if necessary. The U.S. response to the crisis was a spurt of shuttle diplomacy by U.S. Secretary of State Alexander Haig. Haig—whose mentor was Henry Kissinger—made the diplomatic rounds of London and Buenos Aires, promoting an agreement calling for a cease-fire, Argentine withdrawal, and a commitment to negotiate on the long-term status of the islands. Further complicating the situation was Argentina's call for a meeting of consultation under the provisions of the Rio Treaty of 1947. The meeting produced only a mild resolution criticizing the economic sanctions of the European Economic Community and calling for an end to the fighting.

Haig's shuttle diplomacy was also coming unraveled. The negotiations increasingly showed the pro-British position of the United States, and Haig labeled Argentina the aggressor at the Rio Treaty meeting. U.S. efforts to mediate came to a definitive end when the United States announced on 30 April that it was imposing economic sanctions on Argentina and would provide military assistance to Britain, although there would be no direct U.S. military involvement. The rapid switch of the United States from mediator to military ally of Britain raised doubts about the honesty of the U.S. position from the start. British forces landed in the Falklands on 21 May, leading to another meeting of consultation under the Rio Treaty. The meeting passed a resolution, with the United States abstaining, which condemned Britain for its attack on Argentina and called upon the United States to end its assistance to Britain and lift its sanctions on Argentina. With little substantive diplomatic action, the battle for the Falklands was settled by military action; the uneven struggle came to a predictable conclusion with the surrender of Argentine forces on 14 June.

The Falklands/Malvinas controversy damaged Reagan's Latin American policy and U.S.-Latin American relations in general. The Reagan administration lost one of the strongest supporters of its Central American policy and unintentionally strengthened ties between Argentina and Cuba, a prominent supporter of the Argentine position. There was also widespread doubt about how honest a broker the United States had been in its mediation efforts, given the rapid U.S. transition from mediator to supporter of Britain. The role played by the Rio Treaty also undermined good relations. Many Latin Americans were horrified at the prospect of the United States actively aiding a European country in an attack on a Latin American nation. U.S. actions also made it clear that East-West relations continued to enjoy a higher priority than North-South relations. The role played by the United States also confirmed its continuing preference for bilateral, rather than multilateral, approaches to hemispheric crises; when the United States took a multilateral approach, it favored the United Nations over the OAS as a forum.

Intervention in Grenada

The United States largely ignored the Caribbean island of Grenada until March 1979 when the leftist New Jewel Movement led by Maurice Bishop overthrew Grenada's long-time ruler, Eric Gairy. The United States responded by urging the revolutionaries to honor their promise of early elections and by offering financial aid; early on there were fears of Grenada "drifting into the Cuban orbit." These fears took on reality with reports that the Cubans were supplying arms to the new government less than three weeks after it took power. The New Jewel government increasingly aligned itself with Cuba and the Soviet Union on international issues, including support for the Soviet invasion of Afghanistan in December 1979.

When Ronald Reagan took office in January 1981, he increased U.S. efforts to isolate Grenada; for Reagan, Grenada was yet another example of the spread of Soviet and Cuban influence in the hemisphere. Reagan broke relations with Grenada and staged military and naval exercises in the area. By early 1982 the Reagan administration was publicly describing Grenada as a "Cuban satellite." In early 1983 the United States became disturbed over the construction by

Cubans of a new airport, claiming that it would be used to project Soviet power in the hemisphere. U.S.-Grenadan relations took a new turn as the result of a split within the New Jewel Movement, leading to the overthrow and death of Bishop on 19 October 1983. Claiming that the lives of U.S. citizens were at risk in Grenada and that the Organization of Eastern Caribbean States had requested U.S. intervention, the United States sent in troops on 25 October. U.S. forces secured the island within three days, although they would remain for a year until a moderate, pro-U.S. prime minister took office. For the first time, Grenada received economic aid from the United States, totalling $48 million in 1984, making it the largest recipient of aid on a per capita basis in the hemisphere.

The Lost Decade: The Debt Crisis of the 1980s

While Reagan continued the traditional U.S. concern with military and strategic matters, the Latin American nations were preoccupied by traditional concerns of their own: finance and economics. Despite the energy crisis of the 1970s, Latin American economies continued to grow, with much of the growth dependent on loans from commercial banks in the United States and Europe which were recycling "petrodollars." The rapid increase in oil prices in the 1970s produced a big increase in profits for the oil exporting countries. Since no new international agency was established to deal with this dramatic shift in capital flow, these petrodollars made their way back into the international financial system through private commercial banks who were eager to lend to Latin American governments concerned about maintaining growth levels. While some of this borrowed money found its way into investment endeavors promoting long-term growth, much of it went into questionable projects, was lost through corruption, was used to finance a higher level of importation, or found its way into a variety of government subsidies.

Maintaining growth through external borrowing came unraveled with the onset of an international recession in 1980 and the advent of new U.S. economic policies in 1981. The recession reduced demand for Latin American exports at the same time that the terms of trade were turning against Latin American exports. The new economic policies of the Reagan administration helped to produce an increase in international interest rates. This had a double negative effect on Latin American economies. First, many of the old loans to Latin American governments were at variable interest rates which rose along with current rates. Second, many Latin American governments needed new loans to pay old loans; these new loans also reflected the latest rise in interest rates.

As governments encountered greater problems in servicing their debts, major commercial banks cut back on lending while smaller banks ceased lending altogether. When problems mounted, even the major banks became reluctant to extend new loans. The transformation of the debt problem into the debt crisis came in August 1982 with the Mexican government's announcement that it could not service its debt.

Mexico had discovered large new oil deposits in the mid-1970s, just in time to take advantage of the rapid increase in oil prices. Mexico financed development by investing its oil profits and by borrowing heavily from international banks and multilateral institutions, with the loans implicitly secured by future oil profits. Poor management and corruption siphoned off much of the borrowed capital, and Mexico based its borrowing and spending on the incorrect assumption that oil prices would continue to rise well into the 1980s. The U.S. government moved quickly to prevent a formal default by Mexico, fearing that the default of a high-profile borrower like Mexico might have a domino effect among third world borrowers and threaten the entire international financial structure. The United States provided a prepayment of $1 billion dollars for oil imports from Mexico, dispensed $1 billion in agricultural aid, and furnished $925 million as a "bridge" loan to gain additional loans for Mexico from the Bank for International Settlements. The U.S. government also pressured U.S. commercial banks to continue lending to Mexico until debt rescheduling could take place.

The United States—fearing economic and social upheaval on its border—had a special stake in keeping Mexico afloat. However, the debt crisis extended beyond Mexico to include most Latin American nations. Heavy borrowers, like Argentina and Brazil, were also experiencing problems servicing their debts, and it was hard to find a Latin American country that was not involved in the spreading crisis. As Latin American nations lined up to try to reschedule their debts, the United States, the commercial banks, and multilateral agencies typically insisted that any rescheduling include an agreement by the country involved to adhere to an austerity program prescribed by the International Monetary Fund (IMF). A typical program included reduced government spending, increased taxes, currency devaluation, restrictions on imports, encouragement of foreign investment, and the sell-off (privatization) of unprofitable government corporations. Such a program exacted an economic and political price from the Latin American nation involved. Economically, austerity was recession by government plan; it also required many governments to abandon fundamental parts of development strategies followed since World War II. Politically, austerity ran counter to the growing nationalism of the region by injecting outside forces into basic decisions affecting the national economy. Austerity also required governments to take the political heat for bringing about a broadbased decline in the standard of living. The timing of the program was also difficult for many Latin American countries, such as Argentina and Brazil, which were trying to make the transition from military regimes to democracies.

In the face of these internal and external pressures, the debtor governments of Latin America worked to develop a united political front on the issues of austerity and debt rescheduling. After preliminary study, the Latin American nations met at an economic conference at Quito, Ecuador, in January 1984. Pointedly, the United States had not been invited to the meeting. The basic thrust of the conference was that the debt problem was a political issue, not a financial one. It spread the blame for the debt crisis to include the developed countries, the commercial banks, and the multilateral lending institutions. The conference called for all debt negotiations and agreements to reflect the need to harmonize debt servicing with development. By the time the Latin American nations met again at Cartagena, Colombia, in June 1984, there were growing fears in the U.S. government and the international banking community that the meeting might produce a debtors' cartel, with the members forcing a joint renegotiation on creditors. The conference ruled out a collective approach to rescheduling debts but continued the criticism of the role played by the developing countries and the IMF in dealing with the debt problem.

With the debtor group increasingly restive and the debt crisis merging into the worst economic downturn in Latin America since the depression of the 1930s, the United States responded by presenting a proposal at the joint annual meeting of the IMF and World Bank in Seoul, Korea, in October 1985. Dubbed the Baker Plan after U.S. Secretary of the Treasury James Baker, the plan called for a substantial increase in lending by commercial banks and multilateral financial institutions to help debtor nations move beyond austerity to economic development. In return Baker asked the debtor countries to make comprehensive macroeconomic and structural reforms. While the greater em-

phasis on economic development and additional lending was good news for
Latin American debtors, the structural reforms envisioned were simply a
repackaged austerity program.

The lack of response to the Baker Plan by both the Latin American countries and the commercial banks left each Latin American debtor to pursue its
own individual settlement with its creditors. A decline in interest rates relieved
some of the pressures of the debt crisis; the fact that several years had passed
without the debt dominoes falling calmed fears that the entire international
financial structure might be at risk. The commercial banks, debtor countries,
and multilateral lending institutions adjusted to the routine of negotiating
and renegotiating debt settlements. Although financial collapse had been
averted, most of the Latin American nations carried with them into the
post–Cold War era debt loads that were essentially unworkable and unpayable.

CHAPTER 7

AFTER THE COLD WAR, 1988-1999

Vignette: NAFTA's Nuts and Bolts — The Avocado Controversy

Despite revolutionary upheavals, expropriations, and natural disasters, at least one thing remained constant in U.S.-Mexican relations: the U.S. ban on the importation of Mexican avocados. For eighty-three years, Mexican avocados were shut out of the U.S. market on the grounds that they were infested with weevils which could be transmitted to U.S. avocado fields. Although NAFTA provided for the phasing out of both tariff and non-tariff barriers in agricultural products, the agreement still permitted the banning of imports for sanitary considerations. Mexican producers complained that the ban was designed to protect California avocado growers — who account for ninety percent of the U.S. market — from the competition of much cheaper Mexican avocados.

Rather than launch a full-scale attack on the ban, Mexican negotiators opted to try a partial approach, offering to limit the areas in Mexico from which avocados would be shipped as well as the areas in the United States where they would be sold. Mexican officials also promised to intensify their efforts to eradicate the weevils at the center of the controversy. In late 1997 U.S. officials relented and agreed to a partial lifting of the ban, but with several conditions. On the assumption that cold weather would reduce the risk of infestation, avocado imports would be permitted only from November through February and confined to nineteen states stretching from Maine to Illinois. Only sixty-one orchards in Mexico were eligible to participate in the program. Officials from the U.S. Department of Agriculture would inspect the avocados at three stages: at the packing plant in Mexico, at the U.S.-Mexico border, and at the point of sale. Mexican avocados sold outside the designated market area were subject to seizure and destruction. Despite the restrictions, Mexican exporters were optimistic about the long-term possibilities of penetrating the U.S. market. Mexican avocado exports had already increased dramatically to Mexico's other NAFTA partner, Canada, by more than 200 percent between 1992 and 1996; in 1997 the retail cost of a Mexican avocado in Canada was less than half the price of a U.S.-produced avocado in the United States.

While the avocado controversy showed the limitations of NAFTA, it also demonstrated the positive aspects of the agreement. One of the factors influencing the change in the official U.S. attitude was the growing presence of U.S. companies in Mexico's avocado industry. Calavo Growers of California, the biggest avocado cooperative in California, invested $10 million in a new packing plant in Mexico; another major California packer, Mission Produce, spent $2 million upgrading its Mexican operations. This was exactly the type of cross-border trade and investment activities that supporters of NAFTA had envisioned. Guacamole lovers in the southern and western areas of the United States, however, would have to wait and see if the sale of Mexican avocados would expand to new areas.

From the Wall Street Journal, *31 October 1997, p. A18.*

The U.S. presidential campaign in 1988 provided only minimal focus on U.S.-Latin American relations. The resurrection of the Central American peace process helped to deflect criticism of the Republican nominee, Vice President George Bush. The conflict in and with Nicaragua was winding down; the contras and the Sandinistas signed a cease-fire in March 1988, looking to a peaceful political contest for power in 1990. The Iran-Contra scandal made its way into the campaign, but the Democrats found it difficult to link Bush directly to the operation. One specific election issue that troubled the outgoing Reagan administration and constituted unfinished business for the incoming Bush administration was the status of relations with Panama and its unsavory ruler, General Manuel Noriega.

The United States had known for years that the Panamanian military was deeply involved in narcotics trafficking and gun running. The death of General Omar Torrijos in a plane crash in 1981 led to the rise to power of General Manuel Noriega. Noriega was an opportunist of the first order, dealing profitably with such diverse interests as the CIA, Fidel Castro, the Sandinistas, the contras, the U.S. Drug Enforcement Agency, and assorted international drug dealers. The U.S. government also disliked Noriega's casual attitude toward democracy. Noriega interfered in the presidential elections of 1984 to secure the election of his candidate, Nicolás Barletta, and then removed Barletta when the president talked about investigating the Panamanian military's connection to the death of a prominent opposition politician. The United States responded by suspending all aid to Panama in July 1987. As the confrontation intensified, the U.S. government in December 1987 cut Panama's quota for sugar exports to the United States. After years of praising Noriega for his anti-drug efforts, the United States indicted him in February 1988 on multiple counts of drug trafficking. The following month the U.S. government took the important financial and symbolic move of suspending payments for use of the canal.

After Bush took office in early 1989, U.S. attention focused on elections in Panama scheduled for May 1989. When the vote unexpectedly went against Noriega, the general simply nullified the election and escalated the violence against his political opponents. A U.S.-encouraged coup in October failed, leading to further pressure on the Bush administration to take action. Also influencing Bush was the treaty provision that a Panamanian was to be selected to head the Panama Canal Commission in January 1990. Attacks on U.S. military personnel further heightened tensions. Bush responded by launching "Operation Just Cause," a massive U.S. military intervention to arrest Noriega and to protect U.S. personnel in Panama. On 20 December 1989, some 25,000 U.S. troops crossed into Panama, quickly subduing the Panamanian defense forces and forcing Noriega to seek sanctuary with the Vatican representative to Panama. Noriega—blasted around the clock by rock music played by U.S. forces—finally gave up his asylum and surrendered on 3 January 1990.

Following a rapid extradition hearing, Noriega wound up in Miami where a lengthy trial finally resulted in his conviction on drug charges in April 1992. The initial U.S. enthusiasm for the ouster of Noriega gave way to concern about loss of civilian lives and "collateral damage" caused by the invasion. The intervention produced a predictably negative reaction in other Latin American countries. Although the OAS had earlier condemned the abuses of Noriega and had even tried to negotiate his departure, traditional Latin American opposition to U.S. interventionism surfaced immediately after the operation.

President Bush, however, was willing to take the diplomatic criticism in order to rid himself of Noriega. The Bush administration never invoked the anti-communist rationale in justifying the intervention.

Neither the United States nor Latin American nations were prepared for the dramatic changes about to take place in global relations. In 1989 the European communist bloc began a rapid disintegration, followed in 1991 by the splintering of the Soviet Union. Also in 1991 the Warsaw Pact, the Soviet bloc counterpart of NATO, officially disbanded. The basic dynamic of the Cold War—the threat of Soviet expansion—suddenly became irrelevant. This end to the Cold War and the beginning of a "new world order" held both promise and peril for Latin America. The end of the "Soviet threat" created an opportunity for the United States to deemphasize international strategic and military concerns and give greater attention to social and economic problems, a change in emphasis sought by the Latin American countries since the end of World War II. The downside was that much of the attention and aid given to Latin America by the United States had been predicated on heading off the communist challenge; with no external threat, many in Latin America feared that the United States might ignore the area as it frequently had in the past.

Cuba and the United States

U.S.-Cuban relations have remained hostile for more than three decades, as Fidel Castro has maintained his power. Hundreds of thousands of Cuban exiles have made their way to Florida and other parts of the United States, and Cuban immigration has often been an issue in U.S.-Cuban relations. Only recently has there been an agreement to begin to regularize the movement of Cuban immigrants to the United States. Cuba under Castro has been an important spur to leftist movements in other parts of Latin America, but probably played a less significant role than U.S. policymakers believed. Both sides have used propaganda against the other. The United States, for example, financed Radio and TV Martí to beam anti-Castro programs to the island. The United States has also been concerned by the possible involvement of officials in Cuba in the drug trade coming out of South America. A tentative thaw in relations during Jimmy Carter's presidency in the 1970s was cut short by Cuban involvement in African revolutionary struggles.

In recent years, U.S. policy as mandated by the Congress has become even more stringent. In 1992, the Cuban Democracy Act, sponsored by Representative Robert Torricelli, Democrat of New Jersey, made the trade embargo tougher by banning commerce with Cuba by U.S. subsidiaries in third countries and blocking access to U.S. ports by ships which had recently visited Cuba. At the same time, pressure from unexpected sources in favor of relaxing barriers against trade and business began to surface. Castro, faced with declining aid after the collapse of Soviet hegemony in Eastern Europe and then with the collapse of the Soviet Union itself, opened Cuba to foreign investment in many attractive sectors—tourism, mining and oil, cement, and textiles. U.S. businesspeople, fearful that European and other competitors would get a jump on them, began to urge the administration of President William Clinton to ease trade barriers.

A powerful lobby of anti-Castro Cubans led until his recent death by Jorge Mas Canosa and the Cuban American National Foundation (CANF) has been effective in preventing major change in U.S. policy. This group has encouraged a hard line toward Castro's government. During the Reagan presidency, their anti-communist agenda was directly in tune with Washington's. In 1985, the United States began broadcasts to Cuba from Radio Martí, and the administration regulated travel to Cuba and denied visas to Cubans wishing to attend international meetings in the United States. In 1986, the administration tightened even further the trade and financial embargo on the island. The new restrictions were not enough for the CANF. In 1992, they strongly supported the passage of the Cuban Democracy Act, the intent of which was to "promote peaceful transition to democracy in Cuba through the application of appropriate pressures on the Cuban government." The act passed, barring trade between Cuba and foreign subsidiaries of U.S. companies, prohibiting ships trading with Cuba from docking at U.S. ports, and giving the U.S. president power to deny certain benefits to third countries trading with the island.[1]

The influence of CANF in the 1992 elections was clear. President George Bush was initially inclined to oppose the passage of the legislation because of his concern about its effects on U.S. allies. He came around when then-presidential candidate Bill Clinton publicly came out in favor of it while campaigning in south Florida. In the election Clinton lost Florida, but by a narrow margin.

Later, another anti-Castro exile group created an incident leading to even stronger measures, the Helms-Burton Bill of 1996. This group, Brothers to the Rescue, had conducted a number of overflights of the island, leading Cuban officials to complain formally to their U.S. counterparts on four occasions. In

Monument constructed by Cuban refugees outside of Camp Alpha, one of the all-male camps at Guantanamo, reads, "American friends, we the Cuban rafters want to thank you for rescuing us from the dangers of the sea." The boat below the "Liberty" sign was of much better quality than the majority of those that Cubans used in attempting to reach Florida.

Photograph by M. L Horner

late February 1996, while flying in international waters, two of its planes were shot down by the Cuban Air Force. Senator Jesse Helms, a long-time supporter of harsh measures toward the Castro regime, quickly took advantage of these circumstances to push through a new, even more stringent bill, denying U.S. visas to anyone with a stake in property confiscated after the 1959 revolution from persons now U.S. citizens. Another provision permitted former owners to file suit in U.S. courts against any foreign company using such property. Clinton, facing a reelection campaign, quickly signed the bill into law despite the adamant concerns of U.S. allies such as Canada, Mexico, and France, whose nationals have sizable investments on the island.[2] A serious additional concern was Clinton's ceding of authority on Cuban affairs to Congress: he agreed on 1 March, seven days after the planes were shot down, to transform all executive orders dealing with Cuba into law, with any modification or change subject to congressional action.³

Many Cubans in the United States favored less restrictive measures. Ramón Cernuda, the head of the anti-Castro Coordinated Group of Human Rights Organizations, testified in 1992 that the Cuban Democracy Act was "a virtual global embargo against our people, to starve them to death in the name of Cuban rights." Within the context of national presidential election years, it was the strong anti-communist organizations which were able to have the most influence on policy.⁴ And Castro contributed directly to that influence by maintaining a communist hard line even as Eastern Europe and the Soviet Union crumbled.

Painted in the wake of the March 12, 1996 signing of the Helms-Burton Bill by President Clinton, cartoon wall-paintings such as this one lined busy Calle 23 (popularly known as La Rampa) in Havana, Cuba. The box on the lower left of the painting is labeled "Carnicería [slaughterhouse] Helms-Burton." Photographed July 1996.

Photograph by Tiffany Thomas

Another interpretation of the Helms–Burton Bill on the wall of Havana Cuba's Calle 23. The cartoon satirizes bill co-sponsor Senator Jesse Helms. FCA refers to the Cuban exile organization, the Cuban American Foundation. Photographed July 1996.

Photograph by Tiffany Thomas

Still, a number of voices within the United States were calling for change. The *Wall Street Journal* of 12 August 1994, in its "Review and Outlook" column, reiterated its longstanding support of a hardline policy toward Castro; just fourteen days later, however, in the same column, it suggested, "We suspect the time has arrived, indeed, when lifting the embargo would help precisely those forces that are most likely to liberalize Cuba's economic and political power structure."[5]

Other voices quickly joined that of the *Journal,* despite the introduction of new legislation in Congress to tighten economic sanctions. On 19 March 1995, the *New York Times* in its lead editorial also called for an end to the decades-long trade embargo. It refuted the idea that Castro was about to fall now that his government was no longer able to expect economic support from eastern Europe. Rather, it pointed out that other nations continued to invest in the island and were not participating in the U.S. economic sanctions. Further, in a United Nations vote in 1994, the trade embargo had been condemned by a vote of 101–2, the only country joining the United States being Israel which itself trades with Cuba. The editorial went on to describe a shift among younger Cuban Americans in favor of more communication and trade with the Castro regime. It called for "open communication," "freedom for Cuban Americans to invest in businesses at home," and "access to North American goods." These steps, the editorial asserted, would make it impossible for Castro to continue his repressive policies. The editorial closed by saying, "Cuba, absent the ghosts of the Cold War, is an impoverished neighbor of the United States led by a dictator overtaken by history."[6]

Also on 19 March, Cuba specialist Wayne Smith, in the Opinion section of the *Los Angeles Times,* decried the tendency of U.S. policymakers to "disconnect from reality" in attitudes toward Cuba. He particularly attacked new legislation introduced by Senators Torricelli and Jesse Helms seeking to force the Clinton administration to urge other countries to join the embargo on Cuba. He even indicated the possible illegality of the embargo, on the grounds of Cuba's full membership in the General Agreement on Tariffs and Trade and the prohibition in international law against the inclusion of foods and medicines in embargoes.[7] And on 24 March, the *Washington Post* indicated that some members of the Clinton administration were suggesting the lifting of certain sanctions should there be signs from Cuba of any initiatives leading to free markets and democratic institutions. However, the *Post* noted the strong opposition of Senator Helms and others, and, believing Clinton to be unwilling to take policy chances, suggested that nothing would change.[8]

Senator Connie Mack of Florida replied to the *New York Times* on March 24 that more trade with Cuba would simply strengthen Castro, as his government controlled all industries capable of generating hard currency, and that Russia continued to support an "eavesdropping facility" on the island.[9] The *Wall Street Journal* weighed in again in May, refuting Senator Helms' insistence that additional economic pressure would lead to Castro's downfall.[10] The passage of the Helms-Burton Act did not stifle this sentiment for liberalization of U.S.-Cuban relations, and the Clinton administration has been selective in its enforcement of the act.

Fidel Castro has maintained his power in Cuba through 1999, and no strong internal opposition movement has come forward to challenge him. U.S. policymakers from the 1950s through the 1980s, fearing communism and a Soviet challenge in the hemisphere, had tried and failed to prevent Castro's coming to power and to remove him later. What were the major reasons for this failure?

A major factor was that, in the pre-Castro period, the United States administrations had depended on Cuban surrogates, most recently Fulgencio Batista, who were corrupt, brutal, and unpopular. As a result, anti-Americanism had flourished since the United States forced Cuban leaders to adopt the Platt Amendment in the early years of the century. Disaffected Cubans had become accustomed to calling on American power to solve internal problems. Those becoming alienated from Castro's government expected no less. As the situation deteriorated, many fled to the United States. Over time, widespread anger against the United States in Cuba—particularly in response to the Bay of Pigs and the Cuban missile crisis—permitted Castro to use anti-Americanism as a tool to reinforce his own charismatic leadership. He was also able to replace ties to the United States and Latin America with Soviet bloc aid, new markets, and a new source of expertise and imports. Meanwhile, until very recently, his own charismatic authority and some real benefits to the Cuban people kept his power secure.

Cuban policy continues to be controversial, with no easy solutions for U.S. leadership. However, in an interesting footnote to history, two younger Kennedys—Robert Jr. and Michael, both nephews of the former president— met in February 1996 with Castro, who shared with them his belief that John Kennedy would have made changes in "the framework" of Cuban-U.S. relations, had he not been killed in 1963. Michael Kennedy confirmed that recently declassified documents indicated that President Kennedy had been considering a move to improve relations. The visit of Pope John Paul II to Cuba in January 1998 brought further pressure for a change in U.S.-Cuban relations. During his visit the Pope criticized the continuing U.S. embargo of Cuba, encouraging its opponents both in the United States and overseas. Castro further complicated the situation by announcing the release of 299 "political prisoners," leading some to conclude that he was softening his position on a democratic transition. Even long-time supporters of the embargo, such as Senator Jesse Helms and the Cuban American National Foundation, were beginning to have second thoughts and were at least considering the possibility of supporting humanitarian aid to Cubans through private agencies. The recent death of the Foundation's forceful leader, Jorge Mas Canosa, also held out the possibility of further changes in that organization's role in influencing U.S. policy toward Cuba. Pushing policy in the opposite direction were the three Cuban-American members of Congress—Florida Republicans Lincoln Díaz-Balart and Ileana Ros-Lehtinen and New Jersey Democrat Robert Menéndez—who continued to advocate a hard line toward the Castro regime.[11]

The difficulty in changing the longstanding policy of the United States toward Cuba was amply demonstrated by a recent U.S. government report that was *not* released. Democratic Senator Bob Graham of Florida requested an assessment of the military threat posed by Cuba. The U.S. Defense Intelligence Agency was to present the report to Congress by 31 March 1998. When word leaked out that the report downplayed the Cuban military threat, anti-Castro forces in the United States feared that it might lead to a softening of U.S. policy. Graham himself criticized the report before it was made public, saying that it failed to take into account Cuba's capability to produce biological weapons and to use "mass migration" as a policy tool. Responding to the criticism, Secretary of Defense William Cohen postponed release of the report, and Pentagon officials indicated that it would be modified to bring it more into line with U.S. policy assumptions about Cuba.[12]

As matters now stand, with Castro in his seventies and in power for four decades, major adjustments in U.S. policy may have to await his death. Meanwhile, the United States remained almost isolated in its Cuban policy.

New Economic Approaches

Almost as dramatic as the collapse of the Soviet Union, but occurring at a slower pace, was the changing attitude of many Latin American governments toward economic development. There was growing disillusionment with the development approaches that had characterized the immediate post–World War II era: central planning, state ownership of key economic activities, forced industrialization coupled with import substitution, and protectionist trade policies. The initial success of the "Chicago boys" — a group of Chilean economists who embraced the market-guided economics of Milton Friedman of the University of Chicago — in turning around the Chilean economy encouraged a second look at development thinking. Mexican presidents Miguel de la Madrid (1982–1988) and Carlos Salinas (1988–1994) challenged the economic assumptions that guided Mexico's postwar development by introducing a series of reforms reducing the role of the state in the economy. Latin America embraced a new fashion in development planning: market-guided economies, privatization, encouragement of foreign investment, and the removal of trade barriers. Just as the United States could claim "victory" in its strategic struggle with the Soviet Union, it had also "won" the development argument with Latin America; governments in the region were moving to the kind of development policy the United States had been urging since 1945.

The new approach to development was linked to the old problem of the debt. The austerity programs of the International Monetary Fund (IMF) had required debtor nations to make adjustments reflecting the principles of the new approach. Reformers such as Mexico's Carlos Salinas drew another connection: economic restructuring could not continue without debt relief. In March 1989 the Bush administration offered a new method of dealing with the debt problem: the "Brady Plan," named for U.S. Secretary of the Treasury Nicholas Brady. Under the plan commercial banks would write down the loans owed them by the debtor nations and provide new loans for debt servicing and development purposes. Presumably the banks would see the wisdom of reducing the debt and increasing the likelihood of being paid. This would be accompanied by a major increase in lending by the IMF and the World Bank to those debtor nations engaging in major structural reforms. The banks responded initially by "writing off" not "writing down"; major international banks such as Chase Manhattan and Manufacturers Hanover increased their reserves for possible losses, rather than agree to reduce the amount of debt owed by Latin American nations.

Mexico finally reached a complex agreement with its creditors in January 1990. Creditors had three options: (1) exchange their loans for an equal amount of new Mexican bonds, paying a fixed rate of 6.25%, far below existing rates; (2) exchange their loans for new Mexican bonds at a 35% discount but with a variable interest rates more reflective of market conditions; or (3) retain current loans but with the requirement to provide new loans equal to twenty-five percent of the creditor's current exposure to Mexican government debt. Banks holding approximately ninety percent of the debt took either the first or second option, meaning that there would be little in the way of new loans for Mexico. With most of the major commercial banks heading for the exit, the Brady Plan did not produce the long-term commitment hoped for in solving Latin America's development problems. The Mexican settlement also did not lead to a series of similar agreements with most Latin American countries, each of which was left to go its separate way in dealing with international creditors. The actions taken by the banks since 1982, however, had effectively transformed the "crisis" back into a "problem" by the early 1990s — at least as far as the creditors were concerned. Despite fears that the debt crisis of the 1980s would sour creditors on Latin America for years, by 1997 a combination of economic reforms and improved growth rates provoked new interest in the region on the part of lenders. By the fall of 1997, seven Latin American countries — including Mexico, Brazil, and Argentina — had issued more than $17 billion in new bonds. Latin American bond markets — which had practically ceased to function in the 1980s — were now among the most active in the world. Foreign creditors also showed renewed interest in lending to corporate and private borrowers in the region.[13]

With the limited initial impact of the Brady Plan, the Bush administration took an additional step in linking debt, development, and structural reforms in Latin America with the announcement of the Enterprise for the Americas Initiative in June 1990. Designed to create a "new partnership to encourage and support market-oriented reforms and economic growth," the Initiative was a grab bag of economic proposals, including debt reduction, tariff reduction, U.S. aid to facilitate privatizations, environmental improvements, new investments, and the establishment of a hemispheric free trade zone. The proposal was eagerly embraced by the Latin American countries but encountered problems in the U.S. Congress which endorsed the Initiative but was slow to pass the legislation needed to implement it.[14]

The part of the Initiative evoking the greatest response was the call for a free trade area. The Latin American nations had been seeking greater access to the U.S. market throughout the postwar period. President Carlos Salinas of Mexico, under intense political and economic pressure at home, seized the opportunity and proposed a free trade agreement with the United States. Since the United States had signed a free trade agreement with Canada in 1988, Canada officially joined the process in early 1991, leading to negotiations for a North American Free Trade Agreement (NAFTA). Negotiators produced a lengthy and complicated agreement in August 1992, only to have the road to NAFTA take an unexpected turn when President Bush lost his reelection bid in November 1992. The new president, Bill Clinton, had reluctantly and cautiously supported NAFTA during the election. Once in the presidency, however, Clinton embraced the agreement as his own and got congressional approval for the treaty in November 1993, aided by supplemental agreements on labor and the environment which quieted domestic opposition. The numerous provisions of the agreement would be phased in over an extended period. Some provisions—such as the elimination of the U.S. tariff on Mexican autos—would go into effect immediately. Others—such as tariffs on certain agricultural products—would not be removed for fifteen years. NAFTA also eased restrictions on U.S. investment in Mexico, established rules of origin for products, and provided protection for intellectual property such as copyrights and patents.

Point-Counterpoint: Debt Relief and the Brady Plan

"When economic policy makers are the prisoners of circumstances and lack the resources to control events, they are well advised to be vague about their proposals. In searching for a solution to the third world debt problem, Treasury Secretary Nicholas F. Brady is employing the economics of vagueness.

"But that is not to stay he has done nothing. On the contrary, in declaring that the fundamental solution to the debt problem requires not more loans from the rich to the poor but a reduction in outstanding debts, Mr. Brady has taken a big step forward. . . ."

—*Leonard Silk, Financial Columnist,* New York Times, *31 March 1989.*

"With respect to Mexico, the plan only works on the $70 to $75 billion owed as private debt to the banks. Suppose with the plan you get a 20 percent discount on that debt—which I am not sure you could get since banks won't give all the discount to the debtor country. Then you would have a drop of about $12 billion in the debt. This would reduce debt-service payments by $1 billion a year. That's not bad, but Mexico pays $11 billion a year in debt service, so it really is only 10% in relief. And that is if all the banks go along."

—*Jorge Castañeda, Professor, National University of Mexico,* New York Times, *19 March 1989.*

"The plan is a positive development and a beginning.... My biggest concern is that because you've got so many players—banks, creditors, countries—a framework has to be put in place for some central leadership to make the plan happen."

—*James Robinson III, Chairman, American Express Company,* New York Times, *19 March 1989.*

"It's not clear to me that a gradualistic, muddling through approach will work. But some banks, like Citicorp, will love the plan. It will allow them to have more business. Trading in third world debt will boom, and it will make a lot of money for Citicorp."

—*Shafiquil Islam, Senior Fellow, Council on Foreign Relations,* New York Times, *19 March 1989.*

"It is not yet a detailed plan, and it doesn't have a clearly identifiable individual who is responsible and will do the 20 hour-a-day work that is needed to avert a crisis.... I have had conversations with bankers—they want leadership and someone who is in charge.
In the past the feeling was that either you present new money or debt reduction. The plan is a recognition that you need both."

—*Bill Bradley, Chairman, Senate Subcommittee on International Debt,* New York Times, *19 March 1989.*

NAFTA was viewed as the first step toward the creation of a hemispheric trading bloc. The United States promised to expedite a free trade agreement with Chile after NAFTA was in place and already had "framework" agreements with sixteen other Latin American countries which would provide the basis for an expanded free trade area. In December 1994 hemispheric leaders met at the "Summit of the Americas" in Miami and enthusiastically endorsed the concept of a hemispheric free trade area. This summit euphoria soon collided with hard political and economic reality. When a new U.S. Congress convened in January 1995, the Republicans were in control of both houses of Congress and were eager to enact their own political agenda, in which free trade did not figure prominently. Many Democrats—with strong ties to organized labor— were also unenthusiastic about expanding NAFTA. Resistance grew as Mexico's economy entered a new crisis, featuring a drastic decline in the value of the peso. As a result the predicted economic benefits of NAFTA were dramatically reduced, dampening enthusiasm for further free trade agreements.

The approach being used by the Clinton administration of expanding NAFTA was also drawing opposition from Latin American governments worried about its strict labor and environmental standards. When Clinton submitted a request to Congress for "fast track" trade legislation, he was forced to withdraw it in November 1997 when a large majority of the Democratic members of the House of Representatives indicated that they would not support it. At the second "Summit of the Americas" meeting at Santiago, Chile, in April 1998, President Clinton reaffirmed his commitment to receiving "fast track" authority from the U.S. Congress and extending NAFTA. Many Latin American representatives at the conference were skeptical of Clinton's ability to deliver, particularly since 1998 was a congressional election year in the United States.

With the expansion of NAFTA stalled, Latin American nations began to pursue their own regional trade agreements. Chile signed an agreement with Mexico and opened bilateral negotiations with Peru and Ecuador. Argentina, Brazil, Paraguay, and Uruguay created a common market known as Mercosur which went into operation in 1995; Mercosur later offered associate membership to Chile and Bolivia. Mercosur quickly moved in the direction of a South American free trade area, with talks scheduled with Colombia, Ecuador, Peru, and Venezuela. There were also renewed signs of life from two existing regional groupings: the Andean Pact (Bolivia, Colombia, Ecuador, Peru, and Venezuela) and the Central American Common Market (Belize, Costa Rica, El Salvador, Guatemala, Honduras, Nicaragua, and Panama). These regional groupings affected U.S.-Latin American economic relations in two ways. First, the United States was excluded from them; in fact, some of the nations in-

volved cited reducing dependency on the United States as an important benefit of the new arrangements. Second, these groups were seeking closer ties
with Japan and the European Economic Community, increasing the potential
for competition with the United States. Soon after its formation, Mercosur
opened discussions with the European Union concerning a free trade pact.
If these regional groupings succeed, it will retard the creation of a hemispheric
free trade area and undercut the leadership role of the United States in hemispheric economic relations.

Intervention in Haiti

Except for its efforts to expand NAFTA, the first Clinton administration
(1993–1997) showed little interest in Latin American affairs; indeed, there was
early criticism that the new administration was largely ignoring foreign affairs
in general. Clinton attributed his electoral victory to an emphasis on domestic problems, especially the state of the economy. Clinton had not called for
dramatic changes in foreign policy during the campaign; the fact that he received only forty-three percent of the popular vote in the election indicated
that he had no mandate to make such changes. Clinton appointed as his secretary of state Warren Christopher who had extensive dealings with Latin
American issues during the Carter administration; as secretary, however,
Christopher showed the traditional emphasis on East-West relations. Except
for the deteriorating situation in Haiti where the military had overthrown a
democratically-elected president, the major foreign policy problems inherited
by the Clinton administration did not include any relating to Latin America:
American troops in Somalia, coping with Saddam Hussein in Iraq, relations
with the former Soviet Union, and warfare in the Balkans.

Clinton finally committed U.S. troops to a solution of the Haitian situation,
launching a major intervention in fall 1994 aimed at "restoring democracy"
(the democratically-elected president, Jean-Bertrand Aristide) and "rebuilding the economy" which had declined even further as a result of U.N. sanctions. Even then, Clinton stressed the importance of the Haitian situation to
U.S. domestic affairs, emphasizing the intervention as a way to stop the flow
of Haitian refugees to the United States. The United States tried to cast the intervention as a multilateral operation, but U.S. troops numbering more than
20,000 dominated numerically and operationally. While the usual Latin
American outcries against intervention were muted, the composition of the

multinational force spoke volumes about the traditional Latin American opposition to intervention, whether unilateral by the United States or multilateral under U.S. leadership. The token forces of the Haitian intervention which
were not from the United States all came from former British colonies; no
Latin American nation provided troops.

Aristide had little time to deal with Haiti's problems before new presidential
elections in December 1995 resulted in victory for his close political associate,
René Préval. U.S. relief at the election results soon gave way to uncertainty
about the future of the "new Haiti." The ruling Lavalas Party quickly split into
rival factions supporting Aristide and Préval. U.S. military forces were substantially reduced, and the multinational intervention was converted into a
U.N. peacekeeping force. Local and national elections held in April 1997 led
to widespread charges of electoral fraud against the supposedly democratic
government. The resignation of Prime Minister Rosny Smarth the following
June produced political stalemate and government paralysis. While Haitians
and foreigners alike speculated on Aristide's commitment to democracy and
plans for the 2000 presidential election, signs of any "rebuilding of the economy" were hard to find. The U.N.-trained police force created to replace the
Haitian army showed signs of partisan political influence in its command
structure and the creation of special units which were accused of political in-
timidation. The U.N. mandate under which various international groups operated in Haiti ended on 30 November 1997, although there was a last-minute
agreement to keep a civilian police mission which would continue to train
the new Haitian police force until November 1998. This latest intervention in
Haiti invited comparison with a much earlier one by another Democratic
president who wanted to stress domestic reform: Woodrow Wilson in 1915.

Toward the New Millennium

As futurists tried to predict what the new millennium would bring, one historic deadline in U.S.-Latin American relations was rapidly approaching. The
Panama Canal treaty ratified in 1978 called for the complete transfer of the
control of the canal to Panama in the year 2000, bringing to an end almost a
century of direct U.S. involvement in Panamanian affairs. As a new era in U.S.-
Panamanian relations was about to begin, the old familiar problem of political instability resurfaced. After the ouster of General Noriega in 1990, the

civilian Guillermo Endara served as president until 1994. Prohibited by the constitution from seeking reelection, Endara turned over the presidency to Ernesto Pérez Balladares for the 1994–1999 period. Pérez Balladares, however, announced that he will attempt to get the constitution amended and then run for reelection in May 1999. If the effort to amend the constitution fails, Pérez Balladares indicated that he will run his wife for the presidency instead. This maneuvering has led various opposition groups to try to form an alliance to block the incumbent president's plans. Regardless of which political path Pérez Balladares eventually takes, his effort to continue in power will likely provoke a political crisis on the eve of the transfer of the canal.[15]

As U.S.-Latin American relations moved toward the new millennium and—possibly—a new world order, a recent poll sponsored by *The Wall Street Journal* and sixteen major Latin American newspapers indicated both problems and promise. The survey indicated that a large majority of the Latin Americans polled (sixty-five percent) favored U.S.-imposed sanctions on countries that were designated as not doing enough to combat drug production and trafficking, a view not shared by most Latin American governments. The issue of free trade provoked similar contradictory positions. Almost eighty percent of those polled in both Latin America and the United States favored the general principle of free trade; only a minority of U.S. respondents, however, supported the creation of a "Free Trade Area of the Americas." While Latin Americans rated the United States as their most trusted trading partner, the highest rating U.S. respondents gave to any major Latin American country was Brazil's thirty-one percent. Perhaps of greatest interest to the future conduct of U.S.-Latin American relations was the response to the following statement: "The United States only pursues its own interests and interferes too much in the affairs of other countries." Seventy-five percent of Latin American respondents agreed with the statement; even more intriguing, sixty-one percent of U.S. respondents did also.[16]

CHAPTER 8

THE LATINO DIASPORA
IN THE UNITED STATES

Vignette: Immigrants and the Underground Economy

S. T. C. Knitwear in Long Island City started out as a "model,
non-union shop," according to a 1993 article in the *New York Times*.
However, the same article indicated that the situation didn't last long.
When the management changed at the end of 1991, the shop began to
go underground. Medical benefits were canceled, then holidays disappeared, and finally rest breaks vanished as well. Paycheck stubs no longer
showed withholding for taxes. On 2 May 1992, the final blow fell. The
forewoman proclaimed a "Korean work week," which turned out to be
a mandatory 49 hours without overtime. The workers, mostly Latina
immigrants without documentation, walked out. Shortly thereafter,
and despite their undocumented status, they contacted the International
Ladies Garment Workers Union. Joseph Lombardo, a union official im-
pressed with their courage, returned with them to the factory, where the
manager insisted that he had never approved changes and that workers
would be well treated if they returned.

Conditions did not improve. Blanca Julian, an Ecuadoran, gave a fla-
vor of factory relations when she said, "We were barely allowed to talk to
each other, and when the boss came by we were supposed to salute him
like a king." The union won the election to represent the workers in
September, but a month later, on the eve of contract negotiations, U.S.
immigration agents appeared at the factory after being called by the

owner. Eleven union activists were called forward; ten appeared and were handcuffed and taken into custody. The eleventh hid under a table.

The story did not have an entirely unhappy ending. The Immigration and Naturalization Service, angry at being used by S. T. C., gave the women temporary work permits, and their deportation hearings were postponed until August 1994. As of 1993, five had found steady jobs, one was studying English, and another was taking advanced sewing classes. The arrested women were given a settlement by the company. S. T. C. closed its doors just days before a union contract was scheduled for signing, perhaps to open in a more hidden location.

Based on Deborah Sontag, "Emigrés Battling Abuse Flex Rights as Workers," New York Times, *15 June 1993.*

As the Cold War faded, new issues arose to occupy U.S. policymakers. Two which are currently highly compelling are Latin American migration to the United States, both legal and undocumented, and the illegal trade in narcotics. It is to these issues that we turn in chapters 8 and 9. Both impact the social and economic fabric of the United States, as well as domestic politics. The immigration issue emerged in the Republican presidential primaries in 1996 through the campaign of Patrick Buchanan, who attacked Mexican immigrants as criminals and welfare abusers. Resentment against Mexican immigrants in particular surfaced in 1994 with the passage of Proposition 187 in California, the state most affected by illegal immigration of Latinos. This proposition, currently being adjudicated in the courts, severely limited the access of illegal immigrants to public services. As Latinos provided by far the largest number of undocumented workers in the state, the law was widely perceived as reflecting an anti-Latino bias among California voters. At the same time, Governor Pete Wilson of the same state—who also had hopes of being the Republican nominee—proposed that children of undocumented aliens no longer be granted automatic citizenship. Both Proposition 187 and Wilson's suggestion elicited a storm of controversy. In 1996 the University of California board of regents, with Wilson's blessing, eliminated affirmative action criteria from admission consideration throughout that university system. Was California, the state most impacted by legal and illegal immigration, the bellwether for hardening attitudes throughout the country? What historical process had brought resentments and concerns to the point that major political leaders, aspiring to the presidential nominations of their parties, would take these stances?

The 1986 Immigration Reform and Control Act changed the configuration of Latino residence in the United States in offering amnesty to undocumented workers who could prove continuous residence in the United States starting at any time before 1 January 1982. Many Latinos were able to regularize their status and some, as a result, became eligible to bring in other family members. The law also included provisions for employer sanctions, which, however, have remained largely unenforced.

The 1990 U.S. Census shows a total of more than 14 million native born Latinos, and an additional almost 8 million foreign born, resident in the United States. Although this figure probably reflects a significant undercount, it is a substantial number and growing fast. Latinos comprise more than 10 percent of the U.S. population, and Census Bureau estimates indicate that the figure will rise to 24.5 percent in 2050.[1] In aggregate terms, as of 1979, Latin American migrants had the lowest median male incomes—about $9,000 a year—and median household incomes of around $14,000. Given the significant amount of undocumented migration, it is likely that migrants will maintain this unfortunate position. These low incomes in turn lead to their unjustified stigmatization as abusers of welfare. Taken as a group, Latin American migrants are extremely slow to regularize their status as citizens, with Cubans being a notable exception. As a result, except for the large Cuban community in Florida, they have had little power at the ballot box to protect themselves politically.[2]

This chapter will consider the immigration question, with particular emphasis on three cases. The first, and clearly the largest and most important migration over time, has been the Mexican one. In 1987, 72,531 legal Mexican immigrants arrived in the United States; over 70 percent were exempt from quota limits because of their status as children, parents, or spouses of U.S. citizens, and 16 percent more had close relatives who were either U.S. citizens or legal residents. Because of this large social base of family, the possibilities for Mexicans immigrating legally under family reunification provisions will continue to be high. Legal immigration, however, is dwarfed by the undocumented flow. In 1987, the same year noted above, of more than 1 million deportable aliens apprehended by the Immigration and Naturalization Service (INS), 97 percent were Mexican.[3] Located immediately on a border more than 2,000 miles long, Mexico has sent migrants—documented and otherwise—

ever since that border was created. The motives over time have varied, and certainly each individual may have a variety of reasons for moving northward. Political, social, and especially economic issues have all impacted this flow.

The second case, that of Cuba, has been largely political, although social and economic causes have been significant. Since the advent of Fidel Castro, many Cubans have moved the ninety miles to the U.S. mainland, and most have enjoyed the status of political refugees. Further, they have received extraordinary help from the U.S. government relative to other migrants from Latin America, a result of their symbolic usefulness as opponents of communism in the hemisphere.

Third, we will consider the case of El Salvador. Salvadoran migration to the borders of the United States has been largely a factor of civil war and political repression (tied to U.S. support for the Salvadoran military). However, Salvadoran refugees have found their status questionable, as a recognition of their eligibility for political asylum would have required the U.S. government to acknowledge political repression by a regime regarded as an ally.

We will also briefly consider recent changes in the immigration status of two groups of Caribbean migrants, Cuban and Haitian, by the administration of President Bill Clinton, as well as the changing political and legal climate that is emerging at the end of the century.

Mexican Immigration in Historical Context

Substantial numbers of Mexicans were already resident in the southwestern borderlands—present Texas, California, Arizona, and New Mexico—at the time that this area of the country became part of the United States in 1848 with the Treaty of Guadalupe Hidalgo. Through the end of the 19th century, the flow of Mexicans back and forth across the border continued relatively undisturbed, increasing as rail service north from central Mexico improved. The first major push occurred during the Mexican Revolution in 1910–1920, when approximately 1.5 million persons spent at least part of the decade in the relative safety north of the border. Official figures show that 890,371 persons crossed the border between 2 July 1910 and 1 July 1920, a sum which included both legal immigrants and "non-statistical aliens," workers who came for a significant length of time but did not intend to stay permanently. This large migration went principally to Texas, with more than 70% of legal immigrants indicating that state as their destination. There they formed a network for others coming north. Until 1917, when literacy tests and head taxes were imposed and contract labor prohibited by federal law, little attempt was made to control movement from one country to another.[4]

The migration continued through the 1920s, largely as a result of economic hardship in Mexico and the need for labor in the United States. With the onset of the Great Depression in the 1930s, employers gave preference to U.S. job applicants, and U.S. government agencies actively promoted repatriation for Mexican workers. Nevertheless, Mexican workers continued to come and go in enormous numbers, their status as legal or illegal largely determined by the needs of the U.S. labor market. When U.S. entry into World War II led to labor shortages, the *bracero* program—begun under an executive agreement between the two countries in 1942—brought Mexican workers into the United States for fixed periods of employment in the agricultural sector. In 1951, it was institutionalized by Congress as Public Law 78. Officially terminated in 1964, it had brought almost 5 million workers to the United States.

Over the decades, the focus of migration shifted to California, where more jobs were available than in Texas. Los Angeles, in particular, acquired a substantial Mexican and Mexican-American population. By 1928, it had the largest Mexican population of any U.S. city. In the 1990s, it has a larger number of persons born in Mexico or of Mexican descent than all Mexican cities except Mexico City, Monterrey, and Guadalajara.

Statistics show that of economically active immigrants, more than half of the Mexicans are operators and laborers (53%), with only 6% in the professionals and managers category. With over 2 million workers in the U.S. labor force, only 2.5% were listed as members of "professional specialty occupations."[5] These figures place Mexican immigrants at the lower end of the employment scale. Certainly, the numbers of Mexican Americans in upper categories were much higher. Further, Mexicans have been the most reluctant of all major immigrant groups to become citizens. Although Mexicans were the largest group of immigrants to the United States during the 1970s, in the decade 1976–1986, they comprised only 6.7% of total naturalizations. Only 3% of all Mexicans entering legally in 1970 had become citizens by 1979.[6] Given the increasingly negative political climate toward immigrants in the 1990s and recent moves by the Mexican administration to make dual citizenship possible, this percentage is rising rapidly. Still, various factors, such as ease of return to Mexico with a corresponding desire to maintain citizenship there, along with a pride in Mexican identity, have limited the willingness of these immigrants to seek U.S. citizenship.

However, many Mexicans became legal residents in the United States in the wake of the 1986 Immigration Reform and Control Act. This bill imposed penalties on employers hiring undocumented persons but, at the same time, extended amnesty to many of those workers already in the United States. By 1992, approximately 2.5 million people had taken advantage of its amnesty program to become permanent residents, and the largest group of these were Mexicans. This large number, in turn, made it possible for many close family members to enter the country legally. Legal immigration has changed dramatically since the 1950s, when 68% of entrants came from Europe or Canada. In the 1980s, only 13% came from those sources, while 84% (including those granted amnesty) came from Latin America. The 1990 Immigration Act, which took effect in 1992, seems likely to increase this proportion, as it highly favors family members of U.S. citizens and permanent residents.[7]

Cubans and the "Flight" from Castro

The Cuban situation has been far different. Cubans since the advent of Castro have occupied a privileged position relative to other Latino immigrant groups. [8] As refugees from a regime recognized as hostile to U.S. interests, they received special treatment compared to other immigrants, and particularly in contrast to undocumented workers. Their legal status was more easily resolved, with Washington first easing visa requirements and then, for many years, dropping them entirely. Moreover, large amounts of financial and other assistance were provided. As early as December 1960, the U.S. government established an emergency center for Cuban refugees, which was expanded into a major program providing $73 million in direct subsidies between 1961 and 1971. Dozens of other federal, state, and local programs also provided a variety of educational, resettlement, credit, and health services. As a result, Cuban adjustment to the United States proceeded relatively smoothly, and Cubans became extremely important, both politically and economically, in South Florida. By the mid-1980s, it was estimated that Cubans represented $1 billion in the local economy.[9]

The composition of the early wave of Cuban immigration also contributed to Cubans' acceptance in the United States. The group fleeing immediately after Castro's triumph included the top layers of prerevolutionary society, including former political figures and businessmen. Many of these immigrants already had substantial capital resources and personal connections in the United States. In the early 1960s, migration continued, involving increasing numbers of the middle class. During the early years, for example, Cuba lost over 2,000 practicing physicians, approximately one-third of its total medical establishment, including 141 of 158 senior professors at the University of Havana Medical School. As this suggests, the early migrants were well-educated as well, with 35% of the adult immigrants having achieved secondary school education, while the average figure for the total adult population of Cuba was 4%.

From the time of the Cuban missile crisis in October 1962 until April 1980, Cuban immigration continued at a fluctuating level, depending on the political stances of the two countries. From 1962 to 1965, few refugees were able to exit Cuba, and then only clandestinely or through restricted flights to third countries. Between 1965 and 1973, the flow increased as Cuba generally permitted departure of those citizens whose families could come by boat to take them to the mainland. A twice-daily airlift brought others to Miami. Because of the priority given to those with relatives in the United States and given the nature of the early migration, this phase of departure was racially slanted toward Cuba's white rather than black or mulatto population. From 1973 until 1980, the Cuban government restricted exit, and the number of exiles reaching the United States declined precipitously.[10] During this period, the U.S. government also made various attempts to at least control the entrance of Cubans, but, in almost all cases, when pressured by earlier Cuban exiles would permit entry.

Then, in a move which startled Jimmy Carter's government, in 1980 Castro suddenly permitted Cubans to depart for the United States from the port of Mariel. Apparently exasperated by a flood of Cubans seeking refuge in the Peruvian embassy in Havana, he announced that the port would be opened to those wishing to leave. "Freedom Flotillas" organized in Florida quickly made their way to the island, and in five months 125,000 Cubans had fled to Florida. This new migration was quite different from earlier waves; many were semi- or unskilled laborers, a large proportion were black, and over 20% had some sort of criminal record, although these included minor infractions such as tax evasion and black market operations. The large majority were male, in contrast to pre-1973 migrations which had included more women. This huge influx, with almost 5,000 persons a day swarming through Key West, was impossible to deal with smoothly. Despite the provisions of the 1980 Refugee Act, which required that admissible individuals demonstrate a fear of persecution as their reason for flight, virtually all were permitted to enter with little scrutiny.

The "Marielitos," as they became known, were spread out through the country, many of them to camps set up by the U.S. government, where protests and riots broke out as detention stretched from weeks into months. The Marielitos gained a reputation for causing problems, criminal and otherwise. They continued to be a sore point in U.S.-Cuban relations for several years. However, in 1987, Havana and Washington reached an agreement which permitted 20,000 Cuban émigrés to enter the United States annually, while Cuba agreed to the return of 2,500 Marielitos who had been classified as "excludable aliens" as a result of previous criminal records or severe mental instability. The announcement of the agreement again led to riots, this time among deportable Cubans held at detention centers in Louisiana and Georgia.[11]

Still, Cubans from the pre-Mariel group have fit in more readily to U.S. social, economic, and political life than other Latino groups. In economic terms, they have fallen in the mid-range of all immigrant groups, ahead of both Japanese and English households in median income as of 1979.[12] They also have relatively high rates of naturalization. The 1990 U.S. census shows that of almost 322,000 Cubans entering the United States during the 1965–1979 period, 157,000 had already become citizens. Dade County had almost 1 million residents who were either Cuban born or Cuban American. In Florida, then, this population has become a significant force, one that has gained even national influence.

However, events in mid-1994 led to a major policy shift in the treatment of Cuban migrants. Developments were precipitated by large numbers of Haitian "boat people" headed toward Florida, fleeing a repressive military government which had overthrown elected president Jean-Bertrand Aristide in October 1991. The problem had been building for some time, and had attracted the attention of the congressional Black Caucus, who correctly pointed out that, although most Cubans able to get to Florida were admitted, Haitians were turned away. In June 1993, the U.S. Supreme Court ruled that Haitians intercepted at sea could be returned to the island, where they were at the mercy of the Haitian military. Although many of the craft used were far from seaworthy, leading to the loss of many lives at sea, other Haitians were able to make it to the United States. Responding to the concerns of the Black Caucus, in May 1994 President Clinton ordered that these boat people be intercepted at sea and held at the U.S. naval base at Guantanamo Bay in Cuba and detention camps in Panama, pending an investigation of their potential admissibility on the grounds of political asylum.

Roberto Avendaño Corojo left Havana with four other companions on a raft made from plywood and four inner tubes. After five days and with no land in sight, tensions on the raft became so great that Roberto cut himself free and drifted for an additional ten days before being picked up by the U.S. Navy on August 28, 1994. The poster he holds was used by The Cuban American National Foundation in their efforts to sway U.S. policy in favor of the Cuban refugees. None of Roberto's original four companions was seen again.

Photograph by M. L. Horner

Castro, angry as usual at the United States and facing rapidly deteriorating economic conditions on the island, saw an opportunity to make the situation for the Clinton administration worse: he began to permit departures by a new tide of Cuban refugees, most of whom traveled by raft. Clinton, fearing another Mariel, refused to permit their entry into the United States. Cubans apprehended at sea were also sent to the Panama and Guantanamo camps, where Haitians had already begun to brawl with U.S. troops. The arrival of the Cubans made conditions even worse.

The Haitian problem was dealt with by sending the U.S. Marines into Haiti in September 1994 to reinstall President Aristide (see chapter 7). He returned to Haiti the following month, and all Haitians remaining in the camps were repatriated in December. By this time, however, approximately 20,000 Cubans were detained in the two locations. Worse, in December 1994 and January 1995, the detainees rioted, injuring 160 U.S. troops in December alone. President Clinton, who had repeatedly insisted that none of the Cubans apprehended at sea would be permitted into the United States, had to develop a policy in a hurry. Both Senator Bob Graham, Democrat of Florida, and General John Sheehan, chief of the Atlantic Command, warned the president in March that something had to be done before summer, given the potentially explosive situation in the camps. A deal with Castro was quickly forged—reportedly in a series of secret meetings between a confidant of the Cuban president and a senior State Department official—which provided for the detained Cubans to be accepted into the United States. All Cubans henceforth intercepted at sea were to be returned to the island, where they would be aided in filling out applications for admission under the quota of 20,000 a year. This latter provision, added at the behest of Senator Graham and Florida Governor Lawton Chiles, was designed to prevent another influx of immigrants for which Floridians might blame Clinton and the Democrats. The 20,000 admitted immediately would be subtracted from the first three years of the Cuban quota mentioned above. Of particular interest was the fact that hardline Cuban American leaders such as Jorge Mas Canosa were not consulted. By the end of April 1995, the policy was in place, ending more than three decades of almost automatic entry for Cubans.[13]

Cuban refugees before being admitted to the United States had to submit to a background check. Fingerprinting at the Guantanamo refugee camp enabled the Justice Department to determine whether an individual had been previously deported to Cuba from the United States or had any other criminal record that could bar entrance. Over 95 percent of those Cubans who were detained at Guantanamo were eventually allowed to immigrate to the United States.

Photograph by M. L. Horner

The Salvadoran Case

U.S. policies toward El Salvador also had an impact on immigration, but its character was quite different. Civil unrest, coupled with increasing repression, murders of church leaders, and other incidents of political violence (see chapters 6 and 7) led to a massive outflow between 1979 and 1981. By the latter year, the rate had reached 46 persons per thousand in the population, eleven times higher than the level six years earlier.[14] To be sure, not all of these migrants made it to the United States. The Costa Rican Red Cross, the Ecumenical Committee for Refugees in Panama, and Honduran and Nicaraguan authorities began to note high levels of Salvadoran refugees in their countries during the early 1980s. The way north by land led through Mexico, where Salvadorans frequently met with great difficulties, suffering economic hardship and harassment from Mexican authorities. Nevertheless, by the mid-1980s, 500,000 Salvadorans were estimated to be in the United States.[15] According to one authority, by 1985 almost 500,000 persons (with estimates ranging up to double that number) were displaced within El Salvador, with 250,000 in other Central American countries and Mexico, indicating that about 25% of the Salvadoran population was either displaced or had fled the country.[16] Moreover, huge numbers of Guatemalans, also reacting to political violence and military repression, were on the move, many arriving in the United States at about the same time. Because the information on Salvadoran migrants is more accessible and because they were the larger group, we will focus on the Salvadoran case. Still, it is significant that at this time enormous numbers of Central Americans were fleeing political violence and the accompanying economic disruption in their countries.

Despite Jeane Kirkpatrick's assertion that "traditional authoritarian" regimes such as that in El Salvador would not generate many refugees, in fact exactly that had begun to happen. And it was happening in a context of increasing military aid to that country. (See chapter 6.) Moreover, the policies of the Reagan administration, in which she had an important role, were contributing directly to the increase of migrant flows from El Salvador to the United States. Larger numbers of undocumented Salvadorans were apprehended in the United States following both military sweeps through the Salvadoran countryside and surges in death squad activity in statistically significant patterns. The first of the sweeps, in March 1980, tallied with the proclamation of a new land reform program by the Salvadoran government. Ironically, or perhaps unsurprisingly, it was accompanied by the declaration of a state of siege in rural areas and widespread terror carried out by military and paramilitary groups. Other sweeps took place in October 1980 in Morazán province, and in January and February 1983 in Morazán and Chalatenango. There were three much larger sweeps through eight departments beginning in December 1983. All were followed within three to four months with significant increases of Salvadoran apprehensions in the United States. Reports of large numbers of killings at the hands of death squads also coincided, although not quite as strongly, with later U.S. apprehensions of Salvadoran immigrants.[17] While other motivations for migration certainly existed simultaneously, particularly economic need given the widespread destruction throughout the country, political violence seemed to most observers to be the principal reason Salvadorans fled to the United States. However, this perception was at odds with the policies of political asylum then being carried out by the U.S. government.

In fact, very few Salvadorans were granted political asylum during the 1980s, as the Reagan administration skewed annual allocation figures to favor refugees fleeing from communist regimes. Stories of torture, imprisonment, and killings elsewhere were widely denounced by administration spokespersons as exaggeration or merely local abuses. According to a report in 1987 by the General Accounting Office of Congress, only 4% of Salvadorans claiming torture were approved for asylum, as contrasted with 15% for Nicaraguans, 64% for Iranians, and 80% for Poles. The U.S. State and Justice Departments maintained that Salvadoran migrants were motivated primarily by economic considerations and did not meet the standard of "clear probability of persecution for reasons of race, religion, nationality, membership of a particular social group, or political opinion." The situation changed in 1987, when as a result of legal proceedings, Salvadorans who had entered the country illegally since 1982 were granted the status of "extended voluntary departure." This ruling meant that Salvadorans could enjoy a temporary safe haven in the United States.[18] The change may have been in response to a number of pressures: Salvadoran President Duarte had written to Reagan in April of that year to request such status; Congress was and had been pushing safe haven bills for some time; Reagan's Central American policies were under fire as the Iran-Contra affair unfolded; and U.S. public opinion had never been favorable toward U.S. involvement in that country. In fact, as early as March 1981, a poll showed that two out of every three "informed Americans" were concerned that El Salvador would develop into "another Vietnam." Throughout the Reagan years, opinion polls showed consistently that the public opposed the provision of military aid to El Salvador. Still, the U.S. public had little understanding of Central American issues, with vast majorities ignorant of precisely whom the United States was supporting in El Salvador and Nicaragua.[19]

Nevertheless, a concerned portion of the "informed Americans" mentioned above were becoming radicalized on the question of Salvadoran and Guatemalan refugees in the United States. In March 1982, on the second anniversary of the assassination of Salvadoran Archbishop Romero, a Presbyterian Church in Tucson, Arizona, launched what would become the "sanctuary movement." This movement came to include many church people who, horrified by the carnage in Central America, supported the right to asylum of those seeking safety in the United States. Many individuals and churches, particularly in the Southwest, gave help and protection to various types to refugees, up to and including smuggling them into the country and helping them hide from U.S. authorities. During the decade the city of Los Angeles and the state of New Mexico, along with other communities throughout the country, declared themselves "sanctuaries." In May 1986, six church workers from Tucson were convicted on federal charges of conspiracy to smuggle Salvadorans and Guatemalans into the country; at that time more than 300 churches and twenty cities had endorsed the sanctuary movement.

Finally, during the presidency of George Bush, major changes affecting the status of Salvadoran refugees came about. In July 1990, the INS established an asylum officer corps, who would be better trained to evaluate reports of persecution. Second, the Immigration Act of 1990, incorporating much of previous congressional discussion on safe haven, created a new immigration category called Temporary Protected Status. Salvadorans were the first to receive that designation. In 1992, the year in which peace accords were finally signed by the Salvadoran government and the FMLN, that status came to an end and was again replaced, by President Bush, with protection under Deferred Enforced Departure. President Clinton ordered an extension through the end of 1994, but at that time special status for Salvadorans ended, despite the pleas of Salvadoran President Armando Calderón Sol to Vice President Al Gore.

In fact, Salvadoran workers abroad had become extremely important to the economy of their native country. In the mid-1990s, an estimated one million native Salvadorans in the United States remitted $1 billion so-called "dolares pobres" — or "poor dollars" — back to their country. In 1995, the Salvadoran Embassy began to provide legal aid to its citizens in seeking political asylum in the United States, preparing documents without charge (a service that would have cost Salvadorans $250 apiece from the various non-profit counseling centers helping the immigrants). Strangely, Calderón Sol's government was aiding its own citizens in proving that they had a reasonable fear of persecution from itself. The irony was heightened by the fact that Calderón Sol was a member of the ARENA party which had committed many of the abuses initially frightening Salvadorans into leaving in the first place.[20] Privately, most immigration counselors indicated that few Salvadorans who had arrived before 1990 would be forced to leave.

Some Salvadorans, however, were being returned, in yet another bizarre twist to the story. In the 1990s, immigration authorities had stepped up deportation of convicted felons and other lawbreakers. The INS had formed the Violent Gang Task Force in 1992 to investigate and deport gang members illegally residing in the United States. Even those with legal permanent residence could be deported if they had committed felonies. Among those targeted were Los Angeles gang members, particularly from the notorious Mara Salvatrucha gang and their principal rivals, 18th Street. Although the vast majority of Salvadoran migrants were engaged in legal pursuits, largely at the lowest socioeconomic level, Salvadoran gangs were considered among the "most ruthless and deadly" in the Los Angeles area. In 1993, seventy Salvadoran gang members were deported by the task force; hundreds more left through other deportation programs or on their own. As of 1994, the INS had 600 deportation holds on convicted Salvadoran felons in the California state prison system alone. These members would be deported on release.[21]

By 1994, deported gang members, many only teenagers and without family in El Salvador, had become a major social problem in El Salvador itself. Some barely spoke Spanish. Unsurprisingly, when they returned, they set up similar gangs in El Salvador, often with other members they had known in Los Angeles and individuals recruited locally. Crimes by gang members in El Salvador began to soar just as the country was beginning to recover from its long and destructive civil war. These crimes ranged from muggings of pedestrians to smuggling operations—sometimes in partnership with army officers, now cut off from the flow of U.S. funds—bringing stolen cars from the north into Central America and returning with guns.[22] U.S. policy in Central America in the 1980s had strange consequences for both the United States and El Salvador in the 1990s.

Immigration and the Political Scene, 1994–1998

The volatility of the immigration question emerged well before Patrick Buchanan raised it in 1996. As of October 1994, over 100 immigration control measures were pending in the U.S. Congress. Organizations as different as the Federation for Immigration Reform (FAIR) and U.S. labor unions were vociferous in expressing their concerns, despite the fact that most economists agreed that immigrants, legal and illegal, generally had a favorable impact on economic growth and did not substantially threaten the well-being of native born workers.[23] *Business Week,* in a 13 July 1992 cover story called "The Immigrants: How They're Helping the U.S. Economy," indicated that immigrants paid far more in taxes (approximately $90 billion per year) than they received in social welfare benefits (approximately $5 billion per year.)[24] Still, individual communities, especially those close to the border or with large numbers of impoverished immigrants, might find themselves faced with significant costs related to immigrant populations. Los Angeles County, for example, noted in an October 1992 report that four categories of immigrants — new citizens under the 1986 amnesty program, recent legal immigrants, illegal immigrants and their citizen children — accounted for 25% of the population but used 31% of services. As of the 1991–1992 fiscal year, the net outlay for the County was $807 million.[25]

Additionally, in hard economic times, immigrants furnished a useful scapegoat for economic reverses as well as a target for budget cutting legislators. Buchanan's message was, for a few weeks at least, highly resonant for a significant number of primary voters and seemed to be a factor in his primary win in New Hampshire in 1996.

California is estimated to have absorbed almost 40% of the total of 10 million illegal and legal immigrants entering the country in the 1980s.[26] It has also led the country in anti-immigrant demonstrations, beginning with a series of evening rallies in 1989–1990 called "Light Up the Border." In the evening, immigration opponents gathered at the U.S.-Mexican border near San Diego and shined their headlights in the direction of Mexico. In 1994, former INS administrators gathered sufficient signatures to put a measure known as Proposition 187 on the November ballot. This initiative included a number of measures which would deny publicly-funded social services, health care, and education to illegal migrants. More dangerous, it instructed officials to verify immigration status, thereby forcing untrained public employees to become de facto INS agents and empowering them to deny benefits if they "reasonably suspect . . . that the person is alien in the United States." The proposition passed handily but has been in constant litigation and has not gone into effect. Nevertheless, its passage caused consternation in Mexico, where the government officially decried the measure. It also led to demonstrations among the Latino population in California, which correctly believed the measure to be aimed at them.

Point-Counterpoint: Proposition 187

"It is not fair to take education away from the kids. . . . We could be the future leaders. We could be the ones sitting right where you are some-day. You've got to give everyone a chance."

—*Henry Romero, 10th grade student, remarks to the City Council.* Los Angeles Times, *3 November 1994.*

"I was born in Mexico and my parents came over illegally. . . . When I look at these kids, I am looking at me 23 years ago. And they want me to turn them in?"

—*Leo Valdez, third grade teacher at César Chávez Elementary School.* Los Angeles Times, *4 November 1994.*

"Ever see the 'Grapes of Wrath?' Well, that was my story. If the Colorado River had been the Rio Grande, I'd be illegal, too. But the difference be-tween us Okies and these Mexicans is government assistance. We didn't have it back then."

—*Anonymous store owner, Parlier, California.* Los Angeles Times, *4 November 1994.*

"We check people's driver's licenses. Why can't we check their other pa-pers . . . ? My parents and grandparents came over for work. Now they come over for a free ride."

—*Latino sheriff's deputy.* Los Angeles Times, *5 November 1994.*

"We realize that anti-immigration rhetoric is perceived to bring short-term political advantage. But we believe that in the medium term and the long term, this posture is a loser for the GOP. . . . The anti-immigra-tion boomerang, if it is hurled, will come back to hurt the GOP. The Re-publican Party helped create a Democratic base in many of America's cities with its hostile stand toward the last generation of immigrants from Italy, Ireland and Central Europe. Can anyone calculate the polit-ical cost this time of turning away Asians and Hispanics . . . ? The main target is public education. The initiative would bar children of illegal immigrants from public elementary and secondary schools. And U.S.-born children of illegal immigrants — U.S. citizens — could, in effect, be required to inform on their parents, who would then face deportation. This is not a road we should head down."

—*Excerpts from a two-page advertisement, by Jack Kemp and William J. Bennett, Co-Directors of Empower America. Los Angeles Times, 8 November 1994.*

"What people need to understand is that this issue was never about race or racism. . . . This nation-state is a state of legal immigrants, and proud of it."

—*Pete Wilson, Governor of California. Los Angeles Times, 9 November 1994, on passing of Proposition 187.*

"The voices of intolerance have returned. . . . What will happen to the children? Will they return to Mexico? Wash windshields in California? Sell newspapers on the streets or beg?"

—*President Carlos Salinas de Gortari of Mexico. Los Angeles Times, 10 November 1994.*

"I think there is a general feeling, even though it's not necessarily articulated, that California's loss is Texas' gain. I sure make a point of letting my political and business contacts in Mexico know that Texas is a more inviting atmosphere."

—*José Villareal, San Antonio attorney. Los Angeles Times, 6 February 1995.*

"The objective vision of the migratory phenomenon in some sectors of the United States has taken on frequent distortions, noxious stereotypes, xenophobic attitudes, racism, violence and a growing inclination to use electoral means to achieve those ends."

—*José Angel Gurriá Treviño, Mexico's Foreign Secretary (reaction to Proposition 187). Los Angeles Times, 12 April 1997.*

Meanwhile, regents at the University of California were successful in early 1996 in eliminating affirmative action as a criterion for admission, despite faculty and student protests. At the same time, bilingual education in the state came under attack, with new legislation coming before lawmakers to study the effectiveness of current programs, possibly toward their elimination. At the national level, both parties seemed willing to examine immigration questions with an eye to restriction. Meanwhile, on the border, tougher enforcement by the Clinton administration through programs such as Operation Hold-the-Line in El Paso and Operation Gatekeeper in San Diego, as well as the use of U.S military forces for some operations, made illegal crossings much more difficult.

Two incidents in 1996 brought the tensions over illegal immigration, particularly from Mexico, into high relief. On 1 April 1996, Riverside County sheriff's deputies in southern California were videotaped beating two unresisting illegal aliens, while others scattered, after an hour-long, high-speed chase. One was a woman, Alicia Sotero Vásquez, who was dragged by her hair out of the pickup in which the illegals had been riding. Clearly ill and terrified, she appeared on television the next day with the Mexican consul to protest her treatment. Latino protests in Los Angeles accelerated through the week, culminating but not ending in a 6,000-person protest march in downtown Los Angeles on April 7. The two aliens brought suit against the County, later settling for $740,000.

That same day, seven migrants were killed when another truck in the same County, trying to evade the Border Patrol, plunged down a steep hill, skidded on a curve, and flipped over into a ditch. Officers coming upon the scene reported that eighteen others had been injured, but were unsure how many undocumented workers had actually been packed into the stolen vehicle. In neither case were the drivers — assumed to be the smugglers — immediately identified. Callers to radio talk shows, letters to the editor, and local editorials in general expressed distress and concern about the beatings and the loss of life, but some included anti-immigrant diatribes and demands for even stronger enforcement of border-closing measures. The escalation in the number of accidents involving illegal migrants illustrated, however, that increased enforcement was causing smugglers (known as "coyotes") to adopt more desperate measures. With easier routes closed off, migrants were coming through more dangerous areas and smugglers were taking more chances. At the same time, the prices migrants paid to smugglers were increasing, and coyotes were committing more abuses. News stories linked the stronger enforcement to growth in complex, more sophisticated smuggling rings and to possible connections between immigrant smuggling and drug smuggling operations. It was also reported that some aliens were being forced to transport narcotics in exchange for aid in crossing the border.[27]

The controversy over immigration is likely to continue into the immediate future. The Clinton administration, in the wake of his reelection, persisted in its efforts to control the border. By January 1998, more immigration officers were authorized to carry guns than those of any other federal agency. The largest part of the increase at the INS was in the Border Patrol, where the numbers of armed personnel rose from about 4,000 in 1993 to almost 6,000 in 1996.[28] At the same time Clinton seemed likely to support affirmative action programs and other issues that appealed to Latino voters.

Buchanan's brief success with his attacks on immigrants in the Republican primary battle, in which he was ultimately defeated, led other politicians to embrace restrictions on immigration and affirmative action. New legislation emerging in Congress after the primaries was increasingly restrictionist. A *Wall Street Journal*/NBC News poll, released 26 March 1996, showed that 52% of all adults favored a five-year moratorium on all legal and illegal immigration into the United States, as against 40% opposed. Still, while other polls showed that proposals for denying public services to illegal immigrants and for doing away with affirmative action enjoyed considerable support, Republicans and Democrats feared that adopting these measures would alienate Latino and other voters.[29] Meanwhile, against all odds, a Mexican-American high school teacher in Texas won the Democratic nomination for U.S. senator. He lost, however, to a Republican in the general election.

Budget considerations as well as anti-immigrant sentiment contributed to new state and federal regulations which made many immigrants, legal and illegal, ineligible for many government benefits and contributed to renewed fears of deportation. These new restrictions led to the largest upsurge in applications for citizenship in U.S. history. In 1997, 1.5 million individuals applied for naturalization, up from less than one-third of that figure in 1992. The estimate for 1998 was 2 million new applications, while the inadequate government machinery for dealing with the citizenship process led to a record backlog of approximately the same number.[30] Although not all of these new applications came from Latin Americans, a substantial number certainly were from this hemisphere. Meanwhile, certain kinds of restrictions or conditions in home countries have made U.S. citizenship more attractive. For example, Mexican citizens may now hold dual citizenship, and these new regulations are publicized in the Mexican media.

Despite new U.S. regulations, the influx of Latin Americans is likely to continue. Mexican leaders point out that with the Mexican economy only providing about two-thirds of the job growth necessary to employ the 1 million Mexicans entering the job market each year, workers will continue to cross the border. A recent INS study estimated that Mexican undocumented workers in the United States had increased in number by 150,000 a year since 1988. It claimed that 2.7 million undocumented Mexican nationals were resident in the United States as of October 1996, accounting for more than half of the estimated total of 5 million undocumented workers.[31]

In an interesting twist on the immigration question, President Clinton has recently refused to suspend deportation orders against thousands of undocumented Hondurans. Although Nicaraguans, Guatemalans, and Salvadorans who entered the U.S. prior to 1 December 1995 have received a reprieve from the Nicaraguan Adjustment and Central American Relief Act, Hondurans were excluded because, as Clinton argued, "there was no civil war or widespread violence in Honduras compelling Hondurans to seek the protection of the United States." U.S. Representative Ileana Ros-Lehtinen (R-Florida), whose constituency included many affected Hondurans, argued that they should be rewarded for their anti-communist efforts during the 1980s (see chapter 6), but her argument was rejected. The Honduran Attorney General's office denounced the deportations, claiming that they were retribution for Tegucigalpa's refusal to extradite former Haitian police official Joseph Michel Francois to face narcotics charges in the United States.[32] The themes of immigration and drug trafficking were drawn together, at least in the minds of Honduran officialdom.

Although there have been efforts in many localities to soften the impact of the harsher new laws on noncitizens, the trend seems to be clear. There will continue to be increased efforts to control U.S. borders, and there will be far fewer benefits available from governmental sources. At the same time, there will be continued incentives for immigrants to acculturate, as bilingual and other programs lose budget support. Still, given the increasing number of Latino citizens in the United States, their significance as voters will be shifting political pressures on lawmakers through time.

CHAPTER 9

THE DRUG CONNECTION

Vignette: Cocaine and Peasant Strikes in Bolivia

On 1 April 1998, strikes began throughout Bolivia as participants in talks between the government of President Hugo Banzer and coca growers failed to reach a satisfactory agreement. The dispute with coca growers revolved around the government's reduction in March of the compensation paid per hectare for voluntary eradication of coca crops from US$2,500 to US$1,650. This reduction significantly affected the ability of the 300,000 persons in the Chaparé, the major coca producing area in the country, to make a living. The government's anti-drug trafficking plan called for continuing reductions until the compensation plan could be phased out in 2002.

The issue for protestors was economic survival. Coca growers had seen earlier crop substitution plans fail, and they had suffered from a lack of technical assistance. Bolivian Vice President Jorge Quiroga reported, after a trip to Washington to try to reinstate the funds lost when U.S. anti-narcotics aid was cut from US$40 million to US$12 million, that the aid would be reinstated but designated for interdiction efforts. Money for voluntary eradication programs, technical assistance, and alternative development was to be eliminated or reduced significantly. Critics of this approach pointed out that this shift back to interdiction efforts was counterproductive, and moreover, would be focused on material aid, most particularly weapons and ammunition for the Bolivian military. Rather than providing alternative means of making a living for the peasants growing coca, U.S. funds would be used to stifle dissent.

At the beginning of the strike, coca growers blocked the highways, leading to the deaths of seven strikers during clashes with the police.

Mineworkers on a break at Cerro Rico, Potosí, Bolivia, hold plastic bags filled with coca leaves. Working at elevations of over four thousand meters, miners chew coca leaves to ward off exhaustion, altitude sickness, and hunger.

Photograph by Douglas Hecock

Delfín Olivera, speaking for the Federación de Campesinos Cocaleros (Federation of Coca Farmers), insisted that the government fulfil its agreement of the preceding October calling for the "installation of an agroindustrial complex" and the delivery of alternative development plans in the Chaparé. In this way, according to Olivera, the coca fields could be replaced peacefully. Olivera himself was serving on a congressional human rights delegation which had gone to the Chaparé to investigate government repression of the peasants.

While the Bolivian minister of labor admitted that the government had caused the violence to escalate through its use of force in the first days of the strike, another minister declared that the drug traffickers, not campesinos, were causing the trouble in the Chaparé "not to support the salary demands of the workers but to prevent the government from carrying out its eradication plans." On 8 April, police and military were sent in large numbers into the area to remove the roadblocks. After resistance, they opened the roads to the hundreds of buses and trucks that had been stranded for nearly a week. In a further move, 3,000 troops were sent into the Chaparé to destroy coca fields on 15 April. At least one campesino was killed and a large number wounded. Future U.S. government aid to Banzer would depend at least partly on perceptions that his administration was making significant efforts to reduce coca cultivation in his country.

Based on "Bolivia: Violence Increases as Strike Continues," NotiSur (Latin America Data Base, University of New Mexico, ISSN 1089–1560), 17 April 1998.

With the collapse of the Soviet Union in the late 1980s and early 1990s, anticommunism as a basis for U.S. policy toward Latin America collapsed as well. Quickly, however, it was replaced by a threat far more immediate: narcotics. For many countries in Latin America, the U.S. "war on communism" would be replaced by a "war on drugs."

Narcotics is perhaps the most internally destructive social problem for the countries of the hemisphere. Within the borders of the United States, the economic cost was estimated in the 1980s to be $110 billion a year in drug sales, and $60 billion in other costs from drug abuse and drug related accidents.[1] The toll in quality of life resulting from drug related crime in many U.S. cities is unmeasurable in money terms. The cost has not been borne solely by the United States. Latin American nations such as Colombia and now Mexico have found that the narcotics traffic is a threat to their internal security and even national sovereignty. Faced with the drug crisis, the Bolivian government has become tied more and more firmly to the U.S. embassy because its national enforcement mechanisms have proved inadequate. Peru has seen the development of a pernicious interrelationship between guerrilla groups and drug smugglers in the countryside, with the guerrillas providing "protection" for the traffickers. The head of the Panamanian armed forces has been removed by a U.S. military invasion, ostensibly for his connection to the drug traffic (see chapter 7). Everywhere in the hemisphere, including the United States, the corruption of political institutions and enforcement agencies has weakened the efforts to deal with the crisis.

The fact that most illegal drugs originate outside the United States has led to two major approaches to enforcement: the destruction of sources of supply—both crops and laboratory complexes—and the interdiction of shipments before they can be brought to market in the United States. The problem has generally been laid at the doorstep of the supplying nations, to their chagrin. Efforts to reduce demand within the United States have stressed tougher criminal penalties rather than treatment and have been largely ineffective. Although this focus seemed to be changing somewhat with the Clinton administration, the historical approach has been to encourage other countries to destroy drug operations with the help of U.S. money, equipment, and even agents. As of 1998, that approach seemed to be taking on renewed vigor. (See Point-Counterpoint, "Cocaine, Jobs, and Strikes in Bolivia.") The presence of U.S. law enforcement officials in other nations has caused considerable resentment and has again raised issues of sovereignty. Of course, the position of the host government in dealing with all of these issues has been extremely delicate. Latin American countries have been most extensively affected by these policies, as the region produces or transships over 90 percent of the marijuana and 80 percent of the cocaine entering the United States.[2]

The nature of the problem has varied to some degree with the nature and availability of the current drug of choice. Latin American traffickers have proved able to adjust quickly to the market. The major surge in drug use in recent years began with marijuana in the 1960s. In the 1970s and 1980s, cocaine was the major problem. By the 1990s, heroin traffic was a major concern. The *New York Times* reported in mid-1993 that both the amount and purity of the heroin supply were up, and that heroin use was booming. At that time, 25% of the investigations carried out by the Drug Enforcement Administration involved heroin. In 1988, 28% of New York drug arrests involved heroin, versus 55% for cocaine; five years later heroin accounted for 40%, cocaine 47%, and dual addiction was on the rise. Both Mexico and Colombia, long involved in marijuana and cocaine trafficking, were reportedly getting into the heroin business to meet changing market conditions.[3]

Historical Background

Although the drug problem dramatically escalated from the 1960s to the 1990s, it is by no means of recent origin. Drug smuggling in the hemisphere has existed since colonial times. Countries close to the United States—particularly Mexico and Cuba—have been used by some U.S. citizens, at least since the beginning of Prohibition, as places where societal and even legal controls could be disregarded. U.S.-organized crime syndicates had been involved in Cuba since the 1920s, and Havana was known as a "good liberty port" for the U.S. Navy. By the 1950s, the country was welcoming almost 300,000 tourists yearly, and as one prominent historian of U.S.-Cuban relations has noted, the tourist trade "expanded principally around commercialized vice, largely gambling, prostitution, and drugs."[4] Mexico served much the same purpose with even less travel cost, and a walk across the line to Tijuana or Ciudad Juárez was quicker than a flight or boat ride to Cuba.

U.S. attempts to control negative aspects of drug use began long ago as well. Concern was registered as early as the 1890s. The first federal legislation regulating narcotics, the Pure Food and Drug Act of 1906, required labeling of items containing cannabis, morphine, cocaine, and chloral hydrate. During the 1920s, Mexican agricultural workers in U.S. southwestern fields were linked with marijuana use. This link was used as one excuse among others for forcing them back across the border at the time of the Depression. Marijuana, which could be produced north as well as south of the border, seemed virtually impossible to eradicate. The Federal Bureau of Narcotics was reluctant to become involved in enforcement after the controversial experience with alcohol prohibition, which had been terminated in 1933 after widespread public violation. In 1937, however, a transfer tax on marijuana was imposed on the substance by the U.S. government, and severe penalties for illegal use or possession were eventually adopted. The limited use of this drug during the 1930s prevented these laws from affecting many people outside of urban slums and shanty towns; only in the 1960s did its use become widespread enough that the penalties began to concern the general public.[5]

Mexico — Problems of Proximity

Mexico can be taken as an example of the difficulties caused by the narcotics traffic and the U.S. approach to enforcement. As noted previously, Mexico has been a source of marijuana for the United States for several decades. It also affords a favorable climate for the production of opium poppies used in the production of heroin, and has been used regularly as a transshipment point for other controlled substances. Questions of sovereignty surfaced as early as 1941, when U.S. officials asked the Avila Camacho government to formalize an agreement on the use of American drug enforcement personnel in Mexican territory. Although U.S. agents were already operating there, concerns were raised about the political consequences of formalization (interestingly, by the State Department rather than by the Mexicans), and the earlier informal arrangement continued.[6]

As use rose in the 1960s, and as the heavy penalties began to be applied to children of affluent families as well as to the poor, interest in interdicting the supply of narcotics from Mexico grew. By 1969 with Richard Nixon in office, the problem had attracted the attention of Deputy Attorney General Richard Kleindienst, a resident of Arizona on the U.S.-Mexican border and father of four. Particularly concerned about the problem of marijuana supplies, he visited Mexico to encourage officials there to go after smugglers. Frustrated in the attempt, he recommended that border customs enforcement be tightened in order to get the attention of the Mexicans. In this first "Operation Intercept," border traffic slowed to a crawl as customs agents checked every car and truck coming across the line. U.S. army mobile radar units were set up to watch for aircraft. This massive effort did not significantly slow the marijuana trade but did lead to greater cooperation from Mexican officials, including permission for American agents to conduct surveillance of Mexican poppy and marijuana fields. Through the 1970s, the two countries sustained a cooperative effort against production and trafficking. Nevertheless, Mexico replaced Turkey as the source of most of the U.S. heroin supply when the latter country shut down production in 1972. Mexican officials declared a "Permanent Campaign" against drugs, and significant inroads were made in the supply of Mexican marijuana. There was no corresponding drop in U.S. consumption, however, as other sources of supply quickly expanded.[7] This phenomenon — the quick replacement of supply from other sources when any one supplier cuts back — has become characteristic of the struggle against narcotics up to the present time.

Despite a considerable expenditure of time and resources by both countries, the trade continued and grew during the 1980s. In fact, it became the greatest source of tension in U.S.-Mexican relations when an American Drug Enforcement Administration (DEA) agent, Enrique Camarena, was kidnapped in Guadalajara and killed by members of the drug cartel led by Rafael Caro Quintero. American public opinion was inflamed as Mexican officials seemed to be dragging their feet, and a second Operation Intercept was put into place to force Mexican cooperation. When Camarena's body was finally recovered, it was clear that the agent had been tortured before his death, and later tapes were found of his recorded questioning. Caro Quintero had fled to Costa Rica with the aid of some Mexican government officials. Captured and returned to Mexico, he remains in prison. Collusion with at least some authorities continued, since his jailhouse accommodations, for a time at least, were quite luxurious.

Meanwhile, the Mexican government and the Mexican public have been resentful of American attempts to define the problem as Mexican. Relations were further inflamed by the kidnapping and delivery to U.S. authorities of Ruben Zuno Arce, another suspect in the Camarena case, by bounty hunters in Mexico. He was convicted by a Los Angeles jury in 1990 for crimes related to the murder. Still, drug related corruption within Mexican political institutions, the increasing use of drugs in Mexico itself, and the concern of President Carlos Salinas's government to avoid any impediment to the successful conclusion of the North American Free Trade Agreement (NAFTA) led him to create an assistant attorney general position to coordinate anti-drug activities and to expand resource commitments. Both Presidents George Bush and William Clinton pledged to prohibit further kidnappings, but the U.S. Supreme Court's decision in 1992 that nothing in the current extradition treaty prohibited such kidnappings led Salinas to seek a new legal agreement. He also moved at the same time to clean up the Mexican system of law enforcement by appointing a new attorney general, the greatly respected human rights activist Jorge Carpizo MacGregor in January 1993.

The potential destruction of Mexican social and political institutions by the drug trade was brought forcefully home to both countries when, in June 1993, Cardinal Juan Jesús Posadas Ocampo was shot in Guadalajara. The Roman Catholic prelate, who had spoken out against drug traffickers in this western city which had also been the site of Camarena's abduction, was killed when his automobile entered the airport. Apparently not the direct target, he seems to have died in a shootout between drug lords, but questions and rumors continue in Mexico and in the United States. Salinas, furious over the shooting and concerned about the effect on NAFTA negotiations, gave authorities wide latitude to crack down on drugs, but the widespread corruption of both Mexican police and judiciary officials made many on both sides of the border cynical about the possibilities of success. The Mexican attorney general himself was quoted in the *New York Times* as saying that he was "surrounded by traitors," and subsequent events have borne him out.[8]

In the wake of the prelate's shooting, a number of significant discoveries were made, including an unfinished tunnel leading from a Tijuana warehouse apparently to an unfinished cannery on Otay Mesa near San Diego. Complete with ventilating systems and lights, the 65-foot deep tunnel would have stretched 1,400 feet across the border between the two countries. Another tunnel had been found some months earlier between Ciudad Juárez and El Paso. Even worse in its implications was the connection made between a Latino gang in San Diego and the Mexican drug trade. Six members of the gang were apprehended by Mexican authorities in connection with the killing of the Cardinal. More than thirty gang members from the United States were believed to have been recruited by the Arellano drug family, who may have intended to gun down rival trafficker Joaquín (El Chapo) Guzmán rather than the prelate.

Assassinations have continued, threatening the very fabric of Mexican political life. On 23 March 1994, Luis Donaldo Colosio, the presidential candidate of the official party (the Partido Revolucionario Institucional, or PRI) was gunned down in Tijuana at a campaign appearance in a poor barrio. Rumors that his murder involved drug traffickers have swirled ever since, fueled by the subsequent killings of the Tijuana police chief (only five weeks later) and other officials close to the investigation. Another assassination, that of Francisco Ruiz Massieu, the number two man in the PRI, seemed to involve the immediate family of Carlos Salinas, who had yielded the presidency to Ernesto Zedillo in December 1994. Carlos Salinas's brother, Raul, was arrested in connection with the death. Francisco Ruiz Massieu, the victim, was the former husband of Carlos and Raul Salinas's sister, Adriana. Antonio Lozano, Zedillo's attorney general and a member of the opposition PAN party, was also investigating the ties between Raul Salinas and Mexico's drug cartels. Ruiz Massieu's brother Mario, who had been in charge of anti-narcotics efforts during the Carlos Salinas administration — and, moreover, had been in charge of investigating his brother's death — came under suspicion as well and fled to the United States. Reports indicated that Mario Ruiz Massieu had actually put in place a network of narcotics enforcement officials who facilitated movements of large drug shipments into the United States.[9]

Continued drug related violence in Mexican border cities and the seeming inability of the Mexican government to successfully prosecute even flagrant drug traffickers such as Rafael Muñoz Talavera have been discouraging to U.S. drug enforcement personnel and to Mexican government officials. A U.S. official summed up this discouragement when he commented about Mr. Muñoz, "We knew he was going to walk from the date of his arrest. . . . In Mexico, the guy with the biggest pocketbook always wins."[10]

Colombia and Narcoterrorism

The case of Colombia developed somewhat differently. Farther away geographically but still very close to the southeastern United States and particularly Florida, Colombia historically has not been granted very high priority in U.S. foreign policy concerns. Although it enjoyed brief attention in the 1960s, when it was touted as a "showcase" of Alliance for Progress programs, it has more usually been ignored. This situation changed substantially, beginning in the late 1960s, when it became apparent that it was the linchpin of the narcotics traffic from Latin America.

Conditions, historical circumstances, and geography made Colombia a natural site for the growth of drug trafficking. Smuggling had been endemic since the colonial period, when its trade was restricted in deference to the viceroyalties of New Spain (Mexico) and Peru. Smuggling syndicates were regenerated in the late 1950s and 1960s with the tight controls on imports and exports that the government imposed in order to stabilize the balance of payments and to support its import substitution policies. Colombia's social system was particularly unstable in this period, suffering both from the effects of widespread poverty and of a long-term undeclared civil war in the countryside, known locally as "La Violencia." The violent nature of this conflict can be discerned from its name, the capital letters used to characterize it, and estimates of the dead range from 200,000 upwards. Hundreds of orphans crowded the cities, the country suffered from one of the highest kidnapping rates in the world, and crime prevention had largely broken down. Located conveniently at the northernmost point of South America, with coasts on both the Caribbean and the Pacific, it was only 1,000 miles southeast of Miami across the Caribbean.

As the drug trade grew in scale and profits, Colombia not only produced cocaine for trade, but also processed and transported huge amounts from Peru and Bolivia. Its climate was also favorable for the production of extremely high-grade marijuana, also destined for the U.S. market. Exports took off from the Guajira peninsula and initially were flown and/or transported by boat across the Caribbean or through waystations in Central America to the United States. The destination was usually Miami. Crackdowns in Florida by U.S. agents led to the creation of new routes through Mexico, although these required including Mexicans in operations, involved longer distances, and were generally less convenient. The House Select Committee on Narcotics Abuse and Control, which was established in 1976, called Colombia "the single most important staging point for cocaine delivery to the United States."[11]

Initially the Colombian government responded cooperatively, accepting a long-term assistance program developed by the Department of State and enacting a number of anti-drug laws by the end of 1977. Narcotics sales, however, were probably highly beneficial to the Colombian economy, which has unquestionably improved since the 1960s. By the late 1970s it was estimated that illegal drug exports were worth more than the nation's legal coffee trade. Despite U.S. assistance of $16 million in 1979 and 1980, the situation was grave.[12] The Colombian government had largely lost control of its national territory to drug cartels by the early 1980s and has still not regained control.

Although information about the value of the cocaine trade from Colombia is highly speculative, it is likely that it is in the range of at least $1 billion a year. Amounts available to fight the trade, with or without U.S. assistance, have been minimal in comparison. It is not surprising, then, that the trade has continued with little slackening into the 1990s.

At some point in the very early 1980s, two major drug cartels developed, one centered in Cali, in the southern part of the country, and the other in Medellín, very close by plane to Panama. Both cartels were ruthless. The struggle between the cartels themselves brought violence not only to Colombia but to surrounding countries and directly to the United States, where Colombian cocaine wars were played out in the streets of New York and other cities. Further, the cartels set out to intimidate the organs of justice which attempted to control them and the press which tried to shed light on their activities. Dozens of Colombian judges have been murdered, as well as many journalists. Many citizens who had nothing to do with drugs or law enforcement were also killed by car bombs or caught in cross-fires. Cartel hit men, known as *sicarios*, have terrorized the country. Among the dead in the 1980s were Justice Minister Rodrigo Lara Bonilla, Attorney General Carlos Mauro Hoyos Jiménez, and the head of the narcotics unit of the National Police, Colonel Jaime Ramírez Gómez. The Medellín cartel was generally regarded as the more vicious, and most of the political murders have been attributed to them.

Startlingly, the Medellín cartel offered in 1984 to pay off the country's national debt, estimated at between $11 billion and $14 billion, but the government was unwilling to deal and the violence continued. In 1987, the Colombian Supreme Court overturned the Extradition Treaty which, since 1979, had permitted drug traffickers to be sent to the United States for trial,

Casket and funeral procession for Colombian Liberal Party presidential candidate
Luis Carlos Galán, Bogotá, Colombia, August 1989. Many Colombians saw the
forty-five-year-old Galán as a charismatic and dynamic leader, one courageous
enough to confront cocaine cartels and the corrupting influence of drugs within
the Colombian political system. His assassination on the campaign trail intensified
a cruel "drug war" in Colombia and led to increased intervention from the United
States. During the procession, politicians walked beside Galán's casket, and thousands of police lined Bogotá's principal avenue. The close to one million Colombians along the route waved goodbye with white handkerchiefs and chanted,
"Justicia, Justicia, Justicia."

Photograph by Michael Edward Stanfield

leaving the cartels without even the threat of U.S. enforcement as long as cartel leaders stayed in their own country. Only Carlos Lehder among the important cartel leaders had actually been brought to the United States for trial.
A Colombian who had lived in New York as a child, Lehder was deported to
his native country in 1975 after serving a two-year sentence on a drug conviction. Lehder then become a major figure in the transport of cocaine and
marijuana, establishing a small fleet of airplanes and developing Caribbean
refueling stations for his shipments. Before his apprehension in 1987, he had
established his own political party and distributed 1,000 peso notes to those
attending his rallies. Increasingly erratic personal behavior, perhaps caused

by an addiction to cocaine, may have led cartel members to be willing to give him up. Still, his apprehension and extradition led to considerable Colombian resentment toward U.S. President Ronald Reagan as well as the Colombian president, Virgilio Barco. Barco himself was dismayed when the Reagan administration's 1987 budget significantly reduced the money available for anti-narcotics programs within the United States. He complained to a U.S. drug official that while Colombia was "paying a terrible price," the United States was "not serious about the problem." Some Colombian officials were calling for the legalization of drugs in order to undermine the economic basis of the cartels.[13]

Although the Colombian government has made significant progress against the Medellín and Cali cartels in recent years, including the arrests of a number of the principal leaders, in 1996 President Clinton declared that Colombia was failing to cooperate in the struggle against the narcotics trade. The de-certification made Colombia ineligible for U.S. aid and ensured that the United States would vote against loans for that country from international lending agencies. Colombia was further plagued by assertions that President Ernesto Samper had received $3 million or more from drug traffickers during his election campaign. Meanwhile, Mexico was certified despite the problems, corruption, and murders discussed above. Observers felt that political considerations within the Clinton administration made the difference, rather than actual progress or the lack thereof in curbing the drug trade. Clinton, after all, had arranged for almost $13 billion in loans to Mexico after the collapse of the peso in 1994, and Mexico was seen as having special status as an equal member of NAFTA. Colombians, of course, were indignant. President Samper, who has vigorously denied any connection with narcotics traffickers, responded that he would "not accept any foreign intervention in the solution of our crisis." Even the Mexicans, despite having been certified, complained that the process itself was a serious irritant and a hindrance to cordial cooperation.[14]

Point-Counterpoint: Cocaine, Colombia, and
George Bush's War on Drugs

"To suggest that a criminal activity that threatens the whole nation, including the economy, may be tolerated because of its profits is absurd. The real economics of cocaine is the law of supply and demand. This is about the only law the cocaine traffic does not break. More than half the world's supply of cocaine is consumed in the United States. Until this voracious demand is curbed, Colombian men and women will die vainly trying to block the way of a demand-driven tide of illegal cocaine exports."

—*Victor Mosquera Chaux, Colombian Ambassador to the United States,* Washington Post, *4 January 1989.*

"The cocaine cartel does not begin in Medellín. It begins in the streets of New York, Miami, Los Angeles and every city where crack is bought and sold."

—*Nancy Reagan, in a speech to the United Nations (quoted by Mosquera Chaux in his editorial, above),* Washington Post, *4 January 1989.*

"With narcotics, the mestizos, mulattos, and blacks . . . have had the opportunities to enter consumer society and gain substantial wealth. . . . The best vehicles that are driven in the city of Medellín are in the hands of people who have black or dark skins. . . . I consider the drug trade to be the support of a country in crisis. This explains the contradictions in the establishment, which on the one hand denounces it and on the other hand lives with it and benefits from it."

—*Mario Arango, Medellín City Council member and author of bestseller sympathetic to drug barons as "first generation capitalists interested in . . . a better life for their children."* Washington Post, *8 January 1989.*

"Demand remains the crucial front and it is here where Bush's new drug campaign, starting in the nation's capital, must and will be cheered on around the world. This means not only law enforcement but education and treatment. Unlike Latins, we cannot plausibly argue that we do not have the resources to tame the beast. Under the best of conditions, the effort will be time consuming, erratic and often disappointing. Not the least of the new campaign's benefits, however, is the new authority it gives Bush to go back to the Latins and ask them to ratchet up their commitment, too."

—*Stephen S. Rosenfeld, editorial,* Washington Post, *17 March 1989.*

"You're talking about sovereignty issues — here you would have a foreign government bring military forces. . . . We would have a negative impact."

—*John C. Lawn, Drug Enforcement Agency administrator, Washington Post, 27 May 1989.*

"If intercontinental ballistic missiles were being fired at American cities from Peru and Bolivia, surely our government would have devised a plan to knock out the enemy. . . . Why, then, do we treat the threat posed by the international cocaine cartels so lightly?"

—*Representative Stephen J. Solarz (Democrat-New York), Washington Post, 27 May 1989.*

"Those of you who depend on cocaine have created the largest, most vicious criminal enterprise the world has ever known. . . . Colombia's survival as the oldest democracy in Latin America is now at risk, but so is the safety of your streets. . . . They [the drug traffickers] must understand that they are international fugitives, on the run from civilized society everywhere. There is no home for them. . . . There should be no market for them."

—*Virgilio Barco, President of Colombia, in a message given to U.S. broadcast networks for the American public. Washington Post, 29 August 1989.*

The War on Drugs

By the 1980s, many American politicians were sufficiently alarmed by the drug problem in the United States that they were beginning to advocate the increasing use of the U.S. military in interdiction efforts. Advocates of this militarization ranged from liberal to conservative, but were particularly concentrated in areas in which narcotics were causing widespread crime and social breakdown. Examples were New York City's mayor, Edward Koch, and Representative Charles Rangel, both Democrats, and New York's Republican Senator, Alphonse D'Amato. Generally, proponents supported the use of U.S. military forces in interdiction and deployment in foreign countries to destroy drug production at its origins. Not all politicians were enthusiastic about the idea, however. For example, the Department of Defense — especially Secre-

taries Caspar Weinberger and Frank Carlucci—felt that interdiction was unlikely to be effective and that combat readiness for the military's primary mis-
sions would be impaired.[15]

Concern about the drug problem was becoming an important political
issue, as more and more cities were disrupted by the increasing availability
of crack cocaine, which was cheap, easy to use, and devastating to social co-
hesion in the inner cities. In April 1986, with Congress calling for effective action, President Ronald Reagan issued a National Security Decision Directive
addressing the problem. Unsurprisingly, as one prominent historian of U.S.
drug policy has noted, he once again "looked abroad for a solution to the
nation's ills."[16] This document put both drug interdiction and control at the
source within the responsibilities of the U.S. military. Potential for violations
against the sovereignty of other nations were precluded to some degree by
the guidelines set down: (1) the U.S. military would only be sent to participate in drug enforcement measures at the invitation of host governments; (2)
U.S. military activities were limited to support functions; and (3) U.S. civilian agencies (usually the DEA) would direct all operations. Congress responded by significantly increasing the Department of Defense budget for
narcotics control.[17]

The years 1987 and 1988 saw the use of the military in interdiction efforts
increase substantially. Navy ships with Coast Guard officials on board stopped
suspicious vessels, and searches were then carried out by the Coast Guard personnel. These efforts resulted in twenty vessel seizures, more than 100 arrests,
and the confiscation of 225,000 pounds of marijuana—but only 550 pounds
of cocaine. The Navy, the Air Force, and the Army provided assistance with
surveillance. Most of these efforts were focussed on the Caribbean (the obvious route for much of the drug traffic coming out of Colombia), the Gulf of
Mexico, and the U.S.-Mexican border. A 1988 study by the U.S. General Accounting Office, however, found that there was no evidence that the interdiction effort was cost effective in the long term, as supplies in the United
States were not greatly affected.[18]

Attempts to use the U.S. military to destroy the sources of supply were
largely focused on Peru and Bolivia. These Andean countries have been the
major suppliers of the coca which is processed into cocaine and distributed
by the Colombians. In Peru, production has centered around the Upper Hual-
laga Valley and in Bolivia, in the high mountain area of Yungas and the Ama-
zon belt of the Chaparé. Coca growing has been traditional in these areas since

before the arrival of the Spanish, and initially both governments were reluctant to become involved in anti-coca efforts. This reluctance was at least partly due to the potential economic effect on peasant producers. By the mid-1970s, coca paste and cocaine were pouring out of both countries. Although each took some anti-cocaine measures at the national level, including the encouragement of crop substitution, the supply was not diminished significantly if at all. Little U.S. aid was offered or requested in the 1970s, and DEA agents were stationed only in the national capitals rather than in the growing regions. In 1979 Bolivia suffered a coup by military officers led by General Luis García Meza. Members of his government were reported to be profiting heavily from the cocaine trade.[19] By the mid-1980s, however, both countries were more cooperative and the situation in the United States had become so acute that it was affecting the political climate.

Operation Blast Furnace in July 1986 is probably the best-known U.S. military involvement in drug eradication efforts. Lasting four months, the 150-man mission, complete with helicopters, provided air transportation and communications support for Bolivian narcotics police and DEA personnel in the search for and destruction of cocaine laboratories. Although the operation was successful in disrupting coca purchases and processing, temporarily bringing the price peasants received for coca below the break-even point, the supply of cocaine in the United States did not seem to have diminished. Once the Americans returned to the United States, moreover, coca leaf prices quickly recovered their former level.[20]

Operation Just Cause

Despite the relative ineffectiveness of both interdiction and supply reduction efforts, the Bush administration continued to insist on the importance of military involvement in the eradication of the "scourge." In December 1989, President Bush authorized the most heavy-handed American use of the U.S. military in Latin America in more than two decades. Claiming that Panamanian strongman Manuel Noriega was in league with narcotics traffickers —as he certainly seems to have been—and because less direct methods, including CIA covert action plans, had failed to remove him, Bush ordered the invasion of Panama by U.S. forces. (See chapter 7.) Although Noriega's involvement in drug trafficking was not the only reason given for forcibly removing him, it was certainly one of the most often cited.

Operation Just Cause succeeded in its primary mission. Noriega was apprehended when he surrendered to U.S. forces after he had taken refuge at the Papal Nunciature. It was successful as well in destroying the Panama Defense Forces, the military organization which had evolved out of the Panamanian National Guard on which Noriega based his power. The largest combat operation since the Vietnam War, it also seems to have been responsible for the deaths of hundreds of civilians, as the working class neighborhoods of Chorrillo and San Miguelito were heavily bombarded.[21] Still, recent reports on Panama indicate that it remained a major transit point for narcotics, despite the inauguration of a U.S.-sponsored government under Guillermo Endara. Noriega, indicted and convicted in U.S. courts, continued to appeal his case.

More seriously, questions have been raised about Bush's real motives for the invasion. Although Noriega, under indictment in Miami for drug trafficking at the time of the invasion, was certainly a visible irritant, his activities had been known to Washington and tolerated for some time. Noriega himself had served for years as a CIA asset and aided the Republican administrations in the 1980s in their Central American activities. Rumors and accusations have circulated since the invasion that the real purpose was to destroy the PDF so that Panama would be unable to take over the canal on schedule in 1999.[22] It is also rumored that Bush, who had served as CIA director in the early 1970s, feared that Noriega might reveal something about that association and therefore wanted him under U.S. control. If so, nothing new came to light during the trials of Noriega in the United States.

Diplomatic Effects of the War on Drugs

Operation Just Cause itself caused a good deal of indignation throughout Latin America. In order to defuse some of the criticism and to enhance cooperation with the Andean nations, especially Colombia, Peru, and Bolivia, President Bush attended an Andean summit in Cartagena, Colombia, in February 1990. The very fact that Bush attended such a meeting outside the United States and against the advice of those concerned about his security was encouraging to Latin Americans. Although Peruvian President Alan García initially refused to attend as a protest against the U.S. invasion of Panama, Bush's agreement to begin withdrawing troops changed his mind. The summit went well, as the U.S. president promised to emphasize not only military and police action but also economic development (complete with $2.2 billion in development funds to ease the transition away from coca production, which were ultimately not forthcoming). Washington's willingness on this occasion to acknowledge that demand was a major issue, not just supply, also led to better feelings.[23]

However, the spirit of cooperation did not last long, as American actions, including the seizure of two Colombian freighters within that country's 200-mile limit, continued to irritate Andean leaders. President-elect César Gaviria of Colombia explicitly rejected an increasing role for his country's military in the anti-narcotics effort, and asked for expanded trade and international aid to rebuild his country's judicial system instead. He further emphasized that the Colombian government would make the ending of domestic narcoterrorism rather than the control of the international drug trade its first priority. He also announced that he would not extradite Colombia's drug lords to the United States if they would surrender to government authorities and stand trial. Somewhat surprisingly, some of them did, although it proved difficult to keep them in jail, and the level of domestic violence from the narcotics traffic declined.

Bolivia and Peru were more willing to comply with U.S. insistence on a military effort to fight narcotics production and trade. However, they had both declared by September 1990 that they would not accept the assistance offered them by the U.S. government because of the heavy reliance on military rather than economic development strategies. Bolivian President Jaime Paz Zamora was particularly concerned that an increased role for the military might well undermine civilian political control in his country. However, under heavy pressure he eventually acquiesced. Peruvian President Alberto Fujimori was faced with an even more difficult situation. Concerned that a military crackdown on coca-producing peasants would drive them into the camp of the highly effective Sendero Luminoso rebels, he continued to resist U.S. policy suggestions.

Future Prospects

As the region moved into the mid-1990s, prospects for bilateral and/or multilateral cooperation on drug enforcement were increasing. Mexico, Peru, Bolivia, and other countries were faced with increasing problems with drug use, an inability to control even the domestic crime generated by the trade, and continuing problems with the corruption of public enforcement institutions.

The United States was faced with many of the same problems. Many inner cities were descending into violence. Although the Los Angeles riot of 1992 was not directly related to drugs, it is clear that the situation was exacerbated by narcotics problems and the widespread availability of weapons. When the United States sent troops into Somalia to end the fighting between competing warlords in 1992, observers pointed out that U.S. troops might more reasonably be sent into U.S. cities on the same basis. The AIDS epidemic as well was related to drug use; many new cases appeared among drug users and their sexual partners. U.S. prisons were overflowing with drug offenders, incarcerated for long periods of time as a result of mandatory sentencing guidelines. Still, the major traffickers had been harmed very little and drug supplies continued to be plentiful, despite the expenditure of $100 billion in federal, state, and local taxes on drug enforcement programs between 1981 and 1992.[24] The Clinton administration had clearly come to realize that enforcement alone, within the United States or outside of it, was woefully inadequate to deal with the problem. Clinton's appointment of Lee Brown, a Ph.D. criminologist with experience as chief of police of two of the country's most drug-plagued cities, Houston and New York, and his elevation to cabinet status, signaled a focus on the problem. Brown indicated that not only would he move to put more police officers on the streets and encourage moves to more community-based policing, he would also emphasize treatment. The funding for this treatment would be included in the administration's health care package. Meanwhile, Attorney General Janet Reno ordered a review of mandatory sentencing guidelines as a first step to dealing with the severe overcrowding of prison facilities.[25] A recent related issue has been the disparity between sentencing for crimes involving crack cocaine versus powder, with crack involving far heavier penalties. As crack is more closely associated with the African-American population than powder, differing penalties hit Blacks harder.

Although Brown was replaced by General Barry R. McCaffrey in 1996, approaches that included both supply and demand sides seemed likely to continue. Sufficient funding, however, was an issue and continued to be in 1998. Still, these efforts indicated that the Clinton administration was willing to deal with the demand side of the question, which must have been encouraging to Latin leaders who had felt victimized by the U.S. insistence on waging the "war on drugs" on the supply side — within their countries — and letting them face the consequences of retaliation largely alone.

Therefore, Latin American countries as well as the United States were seeing their interests in dealing with narcotics rapidly beginning to converge. The Cartagena meetings had offered a moment of hope; although they were followed by frustration and disillusionment, they pointed the way to future cooperation. Moreover, it seemed likely that the possible linkage of important issues with that of drug control could give impetus to more bilateral or multilateral action. Aid with crop substitution programs in Peru and Bolivia, a settlement of Peruvian debt questions, the establishment of mechanisms for commodity price stability for the Colombians, and the approval of NAFTA for the Mexicans might provide incentives for cooperation on narcotics.[26] The impetus for the nations of the Western Hemisphere to work together, given both domestic and international pressures, seems to be great. However, it remains to be seen whether this relatively favorable climate will lead to any real improvements.

CHAPTER 10

EPILOGUE: THE ISSUES BEFORE US

As we move into the new millennium, relations between the United States and Latin America can no longer be kept at arm's length. What occurs in the countries to the South — economic, social, or political — will impact the United States, whether or not U.S. administrations have relevant policies to deal with the consequences. At the same time, outside influence in the hemisphere is no longer a threat, imagined or otherwise, to U.S. national security. This development has led to the demise of the Monroe Doctrine as the organizing principle of U.S. policy, as problems with Latin America have increasingly involved significant U.S. domestic problems.[1] The historic emphasis on Mexico and the Caribbean basin, a result of proximity in an earlier time, has had to expand to include a far larger area, a result of many factors including easier communications and travel and increased trade (legal and illegal).

U.S. policymakers now must consider domestic issues in formulating policies for the region. Sponsoring surrogate wars in Central America, for example, had severely negative consequences as perhaps 10 percent of Central America's population fled north into U.S. territory.[2] The chaos in the region also made it an area ripe for the development of illegal trade in drugs and, in the case of Panama in particular, money laundering. While the demise of the Cold War has made armed intervention, either with U.S. or surrogate troops, less likely, the possibility of the use of force continues in relation to other problems. At the same time, issues of sovereignty, from the point of view of Latin American nations, remain salient.

Two recent examples illustrate this point. In May 1998, U.S. authorities carried out a sting operation denominated "Casablanca" in which 26 Mexican bank employees were arrested on money laundering charges after being lured across the border. Months later, Mexican Secretary of Foreign Relations Rosario Green Macías was still insisting that this action jeopardized U.S.-Mexican relations as a violation of sovereignty because some of the U.S. investigations were conducted within Mexico itself and without consultation. The secretary commented that, "In the absence of communication, cooperation, confidence, and respect, our relationship will risk going off track. Only with dialogue can we avoid situations that make understanding difficult." She also reiterated that President Ernesto Zedillo intended to prosecute anyone (meaning U.S. enforcement officers) who had broken any Mexican law during the operation.[3] Meanwhile, the corruption of Mexican enforcement agencies made U.S. officials leery of such cooperation in drug cases.

Also during the summer of 1998, negotiations with Panama for the development of a multilateral anti-drug center at Howard Air Force Base began to break down around issues of sovereignty. Despite the fact that polls indicate that a majority of Panamanians favor the establishment of the center, Panamanian President Ernesto Pérez Balladares has been attacked by opposition parties on the basis that such a center would permit the continuation of a substantial U.S. military presence in the country. Pérez Balladares canceled a July referendum on the issue, fearing that opinion was turning and that his own attempts to be reelected to a second term would be imperiled. At the same time, another icon of sovereignty, the Panama Canal, reemerged as an issue. Political opponents hammered away at what they claimed was Pérez Balladares' willingness to leave much control in U.S. hands, while any Panamanian authority over the canal would rest with his family and political friends.[4]

Although U.S. policies must address these problems, there are other more positive areas where cooperation is possible. Latin American countries are attractive trading partners and present opportunities for investment. European economic integration furnishes an incentive for U.S. businesspeople and policymakers to focus on this hemisphere. Stability in the region, based on governments of consent rather than dictatorships, make it a more and more desirable field for direct investment and banking operations.

However, the traditional U.S. domination of trade with Latin America is no longer as unchallenged as in the past. Regional Latin American trade organizations are beginning to seek closer relationships with the European Union and the Far East. Although it seems likely that the United States will continue to be the major trading partner for Latin American nations, they are developing new economic relationships with other world areas. For example, when leaders of the Caribbean Community and Common Market met in the summer of 1998 to celebrate the organization's twenty-fifth anniversary, two major items on the agenda were the European Union's banana import system and further steps toward the creation of a true Caribbean common market. Mexico as well was seeking closer ties with Europe, signing an agreement in December 1997 with the EU establishing the bases for economic cooperation. In the short and long term, Latin Americans seem likely to continue to combine in trade associations among themselves and to develop ties with other world regions.

Moreover, U.S. attempts to isolate Cuba are becoming less and less effective and U.S. leaders are enforcing measures toward that end with less and less zeal. Cuba as well is actively seeking closer business relations with other countries. In 1998 the European Union invited Cuba to attend its September meetings as an observer with the Africa, Caribbean, and Pacific Group. This organization is composed of 71 former European colonies and receives special trade preferences as an EU affiliate. Although Cuba may not succeed in achieving full membership, given the EU requirements for specified goals in human rights and democracy, this acknowledgment is a first step toward some sort of agreement. As of 1998, Cuba is the only Latin American country that does not have a cooperation agreement with the EU.

In fact, despite the continued U.S. strains with Cuba, there were many signs that problems with the island were diminishing. On the U.S. side, as of 1998 President Clinton continued to waive Article III of the Helms-Burton Act, which would provide for U.S. citizens to sue foreign investors using property confiscated from U.S. owners in Cuba during the 1960s. Such a waiver not only pleased the Cubans, but also Canada and Mexico — U.S. partners in NAFTA — as well as other countries. At the same time, Clinton began to work with Congress to revoke Article IV, which permits the Department of State to deny visas to foreign businesspeople whose companies use confiscated property. Such a change is necessary to comply with an agreement made between the United States and the European Union, in return for the EU dropping charges of unfair trade practices against the United States brought before the World Trade Organization. The EU has also indicated that it would continue to pressure Cuba to democratize. Meanwhile, the United States permitted humanitarian aid shipments to Cuba to resume in June 1998.[5]

In addition, the United States and Cuba have been cooperating successfully on immigration issues. With a common goal of avoiding another mass exodus such as the Mariel boatlift or that of the early 1990s, the two countries have found common ground. Currently, Cuban immigrants are subject to most of the same entry requirements applied to other foreigners entering the United States. The Cubans themselves have successfully made illegal departure more difficult. Not surprisingly, the illegal smuggling of Cubans to the United States has become a problem.

Intriguingly, a current strain is caused by Cuban athletes who are defecting and coming to the United States, particularly in the wake of the Florida Marlins' triumph in the 1997 World Series with the help of a Cuban pitcher. The U.S. House of Representatives even introduced a bill in 1998 to waive travel prohibitions for Cuban nationals to come to the United States to play professional baseball. José Ramón Fernández, vice president of the Cuban Council of Ministers and head of the Cuban Olympic Committee, protested that Cuban exiles were luring the country's star athletes to the United States, thus perpetrating "aggression against one of the major successes of the revolution — sports."[6] Given the acrimonious and sometimes lethal conflicts of the past, however, a war of words over baseball players certainly indicated the decreasing tension in U.S.-Cuban relations.

This change of tone, at least, is partly a result of the unwillingness of the rest of Latin America to follow the United States lead in hemispheric affairs. Whether or not U.S. administrations choose to cooperate more equally with Latin American counterparts, it is plain that Latin Americans will take a stronger hand in hemispheric leadership. A recent vote in the Organization of American States left the United States isolated in its policy of sanctions against foreign companies doing business with Castro's Cuba. The United States can in no way depend on automatic support for its policies, in regard to Cuba or other issues, from hemispheric nations.

In addition, Latino populations in the United States seem certain to wield more internal political clout than ever before. Texas, California, and Florida — at a minimum — are already experiencing this phenomenon. Thus far, domestic Latino communities have not been unified in their political efforts, with Cubans (especially in Florida) being significantly more conservative than the largely Mexican communities in the Southwest and elsewhere and the Caribbean communities in the Northeast. As numbers and particularly percentages of Latinos increase, politicians, Latino and otherwise, will pay more attention to their concerns. Current efforts to restrict the access of both legal and illegal immigrants to government benefits, including education, are already being met by increasing organization within Latino communities and reinforced by soaring numbers of Latinos seeking citizenship. Meanwhile,

Latin American workers remain important to the domestic economy, whether or not their contributions are acknowledged by politicians.

The issues involving the United States with Latin America today are complex and difficult. They are international and national at one and the same time. In addition to the issues of immigration and drug trafficking highlighted in previous chapters, other problems loom; environmental protection and public health are only two which deserve careful focus and cooperation.

The challenge, however, will be to maintain a priority for peaceful and consultative relations with Latin America within the context of these increasingly difficult problems. During the Bush administration, we witnessed "a sensible abandonment of reliance on force and covert operations . . . ," albeit a result of the reaction of congressional critics and the American public to the abuse of power in Central America, in particular the Iran-Contra affair. Bush also adopted policies which to some degree improved relationships, particularly in the economic sphere, as illustrated by the renegotiation of Latin American foreign debt and the easing of trade barriers with NAFTA. However, the same administration was responsible for the first use of a sizable U.S. military force in the hemisphere in thirty years: the attack on Noriega in Panama. This invasion was condemned by a vote of 20–1 in the OAS. Still, Bush never invoked the Monroe Doctrine; no foreign threat existed.[7] However, during a visit to Bolivia and Colombia in late 1997, U.S. drug czar Barry McCaffrey struck an ominous note when he seemed to be pushing for an increased U.S. role in counterinsurgency operations. In a major speech in Colombia, he raised concerns when he declared that, "With the unholy alliance between the cocaine industry and the revolutionary guerrilla movement, the drug-trafficker threat to Colombian civil democratic society has again ratcheted up. . . . The melding of revolution and international criminal organizations has created an unprecedented threat to democracy, the rule of law, and the very fabric of society."[8]

President Clinton's administration has seemed to take no consistent policy stance. Although supporting NAFTA and bringing it along to congressional approval, it was obviously not Clinton's initiative. The later bailout of the Mexican government when the peso fell abruptly in early 1995 was characteristic of the Clinton administration's approach: pay attention only in a crisis. The occupation of Haiti as a response to large numbers of refugees attempting to enter Florida in 1994 and the signing of the Helms-Burton legislation further restricting trade with Cuba in 1996 fell into the same category.

A reasonable policy framework toward Latin America is now possible. The problems are large and close at hand, and the consequences for ignorance and evasion substantial. Clearly, however, the asymmetries of power between the U.S. and Latin American nations are changing. No longer can the United States unilaterally enforce political, military, or economic hegemony in Latin America. The opportunities for more equal and consultative relationships, however, are better than ever. It remains to be seen whether this hope will be realized in a post-Monroe Doctrine era.

Appendix

Chronology: To 1848

1776
- U.S. Declaration of Independence

1783
- Treaty of Paris

1795
- Pinckney's Treaty (Treaty of San Lorenzo) with Spain

1803
- Louisiana Purchase

1804
- Independence of Haiti from France

1810–1826
- Wars for Independence in Spanish America

1819
- Adams-Onís Treaty with Spain

1822
- Independence for Brazil
- U.S. recognition of Gran Colombia (Colombia, Venezuela, Ecuador) and Mexico

1823
- U.S. recognition of Chile and the United Provinces of La Plata
- "Monroe Doctrine" set down in U.S. president's annual message

1824
- U.S. recognition of Brazil
- U.S. recognition of Central American independence

1826
- U.S. recognition of Peru
- Inter-American Conference in Panama

1829
- Spanish intervention in Mexico

1830
- Mexican ban on further immigration from United States into Texas
- Gran Colombia splits into Colombia, Venezuela, and Ecuador

1832
- U.S. recognition of Colombia

1833
- British occupy the Falkland Islands (claimed by Argentina as the Malvinas)

1834
- U.S. recognition of Uruguay

1835
- Revolution in Texas
- U.S. recognition of Venezuela

1836
- Texas proclaims independence

1837
- U.S. recognition of independence of Texas

1838–1840
- French blockade of Buenos Aires

1838
- Texas officially withdraws its offer for annexation
- U.S. recognition of Ecuador

1842
- Two brief Mexican invasions of Texas

1844
- U.S. Senate rejects treaty calling for annexation of Texas

1845–1848
- French and British blockade of Buenos Aires

1845
- U.S. Congress approves joint resolution calling for annexation of Texas
- Mexico breaks diplomatic relations with the United States in March
- Texas approves annexation in July
- Slidell Mission to Mexico in November

1846
- General Zachary Taylor moves his troops to Rio Grande in March
- U.S. declaration of war against Mexico on 13 May

1847
- Mexico City falls to U.S. forces in September

1848
- Treaty of Guadalupe Hidalgo signed in February
- U.S. Senate approves Treaty of Guadalupe Hidalgo in March
- U.S. recognition of Bolivia

Chronology: 1848–1898

1848
- U.S. Senate approves Bidlack's Treaty with New Granada (Colombia), which had been signed in December 1846

1850
- Clayton-Bulwer Treaty signed by the United States and Britain
- Compromise of 1850

1851
- Filibustering expedition against Cuba under Narciso López

1853
- U.S. acquires Mesilla Valley from Mexico in Gadsden Purchase (Treaty of La Mesilla)
- Filibustering expedition under William Walker invades Baja California and Sonora in October, returning to the United States in May 1854

1854
- Ostend "Manifesto" on Cuba issued in October

1855
- *Water Witch* incident with Paraguay
- Filibustering expedition under William Walker to Nicaragua; Walker returns to the United States in 1857

1856
- Britain renounces its protectorate over the Mosquito Coast of Nicaragua

1857
- Second expedition by William Walker to Nicaragua fails

1858–1861
- Civil War in Mexico between Liberals and Conservatives leads to Liberal victory under Benito Juárez

1859
- McLane-Ocampo Treaty signed in December

1860
- Third expedition by William Walker to Nicaragua ends in Walker's execution in September

1861
- U.S. Civil War begins in April
- Spanish reoccupation of the Dominican Republic
- Mexico suspends debt payments in July
- Convention of London signed by Britain, France, and Spain in October

1862
- Britain, France, and Spain intervene at Veracruz, Mexico; Britain and Spain withdraw in April

1863
- French forces occupy Mexico City in May

1864
- Archduke Maximilian of Austria arrives in Mexico as emperor
- Spanish intervention in Peru

1865
- U.S. Civil War ends in April
- Spanish occupation of the Dominican Republic ends

1867
- French military withdrawal from Mexico leads to execution of Emperor Maximilian in June
- United States ratifies treaty with Nicaragua providing for a nonexclusive right of transit
- U.S. purchase of Alaska

1868–1878
- Civil war in Cuba

1879–1884
- War of the Pacific pits Chile against Peru and Bolivia

1879
- Ferdinand de Lesseps announces intention to construct canal in Panama

1889
- Failure of the French effort to build canal in Panama
- First Pan-American Conference convenes in Washington in November

1891
• *"Baltimore* Affair" with Chile

1895
• U.S. involvement in boundary dispute between Venezuela and British Guiana
• Combination civil war and independence movement begins in Cuba

1898
• U.S. battleship *Maine* sunk in Havana harbor in February
• United States declares war on Spain on 25 April
• Treaty of Paris signed in December brings war to an end

Chronology: 1898–1945

1899
• General Leonard Wood appointed military governor of Cuba in December

1900
• United States calls for second Pan American Conference in February
• First Hay-Pauncefote Treaty signed in February
• Cuban constitutional convention begins in November

1901
• Platt Amendment introduced in U.S. Senate in February
• Adoption of Cuban constitution in June
• Second Pan American conference convenes in Mexico City on 22 October; adjourns on 31 January 1902
• Second Hay-Pauncefote Treaty signed in November

1902
• U.S.-Cuban Reciprocity Treaty signed
• U.S. occupation of Cuba ends on 20 May
• Spooner Act passed by Congress on 28 June
• British-German naval blockade of Venezuela begins in December
• First statement of Drago Doctrine on 29 December

1903
• Hay-Herrán Treaty signed in January
• British-German naval blockade of Venezuela ends in February
• U.S. Senate approves Hay-Herrán Treaty in March
• Colombian Senate unanimously rejects Hay-Herrán Treaty in August
• On 3 November revolution begins in Panama
• On 4 November rebels proclaim independence of Panama

1903 (continued)
- On 6 November, United States initiates relations with rebel government and Colombian government offers to ratify Hay-Herrán Treaty
- United States extends full recognition to Panama on 13 November
- On 15 November United States and Panama begin negotiations for canal treaty
- On 18 November, United States signs treaty with Panama; approved by Panamanian government on 2 December
- U.S.-Cuban Reciprocity Treaty approved

1904
- Construction of Panama Canal begins
- On 23 February U.S. Senate approves Treaty of Panama
- United States appoints investigative commission to Dominican Republic in April
- "Roosevelt Corollary" to Monroe Doctrine put forward in December

1905
- On 7 February customs receivership treaty for Dominican Republic signed; revised treaty signed on 8 February 1907 which is later approved by U.S. Senate

1906
- Secretary of State Elihu Root tours Latin America
- Third Pan American Conference convenes on 23 July
- Taft delegation sent to Cuba in September
- Second U.S. occupation of Cuba begins on 29 September
- Theodore Roosevelt visits canal in November

1907
- Central American peace conference in Washington in November and December leads to creation of Central American Court

1909
- Second U.S. occupation of Cuba ends in January
- U.S. bankers and Honduras agree on $10 million loan in December
- U.S. expeditionary force sent to Nicaragua in December

1910
- Fourth Pan American Conference convenes in Buenos Aires on 12 July

1911
- United States and Honduras sign customs receivership treaty in January (never approved by U.S. Senate)
- Debt and receivership treaty with Nicaragua signed in June (Knox-Castrillo Treaty; never approved by US Senate)

- In December President William Howard Taft appoints U.S. customs collector for Nicaragua under executive agreement

1912
- In March Secretary of State Philander Knox visits Nicaragua
- U.S. Senate rejects customs receivership treaty with Nicaragua in May
- On 31 May U.S. troops land in Cuba (to leave in late summer)
- U.S. troops intervene in Nicaragua in August
- United States dispatches special envoys to Dominican Republic in October

1913
- Bryan-Chamorro Treaty signed
- U.S. Senate Foreign Relations Committee votes against Bryan-Chamorro Treaty in August
- U.S. President Woodrow Wilson's Mobile Speech given in October
- U.S. President Woodrow Wilson's circular note on Latin American "usurpations" on 24 November

1914
- U.S. financial adviser for Dominican Republic assigned in March
- United States signs indemnity treaty with Colombia in April
- Lansing Memorandum on Monroe Doctrine in June
- Panama Canal opens and World War I begins in August
- In November U.S.-supervised elections in Dominican Republic

1915
- First Pan American Financial Conference in May
- On 8 June Secretary of State William Jennings Bryan resigns
- On 28 July U.S. intervention in Haiti begins (ends in 1934)
- National constabulary established for Haiti in September (operational in early 1916; Haitian control in 1934)
- On 16 September U.S.-Haitian treaty signed
- On 9 October recognition of Carranza government in Mexico by United States and six Latin American countries
- U.S. ultimatum to Dominican government in November

1916
- U.S. purchase of Virgin Islands
- Revised Bryan-Chamorro treaty passed by U.S. Senate in February
- U.S. intervention in Dominican Republic begins on 5 May
- Paris Economic Conference held in June
- On 29 November U.S. military government established in Dominican Republic (rules directly for eight years)

1917

- On 3 February United States breaks relations with Germany
- In April Dominican national guard established
- In summer U.S. troops arrive in Cuba for training (some stay until 1922)

1918

- In June 1918 Haitian plebiscite ratifies new constitution
- In fall new revolts begin in Haiti, continue until spring 1920
- Armistice concludes World War I in November

1919

- Senator Albert B. Fall begins investigation of Mexican affairs in August

1920

- Naval tribunal under Admiral Henry Mayo investigates occupations of Haiti and Dominican Republic
- In January Second Pan American Financial Conference convenes
- Secretary of State Bainbridge Colby visits South America in December

1921

- U.S. Senate investigates occupations of Haiti and Dominican Republic, to continue into 1922
- Guatemala, El Salvador, and Honduras form union in January
- On 20 April U.S. Senate ratifies treaty with Colombia
- On 14 June United States announces its intention to withdraw from the Dominican Republic
- Doctrine of Positive Acts enunciated in Mexico in August
- On 5 December coup in Guatemala brings end to limited Central American union

1922

- On 18 January U.S. issues invitation to Tacna-Arica negotiations
- On 15 May Tacna-Arica talks begin
- President Alvaro Obregón reaches agreement on Mexican debt in June
- On 20 July Tacna-Arica Protocol concluded
- $16 million U.S. loan for Haiti in October
- On 21 October provisional government established in Dominican Republic
- In December Central American governments meet in Washington; meeting continues until 7 February 1923

1923

- In February U.S. Congress approves negotiation of new Panama treaty
- Santiago Conference from 25 March to 3 May
- Bucareli Conference in Mexico City, 14 May–15 August

1924
- Brief U.S. intervention in Honduras in March
- Elections held in Dominican Republic on 15 March
- General Horacio Vásquez becomes president of Dominican Republic on 12 July
- 24 September Dominican Republic occupation ends
- Brief U.S. intervention in Panama in October

1925
- In August U.S. Marines withdraw from Nicaragua
- New Mexican petroleum code passed in December

1926
- Marine landings in Nicaragua in May
- Pan American Commemorative Conference in Panama in June
- In September additional marine landings in Nicaragua
- On 11 November Adolfo Díaz named president of Nicaragua
- Additional U.S. troops to Nicaragua in December

1927
- U.S. intervention in Nicaragua from January to March
- In April Stimson mission sent to Nicaragua
- Tipitapa Accords signed in Nicaragua in May
- Dwight Morrow appointed U.S. ambassador to Mexico in July
- In November Mexican Supreme Court reaffirms Doctrine of Positive Acts

1928
- Havana Conference held from 16 January to 20 February
- Presidential elections in Nicaragua in November
- Clark Memorandum on Monroe Doctrine drafted in December (published in 1930)
- Conference on Conciliation and Arbitration begins in Washington on 10 December (ends on 29 January 1929)

1929
- On 2 March U.S. Congress authorizes survey of Nicaraguan canal route
- Dawes mission arrives in Dominican Republic on 2 April
- Martial law declared in Haiti on 4 December

1930
- Coup in Bolivia in January
- In February Forbes Committee visits Haiti
- Clark Memorandum on Monroe Doctrine made public in March
- Hawley-Smoot Tariff passed in June

1930 (continued)

- Coup in Peru in August
- On 16 August General Rafael Trujillo becomes president of Dominican Republic
- Coup in Argentina on 6 September
- President Herbert Hoover recognizes governments of Argentina, Peru, and Bolivia in September

1931

- Peru defaults on international debt
- In January Hoover administration recognizes revolutionary government in Guatemala
- U.S. statement of policy on Nicaragua in February
- On 13 February United States announces withdrawal from Nicaragua after 1932 election
- On 16 April Secretary of State Henry Stimson announces no general protection for Americans in Nicaragua
- Coup in Ecuador in August
- On 5 August Haitianization agreement reached

1932

- In February World Disarmament Conference at Geneva
- In June renewal of fighting over Chaco region
- New constitution passed in Haiti in July
- On 3 September new treaty with Haiti, replacing 1915 treaty; rejected unanimously by Haitian congress on 15 September
- U.S.-supervised elections in Nicaragua on 6 November

1933

- On 2 January Nicaraguan intervention ends
- On 3 February Augusto Sandino signs peace agreement
- Roca-Runciman Pact signed in May by Britain and Argentina
- In May Sumner Welles appointed ambassador to Cuba
- Executive agreement calling for termination of U.S. occupation of Haiti reached on 7 August
- Sergeants' revolt in Cuba in September
- Roosevelt-Arias accord in October
- Montevideo Conference meets from 3 to 28 December

1934

- Costa Rica and El Salvador denounce 1923 treaty
- On 21 February assassination of Augusto Sandino in Nicaragua
- On 29 March Platt Amendment abrogated

- Reciprocal Trade Act passed in June
- In August United States withdraws from Haiti

1936
- On 21 January Chaco Protocol signed
- On 3 March new Panama treaty signed (not approved by U.S. Senate until 1939)
- Buenos Aires Conference meets from 3 to 26 December

1937
- In March Standard Oil properties nationalized in Bolivia; settlement in January 1942

1938
- On 18 March Mexican oil expropriation takes place
- Chaco Peace Treaty signed in July
- Lima Conference meets from 9 to 27 December

1939
- On 1 September World War II begins in Europe
- U.S. proclamation of neutrality issued on 5 September
- On 23 September Panama Conference convenes
- On 13 December *Graf Spee* incident in Uruguay

1940
- In April Germany invades Denmark and Norway
- In May German invasion of Low Countries
- In June German invasion of France
- On 18 June U.S. Congress passes no transfer of colonies resolution
- On 4 July Britain declares blockade of French West Indies
- From 21–30 July Havana Conference meets
- In November United States signs base agreement with Uruguay
- Inter-American Coffee Agreement signed in November

1941
- In March United States passes Lend-Lease Act
- In April United States signs air transit agreement with Mexico
- Peru attacks Ecuador in July
- In October President Arnulfo Arias ousted in Panama
- On 14 October United States signs reciprocal trade agreement with Argentina
- U.S. Navy receives permission to use Brazilian ports in November
- On 24 November Brazil-U.S. agreement on Surinam (Dutch Guiana)
- On 7 December Japanese attack on Pearl Harbor, leading to U.S. declaration of war on 8 December

1942
- Rio Conference held from 15 to 28 January
- In February U.S. boycott of Argentina begins (ends in 1947)
- U.S.-Dutch-Venezuela agreement on Aruba and Curacao on 7 February
- Lend lease agreement with Brazil signed on 3 March
- Settlement of Mexican oil expropriation in April
- Base treaty with Panama signed in May but not ratified by Panama until May 1943
- In June Argentina recognizes German blockade of U.S. east coast
- In August Brazil declares war on Axis

1943
- Chile breaks relations with Axis in January
- Coup in Argentina on 4 June
- Coup in Bolivia in December

1944
- On 26 January Argentina breaks relations with Germany and Japan
- On 10 March General Edelmiro Farrell takes power in Argentina; not recognized by United States until March 1945
- On 16 August United States freezes Argentine assets; unfrozen in summer of 1946
- In November Secretary of State Hull resigns for health reasons

1945
- Yalta Conference held in February
- Chapultepec Conference meets from 21 February to 13 March
- Argentina declares war on Axis on 27 March
- On 19 April U.S. recognition of Farrell government in Argentina
- From 25 April to 26 June United Nations Conference in San Francisco
- On 20 October conference scheduled for Rio canceled at U.S. request

Chronology: 1945–1998

1945
- Chapultepec Conference held in February and March

1947
- Truman Doctrine enunciated in March.
- Marshall Plan put forward in June
- National Security Act passed in July
- Rio Conference convenes in August and September

- CIA review of Soviet aims in Latin America
- Peru claims 200-mile limit

1948
- General Agreement on Tariff and Trades goes into effect in January
- Bogotá Conference meets from 30 March to 2 May
- United States stops arms sales to Guatemala

1950
- Korean War begins in June

1951
- Jacobo Arbenz takes office in Guatemala in March
- Consultation of Foreign Ministers (Korean War) in March and April
- Mutual Security Act passed
- Inter-American Defense Board's "General Plan" for defense of Western Hemisphere formulated

1952
- Movimiento Nacional Revolucionario gains control in Bolivia in April; U.S. recognition on 2 June
- Agrarian reform law implemented in Guatemala in June
- In September, U.S. purchase of tin from Bolivia
- Tin mines nationalized in Bolivia in October

1953
- Additional U.S. tin purchase from Bolivia in July
- CIA-backed coup in Iran leads to restoration of Shah

1954
- Tenth Inter-American Conference meets at Caracas in March
- Czech arms shipment arrives in Guatemala on 15 May
- Exile "invasion" of Guatemala begins on 18 June; Guatemala complains to United Nations
- Guatemalan President Jacobo Arbenz resigns on 27 June
- Carlos Castillo Armas becomes president of Guatemala on 7 July; recognized by United States on 13 July

1955
- New Panama treaty signed on 25 January; approved by U.S. Senate on 29 July

1958
- Vice President Richard Nixon's trip to Latin America in May
- United States proposes establishment of Inter-American Development Bank in July

1959
- Fidel Castro comes to power in Cuba in January
- Flag demonstrations in Panama

1960
- President Dwight D. Eisenhower visits Argentina, Brazil, Chile, and Uruguay in February
- Sixth Meeting of Consultation in San Jose on 16–21 August
- Seventh Meeting of Consultation in San Jose on 22–29 August

1961
- Announcement of Alliance for Progress in March
- Assassination of General Rafael Trujillo in Dominican Republic on May 30
- U.S. military reserves called up due to Berlin crisis in July
- Berlin wall goes up on 13 August
- Conference at Punta del Este in August
- U.S. Foreign Assistance Act establishes rules for aid to Latin America
- Fidel Castro proclaims himself a Marxist-Leninist on 1 December

1962
- Conference at Punta del Este in January
- Argentina breaks relations with Cuba in February
- President Kennedy visits Mexico in June

1963
- Hickenlooper amendment on compensation for expropriation of U.S. properties goes into effect in October
- Assassination of Kennedy in November

1964
- Riots in Panama in January
- Overthrow of civilian president João Goulart in Brazil on 1 April
- On 11 May, Brazil breaks relations with Cuba
- OAS Council of Foreign Ministers meets in Washington in July
- On 11 August, Chile breaks relations with Cuba

1965
- U.S. intervention in the Dominican Republic in April
- U.S. troops out of Dominican Republic in September (others remain until September 1966)

1966
- Joaquín Balaguer wins presidency in Dominican Republic elections in June
- Last of foreign troops out of Dominican Republic in September

1967
- Drafts of three new Panama treaties revealed in June (none approved)
- Organization of Latin American States Conference in Havana in August
- On 8 October, Che Guevara killed in Bolivia

1968
- Tet offensive in Vietnam in January

1969
- Meeting of Latin American countries only at Viña del Mar in May
- Consensus of Viña del Mar presented to President Nixon in June
- Rockefeller Report on the Americas issued on 30 August
- President Nixon announces "Action for Progress for the Americas" in October

1970
- Marxist Salvador Allende wins presidential elections in Chile in September; confirmed by Congress on 24 October

1971
- On May 26, Allende nationalizes Chiltelco

1972
- On 19 January, Nixon announces "credit blockade" of Chile
- Charter of Economic Rights proposed at UNCTAD meeting in Chile in April; charter approved by UN vote in December
- Peru renews relations with Cuba on 8 July

1973
- Coup in Chile on 11 September leads to death of Allende
- War Powers Act passed by U.S. Congress

1974
- Eight-point agreement for new Panama Canal treaty announced on 7 February
- Secretary of State Henry Kissinger attends Mexico City conference in February
- President Nixon resigns in August
- Meeting of OAS foreign ministers at Quito in November

1975
- President Gerald Ford signs U.S. Trade Act of 1974 in January

1977
- Panama negotiations completed on 10 August
- On 7 September, signing of two new canal treaties
- In October, national plebiscite in Panama approves new treaties

1978

- Assassination of Pedro Chamorro in Nicaragua in January
- President Jimmy Carter visits Venezuela and Brazil in March
- U.S. Senate approves canal treaties on 18 April
- Joint Declaration of Panama on 16–17 June
- Sandinista rebels in Nicaragua seize National Legislative Palace on 23 August

1979

- President Carter visits Mexico in February
- President Carter cuts aid to Somoza on 8 February
- New Jewel Movement takes power in Grenada in March
- On 17 July, Anastasio Somoza resigns as president of Nicaragua
- Castro hosts Non-Aligned Movement in September
- Iranian hostage crisis begins on 4 November
- Soviet invasion of Afghanistan in December

1980

- SALT II treaty withdrawn in January
- Agrarian reform decreed in El Salvador in March
- Marielitos boatlift from Cuba, April-September

1981

- Resumption of U.S. military aid to El Salvador in January
- President Ronald Reagan ends aid to Sandinistas on 1 April
- Death of Panamanian ruler, General Omar Torrijos
- National Security Decision Directive 17 creates contras in November

1982

- Argentina invades Falkland Islands on 2 April
- British forces land in the Falklands on 21 May
- Argentine forces in Falklands surrender on 14 June
- Debt crisis begins with Mexico in August

1983

- U.S. military exercises in Honduras during spring and summer
- Kissinger Commission established in June; publishes report in January
- Conference at Caracas on debt crisis from 5–9 September
- Grenada intervention on 25 October
- Caribbean Basin Initiative trade package approved by U.S. Congress in December

1984
- Kissinger Commission report on Central America issued in January
- Quito Conference on debt crisis in January
- Elections in March and May in El Salvador put José Napoleón Duarte in presidency
- Cartagena Conference on debt in June
- Mar del Plata meeting on debt in September
- Meeting of "Cartagena Group" in Brasilia on debt in November
- Trade Act of 1984

1985
- "Baker Plan" for debt crisis proposed in October

1986
- Jean-Claude Duvalier ousted from presidency in Haiti in February
- Iran-Contra scandal breaks in November

1987
- Congressional investigation of Iran-Contra scandal in May-July
- United States suspends all aid to Panama in July
- Central American peace plan signed on 7 August
- Election scheduled for November in Haiti postponed to January 1988

1988
- In March, Contra-Sandinista cease–fire and Iran-Contra indictments
- U.S. economic sanctions against Panama in April

1989
- Disintegration of communist bloc begins
- Central American peace settlement in February
- "Brady Plan" for debt crisis put forward in March
- Panamanian elections in May nullified by General Manuel Noriega
- U.S. intervention in Panama on 20 December

1990
- Mexican debt settlement reached in January
- Sandinistas lose elections in Nicaragua in February
- Iraq invades Kuwait in August
- Reunification of Germany in October

1991
- Disintegration of the Soviet Union begins
- Air attacks begin for Desert Storm on 16 January
- Ground attacks begin for Desert Storm on 23 February
- In June, Warsaw Pact disbanded

1992
- Earth Summit in Rio in June
- U.S. troops to Somalia in November

1993
- U.S. Congress approves NAFTA in November

1994
- NAFTA goes into effect on 1 January
- U.S. intervention in Haiti in September
- "Summit of the Americas" in Miami in December

1995
- Mercosur common market goes into effect
- Elections in Haiti in December put René Préval in presidency

1997
- Local and national elections in Haiti in April
- U.N. mandate in Haiti expires on 30 November; civilian police mission to remain an additional year

1998
- Second "Summit of the Americas" in Santiago, Chile, in April
- Civilian police mission in Haiti ends in November

NOTES

Chapter One

1. Gaddis Smith, *The Last Years of the Monroe Doctrine, 1945–1993* (Hill and Wang, 1994), p. 33; see Wilson quote, p. 29.

2. For quotes, see Walter LaFeber, *Inevitable Revolutions: The United States in Central America* (W. W. Norton & Co., 1993), pp. 22–23.

Chapter Two

1. Quoted in Philip S. Klein, *President James Buchanan: A Biography* (Pennsylvania State University Press, 1962), p. 324.

2. Quoted in James C. Bradford, introduction to *Crucible of Empire: The Spanish-American War and Its Aftermath*, edited by James C. Bradford (Naval Institute Press, 1993), p. xiii.

3. See Edmund Morris, *The Rise of Theodore Roosevelt* (Coward, McCarm, and Geoghegan, Inc., 1979), pp. 613–20, for discussion and quotations.

Chapter Three

1. On this point, see Louis Pérez, *Cuba and the United States: Ties of Singular Intimacy* (University of Georgia Press, 1990), p. 116.

2. Quoted in David McCullough, *The Path between the Seas: The Creation of the Panama Canal, 1870–1914* (Simon & Schuster, 1977), pp. 339–40.

3. Quoted in Thomas F. McGann, *Argentina, the United States, and the Inter-American System, 1880–1914* (Harvard University Press, 1957), p. 222.

4. Quoted in Lester D. Langley, *The Banana Wars: United States Intervention in the Caribbean, 1898–1934* (Dorsey Press, 1988), p. 60.

5. Quoted in Linda B. Hall and Don M. Coerver, *Revolution on the Border: The United States and Mexico, 1910–1920* (University of New Mexico Press, 1988), p. 47.

6. See Mark T. Guilderhus, *Pan American Visions: Woodrow Wilson in the Western Hemisphere, 1913–1921* (University of Arizona Press, 1986), pp. 16–19.

7. See United States Department of State, *Papers Relating to the Foreign Relations of the United States, 1913* (U.S. Government Printing Office, 1914), pp. 820–27.

Chapter Four

1. Kenneth J. Grieb, *The Latin American Policy of Warren G. Harding* (Texas Christian University Press, 1976), pp. 65–66.
2. Samuel Guy Inman, *Inter-American Conferences, 1826–1954: History and Problems* (University Press, 1965), chapter 7, and James Brown Scott, ed., *The International Conferences of American States, 1889–1928* (Oxford University Press, 1931), pp. 207–91.
3. Inman, *Inter-American Conferences*, chapter 9, and Scott, ed., *International Conferences*, pp. 293–444.
4. Quoted in Joseph Brandes, *Herbert Hoover and Economic Diplomacy: Department of Commerce Policy, 1921–1928* (University of Pittsburgh Press, 1962), p. 200.
5. Inman, *Inter-American Conferences*, chapter 11.
6. Quoted in Bryce Wood, *The Making of the Good Neighbor Policy,* (Columbia University Press, 1961), p. 65.
7. Inman, *Inter-American Conferences*, chapter 12.
8. Ibid., chapter 13.
9. See R. A. Humphreys, *Latin America and the Second World War. Volume One: 1939–1942* (Athlone Press, 1981), pp. 42–51.
10. Inman, *Inter-American Conferences*, pp. 199–202.

Chapter Five

1. For activities at the meeting, see Samuel Guy Inman, *Inter-American Conferences, 1826–1954: History and Problems* (University Press, 1965), chapter 17.
2. Donald Marquand Dozer, *Are We Good Neighbors? Three Decades of Inter-American Relations, 1930–1960* (University of Florida Press, 1959), pp. 213–15.
3. See Edwin Lieuwen, *Arms and Politics in Latin America* (Revised: Praeger, 1961), pp. 198–99.
4. Inman, *Inter-American Conferences*, chapter 19. Treatment of economic matters was deferred to a special conference to be held the following November in Rio.
5. Quoted in Tad Szulc, *Fidel: A Critical Portrait* (William Morrow and Co., 1986), p. 408.
6. For U.S. policy during the Castro revolution, see the excellent study by Thomas Paterson, *Contesting Castro: The United States and the Triumph of the Cuban Revolution* (Oxford University Press, 1994).
7. Quoted in Paterson, p. 257.

8. Ibid., pp. 258–59, 261–62, and Morris H. Morley, *Imperial State and Revolution: The United States and Cuba* (Cambridge University Press, 1987), pp. 97–98.

9. Quoted in Morley, ibid., p. 109.

10. Quoted in Peter Wyden, *The Bay of Pigs* (Touchstone, 1979), p. 8.

11. Morley, p. 142.

12. Wyden, p. 218.

13. Ibid., pp. 240–45, on the U.S. Navy. Morley, pp. 135–146, is a good discussion of policy surrounding the Bay of Pigs operation.

14. See the discussion in Morley, pp. 146–57. A comprehensive look at covert action is provided by Warren Hinckle and William W. Turner in *The Fish is Red* (Harper & Row, 1981).

15. Hinckle and Turner, p. 18.

16. Quoted in ibid., p. 99.

17. Szulc, 547–48.

18. Raymond L. Garthoff in James G. Blight and David A. Welch, *On the Brink: Americans and Soviets Reexamine the Cuban Missile Crisis* (Noonday Press, 1990), p. 75.

19. George Ball, quoted in Blight and Welch, pp. 33–34.

20. Quoted in Morley, p. 184.

21. Quoted in Morley, p. 183.

Chapter Six

1. Nelson A. Rockefeller, *The Rockefeller Report on the Americas: The Official Report of a United States Presidential Mission for the Western Hemisphere* (Quadrangle Books, 1969).

2. See Samuel L. Baily, *The United States and the Development of South America, 1945–1975* (New Viewpoints, 1976), pp. 117–28.

3. Ibid., pp. 122–33.

4. John D. Martz, ed., *United States Policy in Latin America: A Quarter Century of Crisis and Challenge, 1961–1986* (University of Nebraska Press, 1988).

5. Walter LaFeber, *The Panama Canal: The Crisis in Historical Perspective*, exp. ed. (Oxford University Press, 1979).

6. An excellent discussion of the Sandinista Revolution may be found in John A. Booth, *The End and the Beginning: The Nicaraguan Revolution* (Westview Press, 1982). This episode is discussed on 161–62.

7. Walter LaFeber, *Inevitable Revolutions: The United States in Central America*, 2d ed. (W. W. Norton & Co., 1993), p. 203.

8. All quotes are taken from Ronald Reagan, address to the nation, March 16, 1986, in Bruce D. Larkin, *Vital Interests: The Soviet Issue in U.S. Central American Policy* (Lynne Rienner, 1988), pp. 113–19.

9. See discussion in Gaddis Smith, *The Last Years of the Monroe Doctrine, 1945–1993* (Hill and Wang, 1994), pp. 68–69.

10. Alexander M. Haig, Jr. with Charles McCarry, *Inner Circles: How America Changed the World: A Memoir* (Warner Books, 1992), 123–24.

11. Alexander M. Haig, Jr., *Caveat: Realism, Reagan, and Foreign Policy* (Macmillan, 1984), p. 124.

12. For example, see Haig, *Inner Circles,* pp. 549–52.

13. LaFeber, *Inevitable Revolutions,* p. 275.

14. Ibid., p. 271.

15. Excellent discussions can be found in ibid., pp. 276–78, and Smith, *The Last Years,* pp. 162–64. The original may be found in Jeane Kirkpatrick, *Dictatorships and Double Standards* (Simon & Schuster, 1982), pp. 23–52, with quotes on pp. 23 and 49–50.

16. Quoted in LaFeber, *Inevitable Revolutions,* p. 277.

17. All figures are from Gabriel Aguilera, *Centroamérica de Reagan a Bush* (FLACSO, 1991), pp. 37–38.

18. Smith, *The Last Years,* p. 191.

19. Philip Shepard, "Honduras," in Morris J. Blachman, et al., *Confronting Revolution: Security through Diplomacy in Central America* (Pantheon Books, 1986), p. 133.

20. Figures are taken from Aguilera, pp. 40–41.

21. Cynthia J. Arnson, *Crossroads: Congress, the Reagan Administration, and Central America* (Pantheon Books, 1989), pp. 212, 228.

22. LaFeber, *Inevitable Revolutions,* pp. 353–55.

23. Ibid., pp. 356–57.

24. Ibid., pp. 355–56.

25. Ibid., p. 296.

26. For a discussion of these points, see ibid., pp. 353–58.

27. Smith, *The Last Years,* p. 185.

28. Ibid., p. 190.

29. Quoted in Peter Kornbluh, "Nicaragua," in *Intervention in the 1980s: U.S. Foreign Policy in the Third World,* edited by Peter J. Schraeder (Lynne Rienner, 1989), p. 241.

30. See ibid., pp. 241–42.

31. Kornbluh, pp. 242–43.

32. Ibid., pp. 244–45.

33. Arnson, p. 100.

34. See, for example, "Statement in the Security Council on the complaint by Nicaragua, March 25, 1982," in "Central America: Nicaragua and Her Neighbors," in Jeane J. Kirkpatrick, *The Reagan Phenomenon—and Other Speeches on Foreign Policy* (American Enterprise Institute for Public Policy Research, 1983), pp. 183–93.

35. Jeane Kirkpatrick, *The Kennedy-Khruschev Pact and the Sandinistas* (The Cuban American National Foundation, Inc., 1985). Quotes on pp. 4, 10.

36. Arnson, pp. 103–07.

37. Ibid., pp. 21, 173.

38. Ibid., pp. 21, 173, 175–85.

39. Theodore Draper, *A Very Thin Line: The Iran-Contra Affairs* (Touchstone, 1991), pp. 24–28. This book furnishes an excellent narrative of the Iran-Contra scandal.

40. LaFeber, *Inevitable Revolutions*, p. 336.

41. Ibid., p. 333.

42. See the text of the document, "Arias Peace Plan," in James D. Cockcroft, *Latin America: History, Politics, and U.S. Policy*, 2d ed. (Nelson Hall Co., 1996), pp. 707–12.

43. LaFeber, *Inevitable Revolutions*, pp. 342–43.

Chapter Seven

1. Cuban Democracy Act, House of Representatives, 102nd Congress, second session, June 25, 1992 (U.S. Government Printing Office, 1992), 1, and Josette Griffiths, "The Cuban Exile Community's Influence on U.S. Foreign Policy towards Cuba," unpublished paper (University of New Mexico, 1993).

2. See *New York Times*, 29 February 1996, and *Los Angeles Times*, 29 February 1996.

3. Wayne S. Smith, "The Debacle that is Cuba Policy," *LASA Forum* XXVII(Spring 1996):19.

4. For Cernuda quote, see Saul Landau, "Tightening the Chokehold on Cuba," *The Nation*, 15 June 1992, 819.

5. *Wall Street Journal*, 12 August and 26 August 1994, editorial page.

6. *New York Times*, 19 March 1995.

7. Wayne Smith, "Washington's Undying Obsession with Castro," *Los Angeles Times*, 19 March 1995.

8. *Washington Post*, 24 March 1995.

9. *New York Times*, 24 March 1995.

10. *Wall Street Journal*, 16 May 1995, editorial page.

11. *New York Times*, 19 February 1996, and *Wall Street Journal*, 15 April 1998, A24.

12. *EcoCentral*, 16 April 1998, Latin American Data Base (University of New Mexico), ISSN 1089–1560.

13. Catherine Gwin, *U.S. Relations with the World Bank, 1945–1992* (Brookings Institution, 1994), pp. 37–54, and *Wall Street Journal*, 22 September 1997, A16, and 8 October 1997, A17. Most of the new bonds represented a swap for bonds issued under the Brady Plan.

14. Jonathan Hartlyn, Lars Schoultz, and Augusto Varas, eds., *The United States and Latin America in the 1990s: Beyond the Cold War* (University of North Carolina Press, 1992), chapter 6.

15. *EcoCentral,* 16 April 1998, Latin American Data Base (University of New Mexico), ISSN 1089–1560.

16. *Wall Street Journal,* 16 April 1998, A19.

Chapter Eight

1. *New York Times,* 11 April 1996.

2. Alejandro Portes and Rubén Rumbaut, *Immigrant America: A Portrait* (University of California Press, 1990), pp. 79–81, 116–24.

3. Ibid., p. 15.

4. See Linda B. Hall and Don M. Coerver, *Revolution on the Border: The United States and Mexico, 1910–1920* (University of New Mexico Press, 1988), chapter 8, for a full discussion.

5. Portes and Rumbaut, pp. 70, 72.

6. Ibid., 118–20.

7. *Business Week,* 13 July 1992, 116.

8. The authors wish to acknowledge the research assistance of Corinna Reyes in this portion of the discussion.

9. Louis A. Pérez, *Cuba and the United States: Ties of Singular Intimacy* (University of Georgia Press, 1990), pp. 253–55, and Alejandro Portes and Robert L. Bach, *Latin Journey: Cuban and Mexican Immigrants in the United States* (University of California Press, 1985), pp. 88–89.

10. See Portes and Bach, 85–87.

11. Pérez, *Cuba and the United States,* p. 261, and Gil Loescher and John A. Scanlan, *Calculated Kindness: Refugees and America's Half-Open Door, 1945 to the Present* (The Free Press, 1986), pp. 170–87.

12. Portes and Rumbaut, *Immigrant America,* p. 80.

13. *New York Times,* 21 May 1995.

14. This discussion relies heavily on William Deane Stanley, "Economic Migrants or Refugees from Violence? A Time-Series Analysis of Salvadoran Migration to the United States," *Latin American Research Review* 22(1987):132–54; Richard C. Jones, "Causes of Salvadoran Migration to the United States," *The Geographical Review* 79(April 1989):183–94; and research carried out by Trena Klohe, University of New Mexico, Fall 1994.

15. See Sergio Aguayo's excellent study, *El éxodo centroamericano* (SEP Cultura, 1985) for a general discussion of Central American migration during the early 1980s. The 1996 figure was obtained from communication with William Stanley, April 1996, and *Wall Street Journal,* 8 March 1996, A11.

16. Stanley, "Economic Migrants," p. 137.

17. Ibid., pp. 141–47.

18. Jones, pp. 183–84. Information provided by Klohe, 1994, and Loescher and Scanlan, p. 216.

19. Quoted in Cynthia J. Arnson, *Crossroads: Congress, the Reagan Administration, and Central America* (Pantheon Books, 1989), p. 64. See also p. 21.

20. *New York Times,* 27 October 1995.

21. *Los Angeles Times,* 16 June 1994.

22. Ibid.

23. See Portes and Rumbaut, pp. 236–39.

24. *Business Week,* 13 July 1995, 114.

25. Robert Corrigan, "The Rising Cost of Immigration," *Investor's Business Daily,* 2 December 1992. Research carried out by Jennifer Cutcliffe, University of New Mexico, 1994, also contributed to this section.

26. Corrigan, "Rising Cost."

27. For example, see *Los Angeles Times,* 7 April 1996, A1, A20.

28. *Albuquerque Journal,* 26 January 1998.

29. *Wall Street Journal,* 26 March 1996, A20.

30. *New York Times,* 20 April 1998.

31. *SourceMex,* 29 April 1998, Latin America Data Base (University of New Mexico), ISSN 1089–1560.

32. *EcoCentral,* 23 April 1998, Latin American Data Base (University of New Mexico), ISSN 1089–1560.

Chapter Nine

1. Peter H. Smith, "The Political Economy of Drugs: Conceptual Issues and Policy Options," in *Drug Policy in the Americas,* edited by Peter H. Smith (Westview Press, 1993), p. 1.

2. Abraham F. Lowenthal, "Rediscovering Latin America," *Foreign Affairs* 69(Fall 1990):27–41.

3. *New York Times,* 1 August 1993, and *Los Angeles Times,* 15 June 1996.

4. Louis A. Pérez, *Cuba and the United States: Ties of Singular Intimacy* (Athens and London: University of Georgia Press, 1990), p. 222.

5. David F. Musto, "Patterns in U.S. Drug Abuse and Response," in Smith, *Drug Policy,* pp. 39–41.

6. William O. Walker III, *Drug Control in the Americas* (University of New Mexico Press, 1989), pp. 161–64.

7. Elaine Shannon, *Desperados: Latin Drug Lords, U.S. Lawmen, and the War America Can't Win* (Viking, 1988), pp. 47–58,and Miguel Ruiz-Cabañas I., "Mexico's Permanent Campaign: Costs, Benefits, Implications," in Smith, *Drug Policy,* pp. 151–55.

8. *New York Times,* 20 June 1993.

9. See the outstanding articles in the *Los Angeles Times,* 15 and 16 June 1995.

10. *New York Times,* 15 April 1998.

11. Quoted in Walker, *Drug Control,* pp. 195–96.

12. Ibid.

13. Shannon, *Desperados,* pp. 100–04, 400–01.

14. New York *Times,* 2 March 1996.

15. See the excellent discussion in Bruce M. Bagley, "Myths of Militarization: Enlisting the Armed Forces in the War on Drugs," in Smith, *Drug Policy,* pp. 129–50.

16. William O. Walker III, "International Collaboration in Historical Perspective," in Smith, *Drug Policy,* p. 275.

17. Bagley, p. 131.

18. Ibid., pp. 132–33.

19. Walker, *Drug Control,* pp. 198–200.

20. Bagley, pp. 135–36.

21. Ibid., p. 137, and John Dinges, *Our Man in Panama: The Shrewd Rise and Brutal Fall of Manuel Noriega* (Times Books, 1990), pp. 303–15.

22. This thesis is put forward most publicly in the documentary film "The Panama Deception," which won the Academy Award for best documentary in 1993.

23. Bagley, pp. 138–39, and Walker, "International Collaboration," pp. 265–66.

24. Mathea Falco, *The Making of a Drug-Free America: Programs that Work* (Times Books, 1992), p. 7.

25. Lee Brown, interview by Roger Mudd, *MacNeil/Lehrer News Hour,* Public Broadcasting System, 10 July 1993.

26. See the excellent discussion in this regard in Walker, "International Collaboration," p. 276.

Chapter Ten

1. This change of policy has been compellingly analyzed in Gaddis Smith, *The Last Years of the Monroe Doctrine, 1945–1993* (Hill and Wang, 1994).

2. See Abraham F. Lowenthal, "Rediscovering Latin America," *Foreign Affairs,* 69(Fall 1990), 35.

3. *SourceMex,* 17 June 1998, Latin America Data Base (University of New Mexico), ISSN 1089–1560.

4. *EcoCentral,* 11 June 1998, Latin America Data Base (University of New Mexico), ISSN 1089–1560.

5. Ibid., 16 July 1998.

6. Ibid., 23 July 1998.

7. See Smith, *Last Years,* pp. 218–20.

8. *NotiSur,* 24 October 1997, Latin America Data Base (University of New Mexico), ISSN 1089–1560.

SUGGESTIONS FOR FURTHER READING

Nineteenth Century Background

Useful works on the independence period are Peggy K. Liss, *Atlantic Empires: The Network of Trade and Revolution, 1713–1826* (Johns Hopkins University Press, 1983), and the classic work, Arthur P. Whitaker, *The United States and the Independence of Latin America, 1800–1830* (Johns Hopkins University Press, 1941). Alexander De-Conde, *This Affair of Louisiana* (Charles Scribner's Sons, 1976) is the fundamental account of the struggle over Louisiana and its ultimate acquisition by the United States. Also recommended is Lester D. Langley, *Struggle for the American Mediterranean: United States-European Rivalry in the Gulf-Caribbean, 1776–1904* (University of Georgia Press, 1976). Aging but not outdated comprehensive works on the Floridas controversy include Philip C. Brooks, *Diplomacy and the Borderlands: The Adams-Onís Treaty of 1819* (University of California Press, 1939), and Isaac J. Cox, *The West Florida Controversy, 1798–1813* (Johns Hopkins Press, 1918; reprint, Peter Smith, 1967).

Any examination of the Monroe Doctrine should begin with the numerous works by Dexter Perkins, especially his *A History of the Monroe Doctrine* (Little, Brown & Co., 1955). An approach that deemphasizes the international background to the Doctrine is Ernest R. May's *The Making of the Monroe Doctrine* (Harvard University Press, 1975).

For Mexico in the early period of independence, two excellent works are Stanley C. Green, *The Mexican Republic: The First Decade, 1823–1832* (University of Pittsburgh Press, 1987) and Barbara Tenenbaum, *The Politics of Penury: Debts and Taxes in Mexico, 1821–1856* (University of New Mexico Press, 1986).

On Texas annexation, the standard work has long been Justin Smith's *The Annexation of Texas* (Barnes and Noble, 1941). For British involvement in the Republic of Texas, see Ephraim D. Adams, *British Interests and Activities in Texas, 1838–1846* (Peter Smith, 1963). Joseph W. Schmitz provides a detailed analysis of the foreign policy pursued by the Republic of Texas in *Texan Statecraft, 1836–1845* (Naylor Company, 1941). See also Vito Alessio Robles, *Coahuila y Texas: desde la consumación de la independencia hasta el tratado de paz de Guadalupe Hidalgo*

(Talleres Gráficos de la Nación, 1946). A good recent biography of Sam Houston which gives great attention to issues of territorial expansion into Mexico is John Hoyt Williams, *Sam Houston: A Biography of the Father of Texas* (Simon & Schuster, 1993). Joseph Milton Nance, *After San Jacinto: The Texas-Mexican Frontier, 1836–1841* (University of Texas Press, 1963) is an extensive exploration of border problems in the immediate aftermath of the Texas independence movement.

A classic study of the attitudes and rationalizations behind Manifest Destiny is Albert K. Weinberger, *Manifest Destiny: A Study of Nationalist Expansionism in American History* (Johns Hopkins University Press, 1935). See also Thomas R. Hietala, *Manifest Design: Anxious Aggrandizement in Late Jacksonian America* (Cornell University Press, 1985). Gene M. Brack, *Mexico Views Manifest Destiny, 1821–1846* (University of New Mexico Press, 1975) is a good survey of the non-U.S. perspective.

On the Mexican-U.S. War, works to consult are Thomas E. Cotner, *The Military and Political Career of José Joaquín de Herrera* (University of Texas Press, 1949); Glenn W. Price, *Origins of the War with Mexico: The Polk-Stockton Intrigue* (University of Texas Press, 1967); Otis A. Singletary, *The Mexican War* (Chicago, 1960); and John S. D. Eisenhower, *So Far from God: The U.S. War with Mexico, 1846–1848* (Random House, 1989). An outstanding collection of pictorial images of the war is the Amon Carter Museum of Western Art's *Eyewitness to War: Prints and Daguerreotypes of the Mexican War, 1846–1848* (Smithsonian Institution Press, 1989).

For thorough and interesting discussions on attitudes held in the United States toward Latin America developing out of this time period, there are three indispensable works: Reginald Horsman, *Race and Manifest Destiny: The Origins of American Racial Anglo-Saxonism* (Harvard University Press, 1981); Robert W. Johannsen, *To the Halls of the Montezumas: The Mexican War in the American Imagination* (Oxford University Press, 1985); and Frederick B. Pike, *The United States and Latin America: Myths and Stereotypes of Civilization and Nature* (University of Texas Press, 1992).

Emerging Imperialism

A standard, if dated, work on the Gadsden Purchase is Paul N. Garber, *The Gadsden Treaty* (University of Pennsylvania Press, 1923). For the Mexican viewpoint, see Luis G. Zorrilla, *Historia de las relaciones entre México y los Estados Unidos de América,* Vol. I (Editorial Porrua, 1965), 335–60. For an excellent discussion of the impact of domestic affairs in the United States and Mexico on the foreign relations of the two countries at the time, see Donothan C. Olliff, *Reforma Mexico and the United States: A Search for Alternatives to Annexation, 1854–1861* (University of North Carolina Press, 1981). A survey of 1850s filibustering is found in Charles H. Brown, *Agents of Manifest Destiny: The Lives and Times of the Filibusters* (University of North Carolina Press, 1980). Two biographies of William Walker are Albert Z. Carr, *The World and William Walker* (Harper & Row, 1963) and William O. Scroggs, *Filibusters and Financiers: The Story of William Walker and His Associates* (Macmillan, 1916).

Early naval affairs are covered in John H. Schroeder, *Shaping a Maritime Empire: The Commercial and Diplomatic Role of the American Navy, 1829–1861* (Greenwood Press, 1985). Information on the later period may be found in Kenneth J. Hagan, *American Gunboat Diplomacy and the Old Navy, 1877–1889* (Greenwood Press, 1973).

For South America, see Lawrence F. Hill, *Diplomatic Relations between the United States and Brazil* (Duke University Press, 1932); Joseph S. Tulchin, *Argentina and the United States: A Conflicted Relationship* (New York University Press, 1990); Harold F. Peterson, *Argentina and the United States, 1810–1960* (State University of New York Press, 1964); Frederick Pike, *The United States and the Andean Republics: Peru, Bolivia, and Ecuador* (Harvard University Press, 1977); Thomas McGann, *Argentina, the United States, and the Inter-American System, 1880–1914* (Harvard University Press, 1957); and Joyce S. Goldberg, *The Baltimore Affair* (University of Nebraska Press, 1986). For a discussion of the relationships between the South American republics themselves, which quite accurately reflects their minimal involvement with the United States and the great significance of intraregional conflict, see Robert N. Burr, *By Reason or Force: Chile and a Balancing of Power in South America, 1830–1905* (University of California Press, 1967).

On the impact of the U.S. Civil War, the classic exposition of Confederate diplomacy is Frank Lawrence Owsley, *King Cotton Diplomacy: Foreign Relations of the Confederate States of America* (University of Chicago Press, 1959). For the United States and Mexico at the time, an excellent source is Thomas D. Schoonover, *Dollars over Dominion: The Triumph of Liberalism in Mexican-United States Relations, 1861–1867* (Louisiana State University Press, 1978). For Central America, see the same author's *The United States in Central America, 1860–1911: Episodes of Social Imperialism and Imperial Rivalry in the World System* (Duke University Press, 1991). An extended account of Confederate exiles in Mexico is Andrew F. Rolle, *The Lost Cause: The Confederate Exodus to Mexico* (University of Oklahoma Press, 1965).

For the French intervention in Mexico within its Mexican context, see Walter V. Scholes, *Mexican Politics during the Juárez Regime, 1855–1872* (University of Missouri Press, 1969). A survey of U.S.-Mexican-French relations is Alfred J. Hanna and Kathryn A. Hanna, *Napoleon III and Mexico: American Triumph over Monarchy* (University of North Carolina Press, 1971).

The new imperialism is well chronicled in Ernest N. Paolino, *The Foundations of the American Empire: William Henry Seward and U.S. Foreign Policy* (Cornell University Press, 1973); William Appleman Williams, *The Roots of the Modern*

American Empire (Vintage, 1969); and Walter LaFeber, *The New Empire: An Interpretation of American Expansion, 1860–1898* (Cornell University Press, 1963). A more traditional view is Charles S. Campbell, *The Transformation of American Foreign Relations, 1865–1900* (Harper & Row, 1976).

For the Spanish-American-Cuban War, sources are Frank D. Freidel, *The Splendid Little War* (Little, Brown & Co., 1958); H. Wayne Morgan, *America's Road to Empire: The War with Spain and Overseas Expansion* (Wiley, 1965); Philip S. Foner, *The Spanish-American-Cuban War and the Birth of American Imperialism* (Monthly Review Press, 1972); Julius Pratt, *Expansionists of 1898* (Johns Hopkins Press, 1938); John L. Offner, *An Unwanted War: The Diplomacy of the United States and Spain over Cuba* (University of North Carolina Press, 1992); and *Crucible of Empire: The Spanish-American War and Its Aftermath*, edited by James C. Bradford (U.S. Naval Institute Press, 1993).

An overview of U.S. involvement in the Caribbean during the entire nineteenth century is Lester D. Langley, *Struggle for the American Mediterranean: United States-European Rivalry in the Gulf-Caribbean, 1776–1894* (University of Georgia Press, 1976).

A comprehensive view of U.S. policy in the Caribbean at the turn of the century is Richard H. Collin, *Theodore Roosevelt's Caribbean: The Panama Canal, the Monroe Doctrine, and the Latin American Context* (Louisiana State University Press, 1990).

The Era of Intervention

An excellent overview of the first Cuban occupation is David F. Healy, *The United States in Cuba, 1898–1902: Generals, Politicians, and the Search for Policy* (University of Wisconsin Press, 1963). For an examination of the second occupation, see Allan R. Millett, *The Politics of Intervention: The Military Occupation of Cuba, 1906–1909* (Ohio State University Press, 1968). The formulation of the Platt Amendment and its long-term effect on U.S.-Cuban relations are covered in Louis A. Pérez, Jr., *Cuba under the Platt Amendment, 1902–1934* (University of Pittsburgh Press, 1986).

For a readable study of the history of the canal, see David McCullough, *The Path between the Seas: The Creation of the Panama Canal, 1870–1914* (Simon & Schuster, 1977). See also Dwight Carroll Miner, *The Fight for the Panama Route: The Story of the Spooner Act and the Hay-Herrán Treaty* (Columbia University Press, 1940).

For U.S. military operations in the Caribbean/Central American area after 1898, see Richard D. Challener, *Admirals, Generals, and American Foreign Policy, 1898–1914* (Princeton University Press, 1973), pp. 148–62, and Allan R. Millett, *Sem-*

per Fidelis: The History of the United States Marine Corps (Rev. ed., Free Press, 1991).

Thomas F. McGann examines the rivalry between the United States and Argentina and its impact on the early years of the inter-American system in *Argentina, the United States, and the Inter-American System, 1880–1914* (Harvard University Press, 1957). Good surveys of U.S.-Argentine relations are Harold F. Peterson, *Argentina and the United States, 1810–1960* (State University of New York, 1964) and Joseph S. Tulchin, *Argentina and the United States: A Conflicted Relationship* (Twayne, 1990). For the interventionist policies pursued by the United States in the decades following the Spanish-American-Cuban War, see David Healy, *Drive to Hegemony: The United States in the Caribbean, 1898–1917* (University of Wisconsin Press, 1988) and Lester D. Langley, *The Banana Wars: United States Intervention in the Caribbean, 1898–1934* (Dorsey Press, 1988).

The impact of the Mexican Revolution of 1910 on relations between the United States and Mexico has produced an extensive literature. For the multi-layered political and military problems that the Revolution caused along the border, see Linda B. Hall and Don M. Coerver, *Revolution on the Border: The United States and Mexico, 1910–1920* (University of New Mexico Press, 1988). The basic work on the Madero administration is Charles C. Cumberland, *Mexican Revolution: Genesis under Madero* (University of Texas Press, 1974). Michael E. Meyer provides in-depth studies of two Mexican leaders who figured prominently in U.S.-Mexican relations in his *Mexican Rebel: Pascual Orozco and the Mexican Revolution, 1910–1915* (University of Nebraska Press, 1967) and *Huerta: A Political Portrait* (University of Nebraska Press, 1972). The battle of wills between Wilson and Huerta is detailed in Kenneth J. Grieb, *The United States and Huerta* (University of Nebraska Press, 1969).

Mark T. Gilderhus examines Woodrow Wilson's efforts to harmonize his missionary diplomacy with his views on the inter-American system in his excellent work, *Pan American Visions: Woodrow Wilson in the Western Hemisphere, 1913–1921* (University of Arizona Press, 1986). For Wilson's problems with revolution and the use of force in international relations, see Lloyd C. Gardner, *Wilson and Revolutions, 1913–1921* (J.B. Lippincott Company, 1976); Arthur S. Link, ed., *Woodrow Wilson and a Revolutionary World, 1913–1921* (University of North Carolina Press, 1982); and Frederick S. Calhoun, *Uses of Force and Wilsonian Foreign Policy* (Kent State University Press, 1993).

For an excellent overview of the Tampico incident and the intervention at Veracruz, see Robert E. Quirk, *An Affair of Honor: Woodrow Wilson and the Occupation of Veracruz* (W.W. Norton & Company, 1962). Jack Sweetman provides a blow-by-blow account of the Veracruz operation in *The Landing at Veracruz: 1914* (Naval Institute Press, 1968).

The origins of the lengthy U.S. involvement in Haiti are detailed in David Healy, *Gunboat Diplomacy in the Wilson Era: The U.S. Navy in Haiti, 1915–1916* (University of Wisconsin Press, 1976). Good surveys of the occupation are Hans Schmidt, *The United States Occupation of Haiti, 1915–1934* (Rutgers University Press, 1971), and Arthur C. Millspaugh, *Haiti under American Control, 1915–1930* (World Peace Foundation, 1931). Millspaugh served as financial advisor and general receiver during the occupation.

The outbreak of war in Europe in 1914 and the U.S. entry into the war in April 1917 had a major impact on U.S.-Latin American relations during and after the war. Friedrich Katz describes the interaction between European developments and U.S.-Mexican relations in his *The Secret War in Mexico: Europe, the United States and the Mexican Revolution* (University of Chicago Press, 1981). For the impact of the war on U.S. business relations with Latin America, see Mira Wilkins, *The Maturing of Multinational Enterprise: American Business Abroad from 1914 to 1970* (Harvard University Press, 1974). Joseph S. Tulchin examines the political and economic consequences of the war in *The Aftermath of War: World War I and U.S. Policy toward Latin America* (New York University Press, 1971).

1920–1945

Good overviews of U.S.-Latin American relations in the immediate post–World War I period can be found in: Joseph S. Tulchin, *The Aftermath of War: World War I and U.S. Policy toward Latin America* (New York University Press, 1971); Kenneth J. Grieb, *The Latin American Policy of Warren G. Harding* (Texas Christian University Press, 1976); and Lester D. Langley, *The Banana Wars: United States Intervention in the Caribbean, 1898–1934* (Dorsey Press, 1988). The wavering Nicaraguan intervention is covered in William Kamman, *A Search for Stability: United States Policy toward Nicaragua, 1925–1933* (University of Notre Dame Press, 1968). Career diplomat Dana G. Munro covers the winding down of U.S. interventions in Haiti and the Dominican Republic in *The United States and the Caribbean Republics, 1921–1933* (Princeton University Press, 1974). U. S. efforts to reform the military as part of the intervention process are covered in Marvin Goldwert, *The Constabulary in the Dominican Republic and Nicaragua: Progeny and Legacy of United States Intervention* (University of Florida Press, 1962), and James H. McCrocklin, *Garde d'Haiti, 1915–1934: Twenty Years of Organization and Training by the United States Marine Corps* (United States Naval Institute, 1956).

Alexander DeConde examines the reappraisal of the Roosevelt Corollary in *Herbert Hoover's Latin American Policy* (Stanford University Press, 1951). For the economic role played by the United States in Latin America, see Joseph Brandes, *Herbert Hoover and Economic Diplomacy: Department of Commerce Policy, 1921–1928* (University of Pittsburgh Press, 1962), and Mira Wilkins, *The Matur-*

ing of Multinational Enterprise: American Business Abroad from 1914 to 1970 (Harvard University Press, 1974).

Useful surveys of the development of the Good Neighbor Policy are Edward O. Guerrant, *Roosevelt's Good Neighbor Policy* (University of New Mexico Press, 1950); Donald Marquand Dozer, *Are We Good Neighbors? Three Decades of Inter-American Relations, 1930–1960* (University of Florida Press, 1959); and Bryce Wood, *The Making of the Good Neighbor Policy* (Columbia University Press, 1961). For the role of reciprocal trade, see Dick Steward, *Trade and Hemisphere: The Good Neighbor Policy and Reciprocal Trade* (University of Missouri Press, 1975). For the application of the Good Neighbor Policy to Cuba, consult Irwin F. Gellman, *Roosevelt and Batista: Good Neighbor Diplomacy in Cuba, 1933–1945* (University of New Mexico Press, 1973). Samuel Guy Inman traces how the Good Neighbor Policy unfolded at inter-American meetings in *Inter-American Conferences, 1826–1954: History and Problems* (University Press, 1965).

U.S.-Mexican relations between the wars continued to be unpredictable. The prominent role assigned to the oil dispute is examined in Linda B. Hall, *Oil, Banks, and Revolution: Mexico and the United States, 1917–1924* (University of Texas Press, 1995); Merrill Rippy, *Oil and the Mexican Revolution* (E.J. Brill, 1972); and Lorenzo Meyer, *Mexico and the United States in the Oil Controversy, 1917–1942* (University of Texas Press, 1977). For general studies of the period, see Robert Freeman Smith, *The United States and Revolutionary Nationalism in Mexico, 1916–1932* (University of Chicago Press, 1972), and John W. F. Dulles, *Yesterday in Mexico: A Chronicle of the Revolution* (University of Texas Press, 1972).

The most comprehensive survey of the impact of World War II on Latin America is R. A. Humphreys, *Latin America and the Second World War, Volume One: 1939–1942* and *Latin America and the Second World War, Volume Two, 1942–1945* (Athlone Press, 1981, 1982). Frank D. McCann, Jr. examines the special relationship between the United States and Brazil in *The Brazilian-American Alliance, 1937–1945* (Princeton University Press, 1973). The antagonistic relations between the United States and Argentina are covered in Guido di Tella and D. Cameron Watt, eds., *Argentina between the Great Powers, 1939–46* (University of Pittsburgh Press, 1990). For a detailed analysis of Nazi influence and activities in Argentina, see Ronald C. Newton, *The "Nazi Menace" in Argentina, 1931–1947* (Stanford University Press, 1992).

1945–1965

Good studies of U.S.-Latin American relations in the early years of the Cold War are David Green, *The Containment of Latin America: A History of the Myths and Realities of the Good Neighbor Policy* (Quadrangle Books, 1971); Leslie Bethell and Ian Roxborough, eds., *Latin America between the Second World War and the Cold*

War, 1944–1948 (Cambridge University Press, 1992); and Donald Marquand Dozer, *Are We Good Neighbors? Three Decades of Inter-American Relations, 1930–1960* (University of Florida Press, 1959).

Abraham F. Lowenthal, ed., *Exporting Democracy: The United States and Latin America, Themes and Issues* (Johns Hopkins University Press, 1991) deals with U.S. efforts to promote democracy in Latin America. For U.S. relations with two long-standing dictatorships during this period, see Paul Coe Clark, Jr., *The United States and Somoza, 1933–1956: A Revisionist Look* (Praeger, 1992), and G. Pope Atkins and Larman C. Wilson, *The United States and the Trujillo Regime* (Rutgers University Press, 1972).

For a general discussion of the impact of U.S. military policy on Latin America, see Edwin Lieuwen, *Arms and Politics in Latin America*, rev. ed. (Praeger, 1961). See also F. Parkinson, *Latin America, the Cold War, and the World Powers, 1945–1973* (Sage Publications, 1974).

Useful comparisons of the divergent ways in which the United States approached the Bolivian and Guatemalan revolutions in the 1950s can be found in Cole Blasier, *The Hovering Giant: U.S. Responses to Revolutionary Change in Latin America* (University of Pittsburgh Press, 1976), and Bryce Wood, *The Dismantling of the Good Neighbor Policy* (University of Texas Press, 1985).

The U.S. role in Guatemala in the 1950s produced a considerable literature. For a bitter denunciation of the United States by one of Guatemala's revolutionary presidents, see Juan José Arévalo, *The Shark and The Sardines* (Lyle Stuart, 1961). For the extent of communist influence on the revolutionary movement, see Ronald M. Schneider, *Communism in Guatemala, 1944–1954* (Praeger, 1959). For the CIA role, see Richard H. Immerman, *The CIA in Guatemala: The Foreign Policy of Intervention* (University of Texas Press, 1982). See also Stephen Schlesinger and Stephen Kinzer, *Bitter Fruit: The Untold Story of the American Coup in Guatemala* (Doubleday, 1982).

In the late 1950s the United States began to address the social and economic needs of Latin America. For an excellent survey of the evolution of President Dwight D. Eisenhower's foreign economic policy, see Burton I. Kaufman, *Trade and Aid: Eisenhower's Foreign Economic Policy, 1953–1961* (Johns Hopkins University, 1982). Jerome Levinson and Juan de Onís provide an "audit" of the Alliance for Progress in *The Alliance That Lost Its Way: A Critical Report on the Alliance for Progress* (Quadrangle Books, 1970). For the intellectual framework of the Alliance, see Robert A. Packenham, *Liberal America and the Third World: Political Development Ideas in Foreign Aid and Social Science* (Princeton University Press, 1973).

There are several excellent studies of the Dominican intervention: Piero Gleijeses, *The Dominican Crisis: The 1965 Constitutionalist Revolt and the American In-*

tervention (Johns Hopkins University Press, 1978); Abraham F. Lowenthal, *The Do-minican Intervention* (Harvard University Press, 1972); and Jerome Slater, *Intervention and Negotiation: the United States and the Dominican Revolution* (Harper & Row, 1970). For the perspective of a U.S. diplomat actively involved in Dominican affairs, see John Bartlow Martin, *Overtaken by Events: The Dominican Crisis from the Fall of Trujillo to the Civil War* (Doubleday, 1966).

1960s to 1989

Good overviews of the period are in John D. Martz, ed., *United States Policy in Latin America: A Quarter Century of Crisis and Challenge, 1961–1986* (University of Nebraska Press, 1988), and Harold Molineu, *U.S. Policy toward Latin America: From Regionalism to Globalism,* 2d ed. (Westview Press, 1990).

The U.S. attitude toward development problems in Latin America is covered in Nelson A. Rockefeller, *The Rockefeller Report on the Americas: The Official Report of a United States Presidential Mission for the Western Hemisphere* (Quadrangle Books, 1969). See also Samuel L. Baily, *The United States and the Development of South America, 1945–1975* (New Viewpoints, 1976), and F. Parkinson, *Latin America, the Cold War, and the World Powers, 1945–1973* (Sage Publications, 1974).

A review of the negotiations over the Panama Canal appears in Walter LaFeber, *The Panama Canal: The Crisis in Historical Perspective,* exp. ed. (Oxford University Press, 1979).

For the struggle over ratification, see William L. Furlong and Margaret E. Scranton, *The Dynamics of Foreign Policymaking: The President, the Congress, and the Panama Canal Treaties* (Westview Press, 1984), and George D. Moffett III, *The Limits of Victory: The Ratification of the Panama Canal Treaties* (Cornell University Press, 1985). For an insider's view of the negotiations and problems with ratification, see William J. Jorden, *Panama Odyssey* (University of Texas Press, 1984).

The emphasis on human rights posed new difficulties for U.S.-Latin American relations. See Lars Schoultz, *Human Rights and United States Policy toward Latin America* (Princeton University Press, 1981).

For a diplomatic/military history of the Falklands/Malvinas crisis, see Max Hastings and Simon Jenkins, *The Battle for the Falklands* (W.W. Norton & Co., 1983). See also Alexander M. Haig, *Caveat: Realism, Reagan, and Foreign Policy* (Macmillan, 1984). For the origins and evolution of the debt crisis, see Stephany Griffith-Jones, *International Finance and Latin America* (St. Martin's Press, 1984), and Robert Wesson, ed., *Coping with the Latin American Debt* (Praeger, 1988). The debt-development tradeoff is examined in William L. Canak, ed., *Lost Promises: Debt, Austerity, and Development in Latin America* (Westview Press, 1989). For an examination of how effective International Monetary Fund programs were (not very), see Paul W. Drake, ed., *Money Doctors, Foreign Debts, and Economic Reforms in Latin America from the 1890s to the Present* (Scholarly Resources, 1994), chapter 10.

An extremely interesting interpretation of the issues explored in this chapter may be found in Gaddis Smith, *The Last Years of the Monroe Doctrine, 1945–1993* (Hill and Wang, 1994), especially chapters 8 and 9. The outstanding source on Central American-U.S. relations is Walter LaFeber, *Inevitable Revolutions: The United States in Central America,* 2d ed. (W. W. Norton & Co., 1993). An important Latin American view is Gabriel Aguilera, et al., *Centroamérica de Reagan a Bush* (FLACSO: San José, Costa Rica, 1991). An indispensable source on the relationship between Congress and the presidency in Central American affairs is Cynthia J. Arnson, *Crossroads: Congress, the President, and Central America, 1976–1993,* 2d ed. (Pennsylvania State University Press, 1993). A fine collection of essays, now somewhat out of date but extremely good for the early 1980s, is Morris J. Blachman, et al., *Confronting Revolution: Security through Diplomacy in Central America* (Pantheon Books, 1986). A general overview of the region is John A. Booth and Thomas W. Walker, *Understanding Central America* (Westview Press, 1989). An extremely interesting collection of essays is *Vital Interests: The Soviet Issue in U.S. Central American Policy,* edited by Bruce Larkin (Lynne Rienner, 1988).

Recent works on more specific topics or individual countries in U.S. foreign relations are Theodore Draper, *A Very Thin Line: The Iran-Contra Affairs* (Touchstone, 1991); Morris H. Morley, *Washington, Somoza, and the Sandinistas: State and Regime in U.S. Policy toward Nicaragua, 1969–1981* (Cambridge University Press, 1994); Donald E. Schulz and Deborah Sundloff Schulz, *The United States, Honduras, and the Crisis in Central America* (Westview Press, 1994); Martha Honey, *Hostile Acts: U.S. Policy in Costa Rica in the 1980s* (University Press of Florida, 1994); Jack Child, *The Central America Peace Crisis, 1983–1991: Sheathing Swords, Building Confidence* (Lynne Rienner, 1992); Dario Moreno, *The Struggle for Peace in Central America* (University Press of Florida, 1994); E. Bradford Burns, *At War in Nicaragua: The Reagan Doctrine and the Politics of Nostalgia* (Harper & Row, 1987); Annette Baker Fox, *Guatemala, Human Rights, and U.S. Foreign Policy* (Pew Case Studies Center, 1989); and Michael McClintock, *The American Connection* (Zed Books, 1985).

The materials on Cuba and the United States are voluminous. The items listed here are suggested only as a starting point. A basic work on the development of U.S.-Cuban relations is Louis A. Pérez, *Cuba and the United States: Ties of Singular Intimacy* (University of Georgia Press, 1990). Works on the post–World War II period include Morris H. Morley, *Imperial State and Revolution: The United States and Cuba, 1952–1986* (Cambridge University Press, 1987); Thomas Paterson, *Contesting Castro: The United States and the Triumph of the Cuban Revolution* (Oxford

University Press, 1994); and Wayne Smith, *The Closest of Enemies: A Personal and Diplomatic Account of U.S.-Cuban Relations since 1957* (W.W. Norton & Co., 1987).

1989 to the Present

For an overview of U.S. foreign policy in the post–Cold War world, see John Lewis Gaddis, *The United States and the End of the Cold War: Implications, Reconsiderations, Provocations* (Oxford University Press, 1992). U.S. efforts to help Latin America get beyond the debt crisis are in Jonathan Hartlyn, Lars Schoultz, and Augusto Varas, eds., *The United States and Latin America in the 1990s: Beyond the Cold War* (University of North Carolina Press, 1992), chapter 6. For the NAFTA negotiations, see Chris C. Carvounis and Brinda Z. Carvounis, *United States Trade and Investment in Latin America: Opportunities for Business in the 1990s* (Quorum Books, 1992), chapter 4. An easy-to-follow guide to the provisions of NAFTA is R. Pardo-Maurer and Judith Rodriguez, eds., *Access Mexico: Handbook and Directory* (Cambridge Data and Development, Ltd., 1993).

An interesting account of recent U.S.-Cuban relations is Andrés Oppenheimer, *Castro's Final Hour* (Touchstone, 1992).

The basic source on Central American-U.S. relations is Walter LaFeber, *Inevitable Revolutions: The United States in Central America*, 2d ed. (W. W. Norton & Co., 1993). For the Latin American perspective, see Gabriel Aguilera et al., *Centroamérica de Reagan a Bush* (FLACSO, 1991). The often antagonistic relationship between Congress and the presidency in Central American affairs is examined in Cynthia J. Arnson, *Crossroads: Congress, the President, and Central America, 1976–1993*, 2d ed. (Pennsylvania State University Press, 1993).

Recent works on more specific topics or individual countries are Donald E. Schulz and Deborah Sundloff Schulz, *The United States, Honduras, and the Crisis in Central America* (Westview Press, 1994); Jack Child, *The Central America Peace Crisis, 1983–1991: Sheathing Swords, Building Confidence* (Lynne Rienner, 1992); and Dario Moreno, *The Struggle for Peace in Central America* (University Press of Florida, 1994). An official who helped implement U.S. policy in Central America evaluates the Nicaraguan scene in Robert Kagan's *A Twilight Struggle: American Power and Nicaragua, 1977–1990* (Free Press, 1995).

Immigration

Two essential books on Latino immigration to the United States are Alejandro Portes and Robert L. Bach, *Latin Journey: Cuban and Mexican Immigrants in the United States* (University of California Press, 1985), and Alejandro Portes and Rubén Rumbaut, *Immigrant America: A Portrait* (University of California Press,

1990). Cuban migration is also covered in Lyn MacCorkle, *Cubans in the United States* (Westport, 1984).

Sources for Mexican immigration in the twentieth century are Lawrence A. Cardoso, *Mexican Emigration to the United States, 1897–1931* (University of Arizona Press, 1980); Harley Browning and Rodolfo de la Garza, *Mexican Immigrants and Mexican Americans: An Evolving Relationship* (Center for Mexican American Studies, University of Texas at Austin, 1986); Rodolfo Acuña, *Occupied America: A History of Chicanos*, 2d ed. (Harper & Row, 1981); and Mario García, *Desert Immigrants: The Mexicans of El Paso, 1880–1920* (Yale University Press, 1981). Recent literature on Mexicans and Mexican Americans in the United States is voluminous, including George J. Sanchez, *Becoming Mexican American: Ethnicity, Culture and Identity in Los Angeles, 1900–1945* (Oxford University Press, 1993); David G. Gutiérrez, *Walls and Mirrors: Mexican Americans, Mexican Immigrants, and the Politics of Identity* (University of California Press, 1995); Ricardo Romo, *East Los Angeles: History of a Barrio* (University of Texas Press, 1983); and Pierette Hondagneu-Sotelo, *Gendered Transitions: Mexican Experiences of Immigration* (University of California Press, 1994).

Book-length works on other Latino groups are much rarer. Useful, although quite specialized, are Thomas W. Ward, "The Price of Fear: Salvadoran Refugees in the City of Angels," Ph.D. diss. (University of California-Los Angeles, 1987), and María Andrea Miralles, *A Matter of Life and Death: Health-Seeking Behavior of Guatemalan Refugees in South Florida* (AMS Press, 1989).

Literature on the Latino population more generally includes *Latinos in a Changing U.S. Economy: Comparative Perspectives on Growing Inequality,* edited by Rebecca Morales and Frank Bonilla (Sage Publications, 1993); L. H. Gann and Peter J. Duignan, *The Hispanics in the United States: A History* (Westview Press, 1986); and Earl Shorris, *Latinos: A Biography of the People* (W.W. Norton & Co., 1992).

Drug Trafficking

Two excellent collections of articles on this topic with a contemporary focus are *Drug Policy in the Americas*, edited by Peter H. Smith (Westview Press, 1992), and *Drug Trafficking in the Americas*, edited by Bruce M. Bagley and William O. Walker (Transaction Publishers, 1994). A more historical study is William O. Walker, *Drug Control in the Americas* (University of New Mexico Press, 1989). A solid but now somewhat dated investigation of the Mexican situation is Elaine Shannon, *Desperados: Latin Drug Lords, U.S. Lawmen, and the War America Can't Win* (Viking, 1988). A good discussion of Manuel Noriega and the Panama situation is John Dinges, *Our Man in Panama: The Shrewd Rise and Brutal Fall of Manuel Noriega* (Times Books, 1990).

INDEX

Adams, John Quincy, 10–11, 13, 14
Adams-Onís Treaty (1819), 9, 11, 13, 15
affirmative action, 213
agrarian reform, 93, 138; El Salvador, 207
agricultural investment, 85
AIDS epidemic, 235
Allende, Salvador, 140
Alliance for Progress, 129–30, 131, 138
American Revolution, 3, 8, 12–13
anti-Americanism, 80, 186
anticommunism, 7; anti-Castro Cuban-
   Americans, 181, 183; authoritarian
   regimes, 151–52; Bay of Pigs, 123; Bogotá
   Conference, 107–08; Bolivia, 112–13; Cold
   War, end of, 180; collapse, 219; Cuba,
   121–29; dictatorships supported, 109–10;
   El Salvador, 156, 158–59; Guatemala,
   113–15; Kirkpatrick, 163–64; Korean War,
   110–11; Latin America, 106; military
   regimes supported, 131; Nixon administration, 137; presidential (U.S.) elections
   of 1960, 129
Arbenz, Jacobo, 113
ARENA (Alianza Republicana Nacionalista), 156, 158, 170, 209
Argentina: bond sales, 85; debt issues, 174,
   175, 189; Falklands War, 170–72; Great
   Britain, 31; human rights, 146, 147; independence, 10, 11; Malvinas (Falkland)
   Islands, 31; Pan American conference
   (1891), 37–38; trade with U.S., 31; *Water
   Witch* incident, 25; World War I, 71–72;
   World War II, 98, 99–100, 102–03

Arias, Desiderio, 69–70
Arias Plan, 158, 168–69
Aristide, Jean-Bertrand, 193–94
assassinations, 224
austerity programs, 174–75, 175–76
authoritarian regimes, 109–10, 151–52
automakers, 85
avocado controversy, 177–78

Baja California, 27
Baker Plan, 175–76
Baltimore Affair, 38–39
Bank for International Settlements, 174
base agreements, military, 97, 99
Batista, Fulgencio, 89, 120, 186
Bay of Pigs, 122–26
Belize (British Honduras), 29
bilingual education, 213–14
blacklists, 72, 100
Blaine, James G., 37, 39
Bogotá, Act of (1960), 116
Boland amendments, 164–65
Bolivia, 10; coca growers, 217–19; drugs,
   219, 225, 231–32; human rights, 146; in
   Peru, 34; militarization, of war on
   drugs, 234; mining, 85; oil companies,
   U.S., 91; Tacna-Arica dispute, 74–76
Bordas, José, 69
border air patrol, 46, 48
border issues, 198–201, 211, 214; drugs, 222,
   223–24; Plan of San Diego, 65. *See also*
   Texas
Border Patrol, 215